Political Speaking Justified

Political Speaking Justified

Justified

Women Prophets and the English Revolution

Teresa Feroli

DELAWARE

Newark: University of Delaware Press

© 2006 by Rosemont Publishing & Printing Corp.

Associated University Presses
2010 Eastpark Boulevard
Cranbury, NJ 08512

The paper used in this publication meets the requirements of the American National Standard for Permanence of Paper for Printed Library Materials Z39.48-1984.

Library of Congress Cataloging-in-Publication Data

Feroli, Teresa.
    Political speaking justified : women prophets and the English Revolution / Teresa Feroli.
        p.   cm.
    Includes bibliographical references (p.) and index.
    ISBN 0-87413-908-2 (alk. paper)
    1. Great Britain—History—Puritan Revolution, 1642–1660—Historiography. 2. English prose literature—Early modern, 1500–1700—History and criticism.   3. English prose literature—Women authors—History and criticism.   4. Politics and literature—Great Britain—History—17th century. 5. Women in politics—Great Britain—History—17th century.   6. Political science—Great Britain—History—17th century.   7. Women prophets—Great Britain—History—17th century.   8. Great Britain—Intellectual life—17th century.   9. Women—Great Britain—Intellectual life.   10. Fox, Margaret Askew Fell, 1614–1702.   11. Douglas, Eleanor, Lady, d. 1652. 12. Trapnel, Anna.   I. Title.
    DA403.F47   2006
    942.06′2′082—dc22   2005014400

For Tom, Esme, and Matthew

Contents

Acknowledgments

MY RELATIONSHIP WITH THE WOMEN PROPHETS CAN BEST BE described as love at first sight. When I first met them, I knew instantly that they had much to contribute to our understanding of literary and feminist history. I consider myself extremely fortunate not only to have been able to study their writings but also to have received so much support for this project.

I could not have written this book without the participation of a number of major archives. Moreover, one of the greatest pleasures of this project has been the opportunity to work directly with so many rare books. I am particularly indebted to the staffs of the Folger Shakespeare Library and the Burke Library at Union Theological Seminary for allowing me to read extensively in their collections. My book has also benefited from shorter reading excursions through the British Library, the Public Record Office (London), Worcester College, Oxford, and the Quaker Collections at Haverford and Swarthmore Colleges. I am grateful both for the opportunity to have worked in these archives, and, on trips to England, to have enjoyed the warm hospitality of Anne and Bran Milijic.

My journey to completing this book began when I was a graduate student at Cornell University and was followed by teaching positions at the University of Tulsa and Polytechnic University. All three of these universities have provided generous funding for my work. In addition, friends and teachers at these three institutions have been extraordinarily helpful and supportive. In particular, I wish to thank Charlotte Sussman, Gordon Teskey, Laura Brown, Todd Parker, Anne Krook, Patricia Wallace, Rich Durocher, and Lars Engle. I am grateful also to Betty Travitsky, Nigel Smith, and Sharon Achinstein for reading chapters of the manuscript. And finally, an American Council for Learned Societies Postdoctoral Fellowship enabled me to pull years of research together and complete the manuscript.

Katharine Gillespie's excellent *Domesticity and Dissent in the Seventeenth Century* came out too late for me to respond

9

fully to its insights here. Her book addresses many of the same authors I consider—Anna Trapnel, Sarah Wight, and Elizabeth Poole—and demonstrates their contributions to the core principles of political liberalism.

I wish to thank the editors at the University of Delaware Press and at Associated University Presses for their enthusiasm and patience. The book was accepted for publication just weeks before the birth of my son Matthew, and Mrs. Christine Retz at Associated University Presses has been a particularly understanding listener to tales of colic and sleepless nights.

I dedicate this book to my husband Tom Graham and to our children Esme and Matthew. A fabulous and absorbing crew, they have each by turns distracted me from completing this book, and yet they are the reason for doing it.

An earlier version of chapter 1 appeared as "The Sexual Politics of Mourning in the Prophecies of Eleanor Davies" in *Criticism* 36 (1994): 359–82, and an earlier version of chapter 2 appeared in *Women's Studies* 24 (1994): 31–49. In addition, parts of the Introduction have appeared in a topic essay entitled "Prophecy" that I wrote for the Renaissance Women Online database of the Brown Women Writers Program.

Note on the Text

WHEN I QUOTE SCRIPTURE THROUGHOUT, I USE THE KING JAMES (Authorized) Version. Although many religious radicals preferred the Geneva Bible, the primary subjects of my study, as the passages of Scripture they quote illustrate, appear to have favored the King James Version. Of the three women I discuss, only Lady Eleanor, on occasion, takes scriptural passages from the Geneva Bible, but she also invokes the King James Version. I have decided to use the King James Version when discussing Lady Eleanor because the two chapters about her tracts address her adherence to traditional ideas of social order.

Political Speaking
Justified

Introduction: Political Speaking Justified

THIS STUDY DEMONSTRATES THAT THE WOMEN PROPHETS OF THE EN-
glish Revolution inaugurate an early phase in the rise of modern
feminist consciousness. Although the women prophets are not
feminists in the sense that they do not intervene in the political
sphere solely to improve the lives of women, they do represent
an important moment in the history of feminism because they
seek to justify a role for women as political activists. I make my
case in two ways. First, I emphasize the relationship between
prophecy and politics. In the tradition of the Hebrew prophets,
the women I discuss claimed that God called them to convey his
word to the leaders of the nation. Their resulting prophecies—
including denunciations of Charles I and Oliver Cromwell, predictions of the imminent apocalypse, and pleas for religious
toleration—placed them in the forefront of political events. Second, I illustrate how prophecy's political imperative promoted
among female visionaries the understanding that they as women
could assume politically significant roles. Commanded by God to
deliver messages of national import, these women needed to be
believed and thus they needed to constitute themselves as politically viable speakers and writers. While this was a difficult task
in a society that equated women's public speech with sexual impropriety, the women prophets successfully proved that their authority as women could be consistent with the terms of political
power. These terms themselves shifted markedly over the
course of the English Revolution, but they ultimately defined a
political order that privileged individual agency over and against
the dictates of a predetermined hierarchy. I chart the ways in
which three women prophets active in the beginning, middle, and
end of the period respectively—Lady Eleanor Davies, Anna
Trapnel, and Margaret Fell—register this broad shift in the
definition of political authority.

What I discover is that female authority evolves from being an
adjunct of patriarchy to an attribute of female sexuality. Where
Lady Eleanor had once predicated her authority upon her

father's name, Margaret Fell would come to argue that female authority derives from the body.[1] These three authors reveal a progressive move away from defining female political identity in terms of their place in a cosmically ordered hierarchy and toward vesting power in the self. In so doing, they anticipate the rise of modernity that Stephen L. Collins defines as "a process whereby men [and women] created the self as the historical and cultural medium for redemption."[2] Because women prophets are the first significant group of women to instantiate the political authority of self-consciously female selves, they represent a foundational moment of modern feminist consciousness.

This book traces the development of three women prophets' strategies of legitimation between the years 1625 and 1667 and then illustrates how the modes of authority they create inform the work of the well-established "first English feminist" Mary Astell. I begin my study with two chapters on Lady Eleanor because she attempts to justify her prophetic vocation through the language of power of a political order—namely, traditional patriarchy—in a state of decline. She repeatedly represents her vocation as the reluctant beneficiary of a patriarchal hierarchy in which men have failed to maintain their traditional roles. While she does not instantiate her authority, in a more recognizably feminist manner, with a positive assertion of female legitimacy, she does construct a political role for women through an established language of power—patriarchy—and anticipates the ways later female visionaries will constitute their authority in terms of female sexuality. I discuss her political treatises in conjunction first with theories of divine right and second with the sensational trial of her brother Mervin, Earl of Castlehaven, for rape and sodomy.

The second part of my study explores the politics of female sexuality that Anna Trapnel and Margaret Fell develop to authorize their prophetic vocations. Both of these women establish their authority in terms of their bodies and not, as had Lady Eleanor, in terms of patriarchy. Chapter three discusses how the Fifth Monarchist Trapnel used fasting to create a model of political order predicated upon the female body. What makes Trapnel's fasting and prophesying remarkable is that she urged the crowds who gathered at her bedside to regard her not as extraordinary but as representative of the abstemious practices they, as God's chosen people, should naturally emulate. Her emphasis on the representative status of her body surprisingly allies her model of authority with that of Thomas Hobbes. My fourth chapter examines the most famous female authored prophetic treatise (and the inspiration for my study's title), *Womens Speaking Justified.* I assess both the originality and influence of this 1667 tract by the Quaker Margaret Fell by examining it within the context of her fellow sectarians' treatises on women's right to preach in the church and women's meetings. I show how, in a radical departure from earlier Quaker writings on the subject of women's speaking, Fell predicates female visionary authority on the physical bond that she insists women, both as mothers and lovers, share with Christ.

The final section, the epilogue, considers Mary Astell's 1706 Preface to her *Reflections Upon Marriage* and how it effectively translates the women prophets' insistence that female sexuality underwrites female authority into a more recognizably modern assertion of feminist concerns. Famous for her treatises on women's education and marriage and for her embrace of rationalist philosophy, Astell appeals to the vatic mode in Preface. There, she does not replicate the women prophets' politics of female sexuality but produces a contingent vision in which the politics of sexual difference serve to engender a new society based on equality between the sexes.

Beyond illustrating the women prophets' unique contribution to the history of feminism, this study emphasizes the literariness of their writings.[3] By this I mean that I use the same types of approaches conventionally applied to canonical texts. I organize my book around close readings and the interconnections between these women's writings and established literary traditions. While I address the writings of some twenty-three female visonaries, I concentrate on the tracts of three prophets and dedicate three chapters to one treatise each. In order to provide a context for close readings, each chapter situates a treatise or group of treatises in terms of both the Bible, the major source text of seventeenth-century English prophecy, and contemporary literary modes. For instance, I demonstrate that Lady Eleanor's complex prose style can be deciphered through the tropes and figures found in the exegetical writings of major biblical scholars; Anna Trapnel's politicized fasting borrows, in part, from sermon literature; and Margaret Fell's defense of women's prophesying is not a singular achievement but part of a tradition of Quaker gender polemic. My point is that the women prophets are not, as they are sometimes portrayed, a group of unhinged and freewheeling ecstatics. They did not write into a void, but, like so many writers before and since, they sought to remake their world and themselves using the materials of received literary traditions. Theirs is a radicalism born not of "an irruption of female speech" but of reconfiguring existing literatures to serve their political agenda.[4]

Finally, this is an account of an extraordinarily determined and dedicated group of women. Each woman I discuss was imprisoned for publicly communicating her beliefs, and not one was daunted by the trials she endured. One particularly striking testimony to the women prophets' stoic pursuit of truth is Fell's plea to Charles II to desist from persecuting her fellow Quakers. As she details the various forms of persecution the Quakers have suffered, Fell hardly adopts a conciliatory tone but rather combines pathos with defiance: "We have been a *suffering people* . . . Even some *persecuted* & prisoned *till death*; others their bodies bruised *till death*; *stigmatized*; *bored thorow the tongue, gagged in the mouth, stockt,* and *whipt thorow Towns & Cities, our goods spoiled,* our bodies *two* or *three years imprisoned,* with much more that might be said, which is well known *to the Actors thereof.*"[5]

Fell's catalogue of atrocities represents not a sect devastated by egregious tortures but one that has triumphed over adversity. Even the Quakers' "bruised" and "stigmatized" bodies become material witnesses to their persecutors' ultimate impotence. While their adversaries have imprisoned their bodies for "two or three years," the Quakers' consciences remain untouched, penetrated only by God's inner light. Such dedication to what they perceived as the absolute truth was shared by Fell's prophesying sisters within and without her sect. Acting upon God's direct orders, these women entered the public sphere intent on bringing about a godly order and, as part and parcel of this goal, they deemed it necessary to create a political realm in which women's voices could be heard. Theirs is a unique literary record that unites religious faith and devotion with an emerging set of secular desires and ambitions.

৻৶

This book examines the texts of Lady Eleanor, Trapnel, and Fell against the backdrop of the revolutionary period's flourishing tradition of women's visionary writing. Perhaps the most significant indicator of the strength of this movement is the number of texts the women prophets produced. According to Elaine Hobby, well "over half the texts published by women between 1649 and 1688 were prophecies." Phyllis Mack has documented the existence of some three hundred active female visionaries in the 1640s and 1650s.[6] Not all of these women's visions appeared as published tracts, but documentary evidence indicates that in the years 1641 to 1660, some fifty women prophets produced roughly 156 published treatises.[7] Given that only thirty-nine female-authored first editions of any genre appeared in the first forty years of the seventeenth century, the women prophets' publishing record represents a major milestone in women's literary history.[8] Further, the numbers suggest that the revolutionary period and, by extension, those women who published prophecies inaugurated a trend that continued through the end of the century: the Restoration did not witness a radical decline in the numbers of women's published works but rather the stabilization of women's literary production.[9] Simply put, the position of women prophets within the history of women's writing in England is pivotal.

When this formidable group of women published, they frequently addressed political topics. Because "prophecy" in the period was defined in broad strokes—a prophecy could represent an inspired reading of Scripture or a direct communication from God—the women prophets' political writings could range from thunderous pronouncements of doom to carefully plotted exegetical calculations. Hester Biddle, for instance, prophesied certain destruction to the city of London: "Oh *London, London*! The dreadful Lord God of Everlasting strength, which faileth not, his notable, terrible, and dreadful Day is coming upon thee as at noon day, and from it thou canst not escape, neither canst thou quench God's Fire which burns as an Oven, which is overtaking thee." Far less dramatically, Mary Cary announced that based on her reading of the account of the little horn in Daniel she had predicted the execution of Charles I in 1649: "this Parliament which were to be the instruments of the Churches deliverance in their measure, were also long ago prophesied of: In which prophesie, it was so long ago declared . . . that they should do justice upon that wicked King."[10] Although they represent expressive modes ranging from impassioned exhortation to analytical statement, the prophecies of Biddle and Cary both consider weighty political matters.

The women prophets' concern with politics did not merely represent a literary exercise; indeed, many female visionaries gained recognition as political players. Evidence for this claim comes from the seriousness with which the ruling authorities regarded these women's pronouncements on matters of national importance.[11] Unfortunately, this did not mean that government

officials routinely consulted women prophets in times of crisis in
the same way King Josiah's officials consulted the prophet Huldah about the authenticity of some newly discovered sacred
scrolls.[12] More typically, seventeenth-century governing authorities imprisoned women prophets because they feared their
words were being heeded by potentially disruptive segments of
society. For instance, Lady Eleanor's accurate prediction of the
death of Charles's chief advisor, the Duke of Buckingham,
earned her popular acclaim and deeply troubled the King. He
subsequently took a personal interest in seeing her imprisoned
in 1633 after she illegally published and distributed some of her
treatises. Charles was not alone in suppressing a female visionary. Under Cromwell's regime, Anna Trapnel was imprisoned
briefly in 1654 on several charges: witchcraft, treasonous decla-
rations against the Protector, and disturbing the peace. Still, at
least one female prophet, Elizabeth Poole, was directly consulted
by the ruling authorities. In late 1648, she was invited to appear
before the Army's Council of Officers, the group who determined
the King's fate, to communicate her prophecy against killing
Charles. She was supported by moderates among the Army officers who hoped that her prophecy would persuade their fellow
officers to preserve the King's life. Her words ultimately went
unheeded, but those of Margaret Fell did not. In 1660, she peti-
tioned the recently restored monarch Charles II regarding a se-
ries of abuses suffered by a group of imprisoned Friends and
through her "unwearied Application" won their release.[13] Hers,
however, proved to be a local and short-lived victory as the
Quakers continued to endure persecution until 1689 when the
Toleration Act was passed. Nevertheless, women prophets did
influence the course of political events, although they did so on
the grass-roots level. They were well regarded in their sects
where their prophecies were, for the most part, received as divinely inspired. And although the sects were not official government organs, their members came to play a prominent role in
the period's politics through their controversial pamphlets and
service in the Parliament and Army.

The female visionaries were both the first major group of
women to insist on their right to participate in political discourse
and the first socially diverse group to do so. While, according to
Barbara Kiefer Lewalski, the writing women of Jacobean England were, by and large, "women of position, education, and
privilege," the class backgrounds of the female prophets, as
Mack notes, "ranged from the impoverished countrywoman Eli-

nor Channel to the aristocrat Eleanor Davies." Indeed, as historian Dorothy Paula Ludlow observes, much of the women's writing that appeared in the revolutionary decades was produced by "less privileged women." As a result, the female prophets participated in a distinct and more democratic moment of women's history: "The very fact that so many of them became historically visible in a twenty year period is itself worthy of the term 'phenomenon,' since women, except for a handful of rulers, royal mistresses, and the eccentric wives of prominent aristocrats or gentry, tend to blend into the seventeenth-century woodwork."[14]

Given women's general exclusion from the public sphere *tout court*, what enabled a significant number of women to prophesy and publish their visions? The first answer is that they could. In 1641, the Long Parliament eased censorship restrictions and thereby made it possible for both male and female visionaries to publish their words. According to Ludlow, the ruling authorities "quickly regretted" this act "but not soon enough to recapture the initiative seized by clamorous writers and their printers, publishers, and booksellers."[15]

Beyond the legal changes that gave women the opportunity to publish tracts on issues of political import, the revolutionary era created a sense of urgency that spurred many women to assume non-traditional roles. Ellen McArthur calls attention to accounts of women participating in warfare: "They raised bodies such as 'the Maiden Troop,' in Norwich and in London; they commanded besieged garrisons, they plunged into the thicket of the fray on more than one occasion and even accompanied husbands and lovers as soldiers." Commenting on the Royalist sympathizer Ann Fanshawe's memoirs, N. H. Keeble observes that she justifies her forwardness in petitioning Cromwell for her imprisoned husband's release as "occasioned and legitimized only by the exceptional and pressing needs of king and husband." This sense of the unique circumstances of the age not only explained women's need to assume activist roles but also to prophesy. For Lady Eleanor, radical times demanded radical solutions, hence God's decision to send her, rather than a man, to convey his word: "The weaker *Sex* preferred more proper for them, requisit for former dayes neither." Although she does not specifically link the revolutionary era with the rise of women prophets, the Quaker prophet Dorothy White suggests that God has turned the world upside down and thus altered the social structure: "the power of God . . . is come to turne the World upside down. That that, which hath ruled over may be brought down under, and that which hath been of low degree, may be raised up by the power of God, to rule and have the dominion."[16] In a world radically transformed by God's hand, those of "low degree," including perhaps women, have been "raised up . . . to rule." The world was not as it had been and almost anything was possible.

Another impetus to women's prophetic speech was the prolif-eration of religious sects, such as the Baptists, Independents, Fifth Monarchists, and Quakers that both flourished in the Revo-lution's more tolerant atmosphere and contributed to the age's distinctive religious politics. The sects proved particularly con-ducive to female advancement because they emphasized the spiritual equality of the sexes. This belief, together with the sects' privileging of the individual's direct relationship with God, meant that women were as responsible as men for their own sal-vation: "Would-be members of a congregation had to give proof of their individual regeneration, women as well as men. There was no reason to believe that women were less likely to pass this test."[17] For the Quaker leader George Fox, as for many other sec-tarians, women's spiritual equality and accountability had politi-cal implications. He defended women's right to assume political roles in the Quaker movement as an extension of women's spiri-tual responsibility: "so they have an office as well as the men, for they have a stewardship, and must give an account of their stewardship to the Lord, as well as the men." Although certainly the most progressive of the sects on gender issues, the Quakers were not the only group to encourage women to assume more expansive roles. The belief in the spiritual equality of the sexes structured many of the "London Independent congregations" that, according to historian Keith Thomas, allowed "all their members, women included, to debate, vote and, if not preach, then usually at least to prophesy, which often came to much the same thing." While the sects were far from ideal models of gen-der equality—they "excluded women from positions of real lead-ership"—they permitted women a share in church government that they could never have dreamed of possessing in the Church of England.[18]

In addition to granting women greater opportunities for partic-ipation in church life, the sects also gave women a sense of iden-tity distinct from their roles as wives and mothers. As Ludlow puts it, "women learned to allot their time and energies to tasks outside the home—missionary work, petitions, demonstrations, perhaps only sewing on badges or streamers—and thus to make conscious choices between loyalties and demands."[19] According to Thomas, Jane Adams was rebuked by her cosectarians for putting her allegiance to her husband before that to her congregation: "In 1658 Jane Adams excused her absence from the Baptist meeting at Fenstanton by explaining that her husband would not let her come. She was sharply reminded that there were limits to the authority a husband could exercise and that she must come unless restrained by force."[20] By effectively endorsing acts of wifely disobedience, the sects participated in the constitution of female subjects who defined themselves in terms not only of their matrimonial obligations but also of their ideological commitments.

Perhaps the most striking example of women whose sectarian identity assumed greater prominence in their lives than their roles as wives and mothers are the Quaker missionaries, Katharine Evans and Sarah Chevers. Imprisoned on the Island of Malta from 1658/9 to 1662 by the Inquisition, these women wrote letters to their husbands and children that are surprisingly devoid of conventional expressions of sentiment. Evans, for instance, does not speak of missing her family but instead agonizes over their spiritual well-being: "Oh my dear Husband and Children, how often have I poured out my soul to our everlasting Father for you, with Rivers of tears, night and day, that you might be kept pure and single in the sight of our God." What matters is not her kinship with them but their relationships, as individual believers, with God. Far from lamenting her separation from them, she exults in her journey and even in her imprisonment: "I could not wish I had not come over Seas, because I knew it was my Eternal Father's Will to prove me, with my dear and faithful Friend [Chevers]." For her part, Sarah Chevers opens her letter to her husband by stating her commitment to her faith: "My Dear Husband, my love, my life is given up to serve the living God." Clearly, her loyalty to her God—who possesses her "love" and her "life"—far exceeds her allegiance to her husband. Evans too implicitly derogates the significance of her marriage bond when she writes her husband that her companion Chevers, in language typically associated with matrimony, is her "dearly beloved Yoakmate in the Work of our God."[21]

Beyond enabling women to define themselves in new ways, the sects also assisted women prophets in publishing their words.[22] According to historian Phyllis Mack, nearly "every important prophet belonged to a congregation that was supervised by male ministers, and most . . . were dependent on male editors who

bracketed their texts by salutations that affirmed their piety, in-
serted supporting biblical citations, and added substantive arguments."[23] Male editors played a prominent role in publishing
early women's writing in general, and their prefaces frequently
extol female authors' modesty. In doing so, they sought to
counter cultural stereotypes that equated women's published
words with sexual impropriety. Similar encomiums to their authors' modesty preface women prophets' tracts but they assume
a less defensive tone as they proudly identify their authors' chastity with the moral character of the entire sect. Hence, when
Hugh Peter, in a preface to the Fifth Monarchist Mary Cary's
Little Horns Doom & Downfall (1651), praises her modesty he
makes her into a representative sectarian: "A holy, modest, and
painfull spirit runs through her endeavours: which I desire may
not be slighted by any, nor thrown by: for good wine may be found
in this Cluster: in this dress you shall neither see naked Brests,
black Patches, nor long Trains; but an heart breathing after the
coming of Christ, and the *comfort of Saints*."[24] As distinct from
the worlds of the court and the aristocracy, Cary's text wears not
the "dress" of promiscuity associated with "black Patches" and
"long Trains" but the modest garb of female chastity. Although,
strictly speaking, Peter cannot be said to define Cary's sexual
behavior in terms of class, he does position her text (and its
"modest spirit") as an antidote to the specifically sexual misde-
meanors of courtly and aristocratic women. Moreover, his preface implies that her text's "modest spirit" authorizes the values
of the primarily "middling sort" membership of the sects over
and against the corruption of the nobility.[25] In short, her modesty
is as much a feature of her sect and class as it is of her gender.

While the emergence of women prophets in significant numbers is due in large measure to the revolutionary milieu, their
roots go back much further—to the longstanding tradition of
women's activism in English Protestantism. As historian Claire
Cross argues, women's enhanced roles in the Civil War sects represent the fruits of their forebears' labors: "Godly women
achieved so much influence in certain churches during the Civil
War period not so much because of the revolutionary nature of
the times as because the whole trend of puritan practice for at
least the previous century had been preparing them for such action." She demonstrates, moreover, that women were active in
reform movements even prior to the 1530s. They played an active
role in the Lollard movement inspired, in the late fourteenth century, by John Wycliffe. Loosely organized and forced to operate

underground, Lollardy never achieved a regularized doctrine but surfaced in fits and starts from roughly 1382 through 1530. As early as 1393, Cross finds evidence of women's active participation in the movement: Anna Palmer was imprisoned for referring to the Bishop of Lincoln (in epithets that anticipate those of seventeenth-century religious radicals) as "antichrist and to his clerks as antichrist's disciples." Cross documents a number of accounts of women imprisoned and even burned at the stake for their beliefs, but perhaps more significant with respect to the history of women prophets is the role women assumed in transmitting the Word. She describes how, in the Chilterns in the early sixteenth century, women played a leading role in memorizing and then reciting Scripture for the Lollard community. (She speculates that they did this "to avoid being found in possession of incriminating books.") In particular, she notes that "Alice Collins was frequently called upon to recite at conventicles the ten commandments and the epistles of Peter and James, and she brought up her daughter Joan to do the same." More broadly, Cross observes that "a reverence for books characterizes women in a majority of communities and in several Lollard women took a major part in organizing book distribution."[26]

Throughout the sixteenth and into the early seventeenth century, women continued to play an active role in the development of radical Protestantism. Again, as with their Lollard forebears, their activism focused on texts. In general, as Diane Willen observes, "knowledge of the Bible characterized and underlay strong piety and religious activism of Protestant women just as it did Protestant men." While acquiring knowledge of the Bible may hardly suggest a radical act to modern ears, it certainly did to the ruling authorities in sixteenth-century England. In 1543, Parliament officially restricted access to the Bible along class and gender lines: Both noblemen and noblewomen could read the Bible in private, but only noblemen could read it aloud; and merchant men could read the Bible in private but women of the same class could not. Willen comments that "the crown saw danger in allowing women, even in the context of the family, unlimited use of Scriptures." In 1545, at her first trial for heresy, Anne Askew articulated the threat embodied by a Bible-reading woman. She tells her examiner that only the Bible contains the substance of her beliefs. Her contemporary and fellow dissenter John Bale explained why her privileging of scriptural authority troubled the clerics who examined her: "Se what an horryble synne here was. She alleged the scripture for her beleve, whych is a sore and a daungerouse matter. For it is against the popes cannon lawes, and agaynst the olde customs of holy churche."[27] Askew proved too threatening to the authorities, and, as part of their campaign against heresy, they burned her at the stake in 1546.

While Askew is by far the best known of the early female Protestant reformers, many other women played an active role in advancing scriptural authority. Women, for instance, figure prominently as signatories to a 1571 petition to the Bishop of London urging that the church emphasize biblical teachings: "that the word of our God may be set to rayne and have the hiest place, to rule & reforme all estates and degrees [o]f men." Sarah Jones, when brought before the Court of High Commission in 1632 for participating in a "private Conventicle," similarly promoted the primacy of the Bible's direct commands. In response to her refusal to take an oath, her examiner insists: "This you are Commaunded to doe of God who saith you must obey your Superiours." Her reply: "That which is of God is according to Gods word and the Lord will not hold him guiltlesse that taketh his name in vaine."[28] For Jones, the authority of "Superiours" mattered very little in comparison to that of God. Appeals to the overriding authority of God's command would become one of the women prophets' favored means for justifying their radical and subversive acts.

In addition to that of the women defenders of scriptural authority, the women prophets inherited a second radical Protestant tradition: the exegetical writings of major scriptural scholars on Revelation and Daniel. Long before 1641, when prophecies began to roll off English presses in record numbers, commentaries on Scripture's apocalyptic books had altered the shape of historical thought. For instance, the idea, prevalent among the Revolution's religious radicals, that events in Revelation corresponded to specific historical events first appeared in John Bale's 1550 *The Image of Bothe Churches*. As Bale himself put it, Revelation contains the history of the Protestant church "from Christ's ascension to the end of the world under pleasant figures and elegant tropes decided." In using Revelation to trace the history of Protestantism, Bale uncovered a narrative that explained the historical domination of the true, Protestant Church by corrupt Roman Catholicism. He, for instance, identifies the "woman clothed with the sun" in Revelation 12 as a figure of the true church because she endures a period of trial and exile but remains under God's watchful eye.[29] In Bale's view, Revelation "containeth the universal troubles, persecutions, and crosses, that the church suffered in the primitive spring, what it suffereth now, and what it shall suffer in the latter times by the subtle satellites of antichrist, which are the cruel members of satan."[30]

Beyond providing an explanatory model for the church's "troubles, persecutions, and crosses," Bale's reading of Revelation emphasizes the role of Antichrist as a persecuting force. For Bale, Antichrist's "subtle satellites" included "the pope with his bishops, prelates, priests, and religious in Europe, Mahomet with his doting dousepers in Africa." The figure of Antichrist assumed great prominence during the Revolution as men and women came to identify the clergy of the Church of England and Charles I with this satanic icon. Antichrist became such a powerful rhetorical figure in the period because, according to Christopher Hill, it was an imprecise symbol that "allowed differing interpretations to be put upon it, either by different people or the same person in appealing to different groups. Antichrist stood for bad, repressive, papal institutions: exactly which institutions was anybody's choice." Bale's use of Antichrist would further the development of the "polarized view of the universe" that characterized apocalyptic thought in Tudor and Stuart England.[31]

In addition to promoting the idea of Antichrist, Bale's commentary on Revelation influenced the development of English apocalyptic thought more generally. According to Paul Christianson, his historical vision was integrated "into the two most popular books of Elizabethan and early Stuart England, the Geneva Bible and John Foxe's *Actes and Monuments*." First published in 1560, the Geneva Bible included a line-by-line commentary that incorporated many of Bale's ideas. In his *Actes and Monuments*, first published in English in 1563, Foxe further elaborated Bale's vision of the "two churches" by documenting the plight of the "suffering" Protestant church from the time of the early Christians through the Marian martyrs of his own age.[32] Toward the end of the sixteenth century, the Scottish mathematician John Napier introduced a modification of Bale's historical vision: while Bale traced a "linear pattern of prophecy and its fulfillment in the past," Napier applied those same principles to predicting future events. For instance, based on his claim that "The first Trumpet or Viall began at the Jubilee, in anno Christi 71," Napier calculates "The last Trumpet or Viall beginneth anno Christi 1541 and should end in anno Christi 1786."[33] Following Napier's lead, Thomas Brightman emphasized Revelation's relationship to future events "by projecting a literal reign of the saints on earth for a thousand years, thereby reviving in respectable circles the millennium pursued by the earliest Christians, by medieval heretics, and by sixteenth-century anabaptists." Brightman's commentary on Revelation is also significant for advancing the idea of England as the "elect nation." According to Brightman, England enjoys prosperity because God has willed it: "Thou by heaping so many good things upon us, hast made the world to know, that thy Gospell is not a beggarly or niggardly guest . . . but a very rich and beautifull one."[34]

Bale, Foxe, Napier, and Brightman represent some of the key figures in the scholarly tradition of early modern apocalyptic thought.[35] Many of their ideas about Antichrist, history, and the millennium surfaced in the popular prophetic writings, including those authored by women, that became a prominent feature of the revolutionary era's intellectual landscape. In 1641, the Independent Katherine Chidley likened the orthodox church to Antichrist in order to justify her call to separate from it: "For my owne part, considering that the Church of England is governed by the Canon Lawes (the Discipline of Antichrist) and altogether wanteth the Discipline of Christ . . . I hold it . . . lawfull . . . to separate . . . from them." Some fourteen years later, the Quakers Priscilla Cotton and Mary Cole similarly denounced the established clergy as "idol-Shepherds" and "Antichrist." The Fifth Monarchist Mary Cary cited Thomas Brightman directly in 1651 when she concluded "that this one thousand two hundred and sixty years, in which the Romish Beast was to be permitted to persecute the Church, and to tread it under foot, is very near come to a period." Indeed, by her estimate, the Beast's fortunes started to wane in 1645 when Christ "began to take his kingdome," and she expects the year 1701 to mark "the finall and compleat deliverance of the Church." Her vision of world history extends beyond 1701 to the millennium in which "Christ having subdued his enemies, shall personally appear on earth, and shall raise up the Saints before departed out of this world to come and reign with him on earth."[36] Although the women prophets wrote popular pamphlets rather than scholarly treatises, they appropriated the key tropes and modes of thought that constituted, in Cary's words, the "judgement of all the learned, and godly men that have written, and publisht" on the Bible's apocalyptic books.[37]

Created through a complex of religio-political developments, the female visionaries emerge as one of the most vibrant and exciting forces in the history of women's activism. They wrote treatises in poetry and prose that challenged the authority of Charles I and Oliver Cromwell, advocated women's right to preach, and envisioned life during the millennium. Hardly a group to stay at home and write, women prophets backed up their words with radical deeds: Lady Eleanor installed herself on the Cathedral of Lichfield's throne and declared herself primate and metropolitan; Elizabeth Hooton traveled to America and the Caribbean to advance the Quaker cause; and Dorothy Waugh was bridled for speaking "against all deceit & ungodly practices."[38]

Feminist scholars have long been impressed by the vitality of the female visionaries, but they have debated how and whether to integrate them into the history of feminism.[39] In particular, Hilda Smith's 1982 monograph *Reason's Disciples: Seventeenth-Century English Feminists* has played a significant role in establishing the origins of feminism in the Restoration rather than the English Revolution. Smith argues that the women prophets do not count as early feminists because they do not devote themselves explicitly to attempting to balance the power relationships between men and women: "Thus by seeing women as a sociological group and by using that vision to establish programs and viewpoints which work to end the inequalities in women's status as a group, feminists separate themselves from those who do not concern themselves with changing the lives of all women."[40] Although the women prophets effectively sought to change the gender hierarchy by advancing their own political authority, their "failure" to address themselves self-consciously to righting the inequities of that hierarchy excludes them from Smith's pantheon of early feminists.

While the women prophets do not measure up to Smith's definition of feminism, she determines that many women writing just after the Revolution do. Most of these women—a group that includes Bathsua Makin, Mary Astell, Elizabeth Elstob, Lady Mary Chudleigh, and Anne Finch, Countess of Winchilsea—were identified with the Tory cause and belonged to the gentry or upper classes. As a group, they are often remembered for their writings on improving the education of elite women. Smith is not the only feminist scholar to emphasize early feminism's close ties with Toryism and gentry and upper-class status but has been seconded by Joan K. Kinnaird, Ruth Perry, Catherine Gallagher, and Carol Barash. With the exception of Barash, these scholars imply that time begins with the return of Charles II and so they only minimally, if at all, register the existence of women prophets.[41] For her part, Barash suggests that later pro-monarchist feminists adopted the tropes of the women prophets: "radical Protestant rhetoric appealed to royalist women writers, enabling them to use political and religious obligation to break rules that required women's public silence."[42] Barash, however, sparingly incorporates this observation into her discussion of late seventeenth- and early eighteenth-century women's writings. Even Smith, who excludes the women prophets from her study because their religious beliefs underwrite their activism, vaguely observes that the rhetoric of Civil War radicals may have figured in the writings of her early feminists: "The impact of the revolution on feminist thought, aside from supplying some adaptable rhetoric, was almost wholly negative, reminding those women who opposed its goals that the leaders of the revolution had little interest in improving the status of women within either the home or the state."[43] Their "adaptable rhetoric" notwithstanding, the women prophets are simply not secular enough to count for Smith: "Despite some studies of women in the radical sects of the Civil War, especially Quakers, and some works on women's treatment by political theorists and Puritan writers, almost no attention has been given to women's having developed an independent criticism of their situation outside of the revolutionary and religious ideologies and groupings formed between 1640 and 1660 and later during the Glorious Revolution."[44] Smith defines feminism as a secular movement and so cannot accept the possibility that sectarian religious beliefs may have given birth to women's political self-consciousness.

On the opposite side of the fence, the feminist scholar Elaine Hobby views the emergence of Restoration "feminists," such as Makin and Astell who emphasized women's education, as marking a decided retreat from the political engagement of the revolutionary era. She deems tepid the "carefully qualified arguments for women's education" that Smith considers the foundation of early feminism, and she laments the "loss of visionary potential of the revolutionary years."[45] More broadly, Hobby observes that the rise of the nuclear family and the relegation of women to the domestic sphere deprived women of the opportunities for collective activism they had enjoyed during the revolutionary era.[46] For Hobby, time in terms of women's visionary and political potential effectively stops with the return of Charles II to the throne.[47] Indeed, as she opines of Bathsua Makin's apology for women's education, *An Essay to Revive the Antient Education of Gentlewomen*, to be associated with the monarch in the Restoration is to be capable of only a limited radicalism: "A close ally of the returned monarchists, Makin in no way supports or identifies with the rebellious women who had fought for the ending of the hierarchy and kingly power, and called for the abolition of the universities and book learning."[48] For Hobby, the religious enthusiasm of the women prophets does not derogate their activism but rather makes it far more "rebellious" than the staid protests of Smith's secular feminists.

As compared to Hobby and Smith, who specify the greatest achievements in seventeenth-century women's political activism as occurring on opposite sides of the historical divide marked by the year 1660, Phyllis Mack pursues the middle way and explores the continuities between these two groups of early women activists. On the one hand, she concurs with Hobby in the sense that she regards the most radical elements of women's prophecy as possessed of a limited historical tenure. For instance, in discussing the deliberate mellowing of Restoration Quakerism, she observes that the ecstasies associated with the sect's early days were only possible for a short time: "their concern for a more sustained experience of walking (as well as resting) in the light meant that the mind must inevitably become more important and the body less so, for the attainment of a perfection that would stand both the test of time and the world's scrutiny depended more on the capacity for self-analysis than it did on the capacity to shed inhibitions." Unlike Hobby, she does not see this development strictly in terms of "loss": the Quakers did not jettison visionary experience altogether but rather attempted "to contain it within a rational and orderly context."[49] Mack's interest in the interplay between enthusiastic and socially conservative elements calls attention to the rationalist and proto-bourgeois overtones that surfaced in the writings of religious radicals even prior to the advent of Restoration Quakerism.[50] As Mack has observed, the rational and enthusiastic are not mutually exclusive. Indeed, in her mind, seventeenth-century Quakerism's legacy to modern feminism rests in that sect's decision to reconcile rational and enthusiastic strains: "Quaker women of a much later period, those who inspired and organized the movements of abolition and women's suffrage, appear to have drawn on both the early tradition of egalitarian worship and the later tradition of formal organization and bourgeois womanhood."[51]

While Mack, Hobby, and Smith assess the feminism of the women prophets in terms of politics, I analyze their politics in terms of the history of female sexuality.[52] Like these scholars, I am interested in identifying the position of the women prophets in feminist history, but I seek to do so by examining how they reconciled their female sexuality with the terms of political power. They develop a politics of female sexuality that enables them to predicate their authority as political speakers and actors not in terms of difference but in terms of the uniqueness of the female body. Their efforts to interpolate female sexuality into the political sphere represent the beginnings of what I take to be feminist consciousness—namely, the recognition that women as women can effect political change. This development is unique to the revolutionary period and is more politically dynamic than the agenda of Smith's Restoration feminists. At the same time, the women prophets' struggle to "engender"—in the sense of both "to produce" and "to write gender into"—political authority directly anticipates Smith's feminism of women's rights. I do not then reject Smith's definition of feminism out of hand but maintain, like Mack, that secular feminism can trace its roots back to the religiously based activism of the women prophets. At the same time, however, I remain committed, like Hobby, to illustrating the women prophets' particular contribution to the history of women's political activism.

In my view, one of the most distinctive features of the women prophets is their representation of female sexuality. Lady Eleanor, Trapnel, and Fell reveal a shift away from defining female sexuality in terms of men and toward comprehending it as ontologically separate. This development evokes Thomas Laquer's theory of the rise of the two sex model. According to Laquer, it was not until the eighteenth century that people began to perceive male and female as sexual opposites. Prior to this period, male and female were viewed as linked by shared sexual traits. The vagina, for instance, was described as an inverted penis, and while related to the male sexual organ, it was believed inferior to the male original. Laquer identifies this older perceptual mode as the one sex model and ties the transition from the one sex to the two sex model to the philosophical shift from traditional ideas of order to the new emphasis on the individual: "the old model, in which men and women were arrayed according to their degree of metaphysical perfection, their vital heat, along an axis whose telos was male, gave way by the late eighteenth century to a new model of radical dimorphism, of biological divergence. An anatomy and physiology of incommensurability replaced a metaphysics of hierarchy in the representation of women in relation to men."[53] Rather than being seen as inferior versions of men, women emerged as distinct beings possessed of an entirely dif-

ferent sex. As for the women visionaries I discuss, Lady Eleanor
views her sexual identity in terms akin to the one sex model,
while Trapnel and Fell consider their sexual identities in terms
closer to that of the two sex model. Still, the politics of sexual
difference cannot properly be said to be theirs. (As I argue in the
epilogue, the politics of sexual difference did belong to the late
seventeenth- and early eighteenth-century feminist Mary Astell.) Rather, they articulate a more fluid politics of female sexuality that privileges the attributes of the female body more as
positive than as differentiating possessions. And this, it seems to
me, is the unique political achievement of the Civil War era female prophets.

As distinct from Laquer's two sex model, the politics of female
sexuality that Trapnel and Fell develop focus on their bodies as
material possessions. Both women viewed their capacity for direct communication with the divine to be related to their female
bodies. Their sexuality, in other words, was a material entity
through which they could lay claim to divine and hence political
authority. Their sense of their bodies as possessions that could
instantiate divine authority evokes C. B. Macpherson's use of
"possession" in his theory of "possessive individualism." He argues that seventeenth-century individualism's "possessive quality is found in its conception of the individual as essentially the
proprietor of his own person or capacities, owing nothing to society for them." Self-proprietorship becomes for seventeenth-
century men and women a form of political self-definition. The
Leveller concept of individualism, for instance, depends upon
their belief that "freedom" is "a function of proprietorship. The
essential humanity of the individual consisted in his freedom
from the will of other persons, freedom to enjoy his own person
and to develop his own capacities." According to Macpherson,
the Levellers saw self-propriety in real, material terms: "One's
person was property not metaphorically but essentially: the
property one had in it was the right to exclude others from its
use and enjoyment."[54] Women prophets appealed to their bodies
for a complex of political reasons. They were sites of power but
they also became for these women real properties through which
they could establish their political identities. In other words,
women who no longer derived their political identity from their
roles as wives and mothers began, in some cases, to establish it
in terms of their bodies.

While Trapnel and Fell appealed to their bodies to establish
their prophetic authority, the earlier Civil War prophet Lady El-

eanor invoked her position in the patriarchal order to justify her right to convey God's Word. Lady Eleanor founded her prophetic vocation on the failure of traditional institutions such as the monarchy to preserve order: she blamed men for England's political turmoil and maintained that God was punishing the nation by sending a female, rather than a male, prophet. In many senses, hers is a prophetic career devoted to mourning the passing of old social structures. And for this reason her story is essential to understanding the ways in which Trapnel and Fell would come to justify their callings. Lady Eleanor gives us insight into the demise of the political structures upon which Trapnel and Fell would constitute new models of authority. I emphasize Lady Eleanor's connectedness to this larger narrative because she is often regarded as an anomaly among women prophets—she did not belong to a sect, she was a member of the aristocracy, and she financed the publication of her tracts herself. Her atypical social circumstances notwithstanding, Lady Eleanor presents an astute commentary on the chaos of her times, and so I begin with this extraordinary prophet.

1

In the Name of the Father: Divine Right and Women's Rights

The King towards his people is rightly compared to a father
of children, and to a head of a bodie composed of divers members.
— James VI, *The True Lawe of Free Monarchies* (1598)

৯ৣ৯

IN 1655, LORENZO PAULUCCI, THE VENETIAN SECRETARY TO ENGLAND,
commented on the public debate over whether the Protector, Oliver Cromwell, should take the crown: "that as England has always been ruled by a monarch and all its fundamental laws are
instituted in consideration of that, the affairs of the realm cannot
proceed with the necessary smoothness in the absence of a king,
and the laws lack the force imparted to them by the royal assent."[1] For Paulucci, as for many English, it did not seem incon-
gruous to suggest that one of the generals who had played an
instrumental role in putting Charles I to death should himself assume the title of king. According to historian Howard Nenner, the
pressure for Cromwell to declare himself king was fueled by anxieties about the nation's political stability: "As long as there were
questions about the constitutional limits of the Protector's power
and a disquieting uncertainty about who would succeed him, confidence in long-term political stability remained significantly im-
paired."[2] Although since 1642 when Parliament refused to cede
control over the Army to Charles, England was moving in the direction of representative government; the transition was far
from smooth and direct. In 1657, Parliament formally offered
Cromwell the crown, and in 1660 a relieved nation greeted
Charles II upon his return.

As the very fact of the Restoration suggests, the heady years
of the English Revolution found many cleaving to the idea that
monarchy was fundamental to political order and individual identity. Writing shortly after Charles's execution in 1649, the Royal-

35

ist poet John Cleveland would wonder how he could exist now that his king was dead:

> If *dead men* did not *walk*, t'would be admir'd
> (The *Breath* of all our *Nostrils* thus *expir'd*)
> What 'tis that gives us *motion*, And can I,
> Who want *my self* write *Him* an Elegie.[3]

While we might expect this sort of lament from a Royalist, we also find profound expressions of allegiance to the idea of monarchy in the works of radicals such as William Sedgwick. Although sympathetic to the Army's cause, he denounced their *Remonstrance* of late 1648 for its assault upon the King: "This love you know not, that embraces God and the King, and King and people in one body." More famously, the poet and republican sympathizer Andrew Marvell expressed ambivalence over the demise of Charles and the rise of new forms of power in "*An* Horatian *Ode* upon Cromwell's *Return from* Ireland." Marvell's image of Charles submitting to the executioner's block as bowing "his comely head,/Down, as upon a bed" while surrounded by "the armed Bands" who "clap their bloody hands" and thus usher in "the forced Pow'r" suggests sympathy for the deceased king and anxiety about the new order that has replaced him.[4]

Clearly, during the English Revolution, holding radical religious or political views did not necessarily imply the repudiation of monarchy. Moreover, even being to varying degrees opposed to the continued existence of a given king or of the institution of monarchy itself did not necessarily preclude one from identifying oneself in terms of monarchy. This was certainly true of one of the most controversial women prophets of the period, Lady Eleanor Davies. She published some 69 prophetic treatises between 1625 and 1652, many of which denounced Charles I. As early as 1633, Lady Eleanor had likened Charles, in her *Given to the Elector*, to the doomed Babylonian king Belshazzar. In a later edition of this same tract, she suggests a variation on Belshazzar's name, "Belchaser," as an anagram for "Charles Be" signifying "Charles Beheaded."[5] Her hostility toward Charles notwithstanding, Lady Eleanor revealed herself to be an ardent admirer of his father, James I. She regarded James, who died in 1625 shortly before she published her first tract, as the muse of her prophetic writings because he epitomized the virtues of divine right. He was, both in his and her eyes, "Gods lieutenant in earth."[6]

The idea of divine right together with Lady Eleanor's admiration for James plays a central role in the way she constitutes her prophetic identity. This is most apparent in her early tracts of 1625 to 1641. Representing a small but crucial part of her *oeuvre*, Lady Eleanor's early tracts illustrate how she invokes James to create her political signature as a prophet. She begins by lamenting James's death and memorializing him as a prophet-king who shares with her an intimate tie to the Word. Over time, however, she makes his the voice that calls her to prophesy. James is no longer merely an inspired king but the embodiment of divinity itself. So powerful is the memory of James that it plays a second role in shaping her prophetic authority. By identifying his daughter Elizabeth, Queen of Bohemia, and not Charles as James' heir, Lady Eleanor begins to imagine herself, the daughter of a noble father, as the heir to the power and privilege associated with her patronymic. In so doing, she counters her contemporaries' dim view of female inheritance rights and confers the capacity to share in the power of the father's name on the broad category of daughters as well as the daughters of kings.[7]

The early years of Lady Eleanor's prophetic career provide a prism through which we can see how old models of political authority continued to inform the establishment of even the most radical authorial positions—that of the female prophet. Lady Eleanor, in essence, takes traditional ideas of divine right and patriarchal inheritance and reshapes them to suit her needs. In this way, she contributes to her contemporaries' growing belief that individuals could construct a political system rather than merely comprehend their position in a predetermined hierarchy. As Donald W. Hanson puts it: "men [and women] were competent . . . they could deliberately undertake the creation of a political system designed to satisfy their preferences and to reconcile or at least contain their differences."[8] Lady Eleanor represents an early stage of this new development, even as she relies heavily on the traditional political forms of monarchy and patriarchy to build her model of female authority. She can be deemed politically creative, nevertheless, because she departs radically from patriarchy's focus on the transmission of power from man to man. Aligned with patriarchy yet advancing a model of female authority, her work marks the earliest stages in the emergence of female political self-consciousness.

PROPHETS AND KINGS

Like the eighteenth-century poet Christopher Smart, Lady Eleanor has been chiefly remembered for being mad and for writing in a nearly incomprehensible idiom. She began to earn a reputation for madness when, in a move that "much unbeseemed her Sex,"[9] she launched her prophetic career in 1625 by professing to have determined the end of time prefigured but not accurately predicted in Daniel. Prior to publishing her revelations, she lived much as a typical aristocratic woman. She was born in 1590 to George Touchet, Baron Audeley, and his wife Lucy. In 1609, her father arranged her first marriage to the poet and prominent barrister, Sir John Davies. She bore three children to Davies, only one of whom, her daughter Lucy, survived into adulthood. Following Davies's death in 1626, she married the professional soldier Sir Archibald Douglas in 1627. These details aside, however, Lady Eleanor led an extraordinary life. She made astonishing predictions regarding the end of time, the death of her first husband, and the demise of King Charles I; she traveled to Amsterdam to publish her treatises; she occupied the bishop's throne at Lichfield Cathedral and declared herself primate and metropolitan; and she spent years in prison. Upon her death in 1652, her daughter Lucy commemorated Lady Eleanor's life with an epitaph testifying to her mother's unswerving commitment to her prophetic vocation: "In a woman's body a man's spirit, In most adverse circumstances a serene mind, In a wicked age unshaken piety and uprightness. Not for her did Luxury relax her strong soul, or Poverty narrow it: but each lot with equal countenance And mind, she not only took but ruled."[10]

Because she pursued her calling with such passion and enthusiasm, Lady Eleanor, like Margaret Cavendish later in the century, would find herself deemed mad by a society that ridiculed and chastised women who deviated from the constraining norms of modest femininity. Joining in the clamor of Lady Eleanor's early modern opponents, some early twentieth-century scholars have identified her as insane.[11] More recent criticism does not emphasize her madness but focuses on her unique status among women prophets of the period. As distinct from the female visionaries who emerged in increasing numbers beginning in the 1640s, Lady Eleanor launched her career earlier (in the 1620s), belonged to an aristocratic family, and lacked a specific church or sectarian affiliation.[12] In addition, she is remembered for being the most prolific female visionary.[13] Finally, she has been deemed a failed apocalyptic writer whose need to authorize her calling over and over again prevented her from producing the sorts of calls to action typical of her male contemporaries.[14]

One of the signature features of Lady Eleanor's prophetic writings is their complex and densely allusive prose style. In the early 1930s, S. G. Wright described her prose as having "achieved an obscurity of meaning and a freedom from syntax" that was caused by "a definite mental weakness." Her biographer Esther S. Cope, however, takes her prose style more seriously and provides a useful analysis of its form and function: "She ordinarily wrote in the third rather than the first person, strung phrases together, often omitted subjects or verbs, shifted abruptly from the biblical to the historical or personal, and so packed the tracts with anagrams, puns, and complex images that their seemingly inscrutable message demonstrated graphically how the unbeliever could not understand the wisdom of the prophet." While her tracts effectively "demonstrated . . . how the unbeliever could not understand the wisdom of the prophet," Lady Eleanor portrayed her writings as clarifying the mysteries of the Bible: "Witness (Cor. 4) *Therefore judge nothing before the time of the Lords coming, who will lighten things hid in darkness.* Namely the same *Spirit* by which they were *Pen'd* or *Written*, to be explained. Of which *refreshing Times* the Spirit again pour'd out."[15] She possesses the "same Spirit by which they [biblical texts] were Pen'd or Written" and so is particularly qualified to unlock their secrets. Of course, professing to clarify Scripture and writing clearly can certainly be two distinct achievements. Lady Eleanor never really characterizes her prose style *per se*, but at one point, she provides the briefest glimpse of how she sees it operating: "And one thus unfolding another."[16] In this particular instance, she catalogues the multiple sins of her enemy Archbishop Laud and suggests they are so intertwined that to speak of one is to begin to address a second, then a third, and so on. For Lady Eleanor, the world is an overladen place, and her capacity to see relationships between apparently disparate topics makes her dense and allusive prose into an echo chamber that continuously resonates her key themes.

The case of Lady Eleanor's literary relationship to the memory of James illustrates one feature of her densely intertwined style: her interest in repeatedly returning to and developing further images she has used previously. (Indeed, the best way to comprehend Lady Eleanor's complex imagery in any given text is to have read all of the treatises that have preceded it.) While Lady Eleanor produces the majority of her texts after the easing of censorship restrictions in 1641, it is in her earliest treatises, published between 1625 and 1641, that the figure of James appears as a seminal influence on the way she constitutes her prophetic identity. James, however, does not initially appear as the muse of her calling. In 1625, in *A Warning to the Dragon and All his Angels*, she simply claims to have been inspired by God and predicts that "There is nineteene yeares and a halfe to the day of Judgement, [from] July the 28. M.DC.XXV."[17] (Her later texts identify the execution of William Laud, Archbishop of Canterbury, in January of 1645 as ringing in the "day of Judgement" anticipated by *Warning*.)[18]

After the publication of *Warning* in 1625, she increasingly makes James the source of her authority. While she had originally insisted that she gained knowledge of future events through laborious study, by the time she produces *The Lady Eleanor, Her Appeale* in 1641, she professes to have learned about the "nineteene yeares" from a "Heavenly voyce." Imprisoned twice between 1625 and 1641, her personal experience of persecution clearly contributes to this new emphasis on her direct contact with a voice from above. Her sufferings teach her that as a woman she must link her authority to a concrete connection with the divine rather than to the workings of her own brain. Still, the "Heavenly voyce" does not come as a simple antidote to her plight but as the product of her meditations on James. Lady Eleanor's mourning for James resembles that of the Hebrew prophet Isaiah who replaces the secular presence of a beloved king with a vision of the face of God. Isaiah receives his call around the time that King Uzziah dies: "In the year that king Uzziah died I saw also the Lord sitting upon a throne, high and lifted up, and his train filled the temple . . . Also I heard the voice of the Lord, saying, Whom shall I send, and who will go for us? Then said I, Here *am* I; send me."[19] Signs of monarchy predominate in Isaiah's vision and suggest that the prophet substitutes God's heavenly "train" for Uzziah's earthly "train." Over time, Lady Eleanor will make a similar substitution as she moves from regarding James as a fellow prophet to making his the divine voice that authorizes her calling.

In her first tract, *Warning*, however, Lady Eleanor invokes James not as the muse of her calling but as the ideal muse of his son's reign. She holds James up to his newly crowned heir, Charles, as an example of the best kind of monarch and dedicates her exegesis of the last six books of Daniel to the new king in the hopes that he, like his father, will serve as the "Defender of the Faith" (6). The shade of James is omnipresent, and, as Cope tells us, Lady Eleanor had planned to present her exegetical treatise on the last six books of Daniel to James himself but was prevented from doing so by his death on 27 March 1625. (Instead, she presented it to Archbishop Abbot "whose evangelical Calvinism and intense opposition to Rome" promised "to make him sympathetic to what she said.")[20] In *Warning*, she celebrates James as a prophet-king who, she implies, kept his nation from falling into the spiritual torpor that has beset others: "for the [British] Isles [under James's leadership] feared the Judgement of the Lord and saw [or responded to] it"(22). She compares James's efforts to suppress the great bugbear of seventeenth-century English Protestants, Roman Catholicism, to the angel Michael's struggle against Satan:

> After these dayes were past, there was warre in Heaven; MICHAEL and his Angells, fought against the Dragon and the Dragon fought, and his Angells the Jesuites, and prevailed not, neither was their place found any more in Heaven.
> Heaven is here taken in this place for the Church of God, the fray is fought by seconds, by MICHAEL is meant King JAMES; The Dragon needs little exposition, It is the Pope, for MICHAEL overcame by the blood of the Lambe, and by the testimony of so many Bishops, and other faithfull, crowned with the Glory of Martyrdome. (32–33)[21]

Lady Eleanor maintains that she compares James's efforts against the Pope to Michael's contention with Satan because the dead king's attacks exhibited a superhuman quality: "this Prince ... fought the battell of the Lord, more like an Angell than a Mortall Man"(33).

In contriving her image of James as a warrior against Papists, Lady Eleanor may have been influenced by his *A Paraphrase Upon the Revelation of the Apostle S. John*. There, James identifies Revelation as "a speciall canon against the Hereticall wall of our common adversaries the Papists."[22] Moreover, his *Paraphrase* is notable if not for identifying him with a superhuman biblical personage, for likening him to the prophet John. James assumes the voice of John in order, allegedly, to make "the Discourse more short and facile," but, in fact, by doing so he gains the ability to transpose the authority of the prophet's name onto his own royal name through the first person pronoun: "it is for the making of the Discourse more short and facile, that I have made JOHN to be the speaker in all this Paraphrase; and not that I am so presumptuously foolish, as to have meant thereby, that my Paraphrase is the onely trew and certaine exposition of this Epistle, rejecting all others: For although through speaking

in his person, I am onely bounded and limitted to use one, and
not divers interpretations, of every severall place."[23] As Jonathan
Goldberg's *James I and the Politics of Literature* has taught us,
James was not one to represent his authority as "bounded and
limitted" in any way. Moreover, he shrewdly incorporates his
unique approach to Revelation within the anti-Rome polemic of
his text: by "speaking in his [John's] person," James may be suggesting that his interpretation eschews the "divers interpretations, of every severall place" espoused by the fourfold method
of the Catholic Church.[24] For James, the polemical objectives of
Protestant scriptural exegesis enable him to enhance his stature
as a sacred and secular authority. By appropriating the "I" of
John as a means of interpreting Revelation, James links prophetic and monarchical authority to assert, effectively, that his
"Paraphrase is the onely trew and certaine exposition of" John.
While James fashions himself as the "prophet-king," he does not
announce himself as such because, as Goldberg argues, his
writings "exercise the discourse of power and the power of discourse."[25] Although "bounded and limitted to use one" interpretation, he speaks in the name of John and juxtaposes the
authority of that name with his own. Even as James stops short
of endowing himself with visionary powers, he does, in his *Paraphrase*, constitute himself as larger than life. Lady Eleanor's portrait of James then expands upon James's own grandiose claims
to divine authority.

While Lady Eleanor imagines the roles of prophets and kings
as overlapping, she still maintains that each accedes to power
through distinct means. Kings, in her view and that of James, receive authority through lineal descent.[26] As she celebrates
Charles's potential in *Warning*, she links his potential for success to his being James's son: "And God make the name and
Throne, of the King of his Sonne, better, and greater then his"
(33). She predicts that Charles will preside over a period of history, as described in Daniel 12, in which "a time of trouble" will
give way to deliverance and the dawning of the millennium. As a
result, Charles like his father before him will assume the role of
Michael: "And at that time shall MICHAEL stand up, the great
Prince that defends the Faith, CHARLES King of Great *Britaine,
France,* and *Ireland,* which standeth for the faithfull Children of
our Nation, the Saints of the most Highest" (48). Clearly, she is
enthusiastic about Charles because she hopes that he, like his
father, will emerge as a superhuman defender of the faith. That
Lady Eleanor sees Charles's potential for greatness in conjunc-

tion with his father's legacy is further illustrated by the anagram "JAMES, CHARLES,—ARE MICHAELSS" (48). Her anagram implies that without the name of James, Charles could not be a Michael.

She reenforces her belief that the best sons resemble their powerful fathers when she represents Christ's death in terms of a state funeral for a beloved prince: "The whole Globe Mourning in Sable blacknesse, except Man, at the dreadfull Funerall of this most mighty Prince . . . the true light of Men, by mankinde was so ungratefully and unkindely extinguished, the expresse Pure Image of the Maker, the Prince of life, The Person of God, (not made) turn'd to a lumpe of Clay, by a shameless accusation, an unjust sentence, and a cursed Executioner" (40). Although in rendering the portrait of Christ's state funeral Lady Eleanor doubtless refers to the funeral for James that has recently transpired, her description uncannily anticipates the way Royalists will liken the circumstances of Charles's execution to those of Christ.[27] For Lady Eleanor, the tragedy of Christ's execution is that he was "the expresse Pure Image of the Maker . . . The Person of God." Similarly, she hopes that Charles will also be the "Pure Image" of his "Maker." Ultimately, Charles will fail her, but she will transfer her portrait of his noble paternity to herself to claim that her father's aristocratic status underwrites her prophetic authority.

In *Warning*, however, Lady Eleanor does not yet establish her right to prophesy in the language of patriarchal power but explicates her authority in the terms of prophetic discourse alone. She emphasizes not her social status but her knowledge as the cornerstone of her legitimacy: "having a perfect understanding" she deems herself called "to roote out, to pull downe, to build, and to plant"(2). Moreover, she is: "Pressed and constrained with obedience to him, and Duty towards you; saying no other things then the Prophets and Apostles did say should come to passe, that yee might know the certainty of those things, wherein yee have beene instructed, whether you will heare or whether you will forbeare" (2–3). In comparison with other female authors of the period, she does not expend a great deal of energy justifying her status as a woman writer. Rather, she insists that her special knowledge leaves her, or any other similarly knowing woman, no option but to speak: "Former things are come to passe, and new things I declare unto you; no age so weake, nor sex excusing; when the Lord shall send and will put his words in their Mouth" (2). The special character of the times, she warns her readers, warrants a kind of gender blind attitude, especially when it comes to messages of apocalyptic doom. She reenforces her point by alluding to the apocalyptic passages in Joel that correlate women's inspired speech with the last days: "He powreth out his Spirit upon his handmaidens; the rich are sent emptie away, even so Father for it seemed good in thy sight" (2).[28]

Although she clearly feels compelled to justify her authority as a female visionary, she does so without apology and with a confidence born of apocalyptic pragmatism. She is so certain of her authority that she prophesies although, as she herself acknowledges, she cannot yet shore up her assertions with a "Signe": "Least any should thinke of me above or better then he seeth me to be, as others to suspect a forged passe; To present you with Pearles of that sort or holy things, I forbeare at this time" (4). (While *Warning* itself did not contain a "Signe," the short text she claims to have appended to the copy she presented to Archbishop Abbot did. In it, as she records in a later treatise, she predicted the end of the plague that besieged London in the summer of 1625: "and with this Signe annext to it, That the great Plague presently should cease, which came but to its height the next Week after.")[29]

Lady Eleanor's definition of prophecy itself bears comment. Nigel Smith describes her prophetic writings as melding traditional forms of prediction with scriptural exegesis: she "follows the popular tradition of using forms of knowledge, astrology, numerology, and the significance of particular letters, as well as scriptural exegesis to interpret contemporary events." He also observes that Lady Eleanor, as compared with later sectarian prophets, is more concerned with knowledge of God than with the experience of God's presence. Still, Lady Eleanor is more scholarly and more radically Protestant than Smith's description suggests. For instance, the popular tradition of numerology she invokes derives from an influential scholarly source. John Napier, known today as the developer of logarithims, applied mathematical methods to the Book of Revelation to calculate that the "day of Gods judgment appears to fall betwixt the yeares of Christ, 1688 and 1700."[30] His emphasis on forecasting future events would significantly influence the millenarian tenor of the apocalyptic writing that gained prominence during the English Revolution.[31]

In the tradition of Napier, Lady Eleanor boldly predicts that "nineteene years and a halfe" remain until the "day of Judgement": "Last of all, the whole world is numbred and those that worke abomination therein, and the delights thereof, weighed in the balances, are found lighter then vanitie it selfe. There is nineteene yeares and a halfe to the day of Judgement, July the 28. M.DC.XXV. Sixe hundred and threescore Moneths [55 years] are excluded, from this last Age of seventeene hundred yeares" (55–56). July 28, 1625 may represent the date when she either receives her call, as it does in later texts, or calculates the year (1645) of the "day of Judgement." Her text corroborates a reading of her dating of the "day of Judgement" as a divinely inspired, intellectual accomplishment by including the interpretation of the final vision of Daniel in a list of the achievements of the modern age: "though many shall run too and fro by the Art of Navigation, discovering an other Hemisphere, Sayling by the Compasse and the Needle, found out by expert men, and knowledge increased, furnishing Magnificent Libraries with printed Bookes, By which two Arts, chiefly the Gospel shall be published to all Nations; yet the Character of this Booke shall not be read, till the time of the end" (50).[32] Although she marvels at the potential capacity of the "Arts" of printing and navigation to convert the heathen, she implies that the achievements of "expert men" pale before hers which marks "the time of the end."[33] Her first treatise locates her reading of Daniel in the forefront of scientific progress and presumes that her special knowledge alone establishes her authority.

Lady Eleanor's self-presentation in *Warning* as an inspired reader of Scripture evokes a second understanding of prophecy: the Puritan belief that prophecy is "the interpretation or expounding of Scriptures." Her emphasis on scriptural exegesis follows in the tradition of prophecy established by such influential commentaries on Revelation as that of Thomas Brightman. In his *Revelation of Saint John*, Brightman sets out, in terms that resemble those used by Lady Eleanor, the prophetic role of adept exegetes: "For the Lord . . . inlighteneth the minds of his servants, that they may be able to search out the hidden truth of his word, and to bring it forth into the open world. Now, he with whom the Lord doth in this manner communicate his counsailes, cannot but see a necessity lying upon him, to declare abroad unto others, what he hath received."[34] In addition to the certainty of its pronouncements, Brightman's text contains one of the more famous typological readings of Scripture to emerge from the early modern English canon of apocalyptic writings. He likens the Church of England to the Laodicean Church described by John and urges the English to pursue the work of reform with greater enthusiasm: to be "either all *Romish*" or "admit a ful *reformation*."[35] Typological readings found in texts such as Brightman's profoundly influenced the radical sectarians of the revolutionary period. Moreover, his view that the seventeenth century represented a dramatic period of history which would see the fall of the Romish Antichrist contributed to the apocalyptic and millenarian fervor that characterized the revolutionary era. Brightman's *Revelation* was first published in Amsterdam in 1615; but once censorship restrictions broke down in England in the 1640s it was reprinted numerous times and widely circulated.[36] Lady Eleanor's *Warning*, with its typological readings and predictions of apocalypse, belongs squarely in the exegetical tradition of Brightman that would underwrite the later work of many of the sectarians. It remains the case that Lady Eleanor's writings lack the emphasis on the experience of divine presence which marks the writings of John Bunyan and Anna Trapnel. Nevertheless, she participates in the tradition of scriptural exegesis that gives rise to those personal readings of scripture. Where Brightman and Lady Eleanor once considered scripture as delineating the course of human history, the sectarians would increasingly come to view it as articulating the order of personal history.

In addition to scriptural exegesis and numerology, the third way Lady Eleanor instantiates her prophetic authority is through anagrams. The most famous of these is "REVEALE O DANIEL" which she derives from the letters of her maiden name "Eleanor Audeley" (6). In *Warning*, she devises a second anagram "O A Sure Daniel" that is based on the letters of her married name, "Eleanor Davies" (5). As Clement Hawes has observed, the use of anagrams by Lady Eleanor and other radical visionaries articulates a "sense of the total immanence of God in language." Thus, Lady Eleanor's anagrams serve to make the point that, by virtue of her name, she simply *is* an heir to the prophetic legacy of Daniel. While Smith rightly describes anagrams as part of a "popular tradition of using forms of knowledge . . . to interpret contemporary events," Hawes, by way of Jackson I. Cope, illustrates how such wordplay can also articulate Puritan reading strategies: "The most crucial authority for such extreme linguistic essentialism is, as Jackson I. Cope observes, the opening of the Johannine Gospel: 'In the beginning was the Word, and the Word was with God, and the Word was God' (John 1:1). It is a dwelling on the Word that leads Puritans to a dwelling on words and their hidden meanings, their homonyms, their roots and punning associations: it both assumes and constitutes a sacred language that claims access to essential reality."[37] Because Lady Eleanor was clearly devoted to close study of the Word, her use of anagrams can also be seen as linking her to radical Protestant modes of legitimation.

In *Warning*, Lady Eleanor strikes out on a markedly different path from that pursued by most women writers of her generation but one that is hardly unusual for late sixteenth- and early seventeenth-century prophets. She focuses less on her gender than on the significance of her message, and she justifies her prophetic authority using means that would have been familiar to major figures—Napier and Brightman—of the English tradition of apocalyptic writing. Perhaps more than any other of her treatises, *Warning* strongly communicates Lady Eleanor's relationship to the canon of apocalyptic writing. This connection is important because critical assessments of Lady Eleanor often regard her as a literary anomaly. A case in point is Megan Matchinske's "Holy Hatred: Formations of the Gendered Subject in English Apocalyptic Writing, 1625–1651." Matchinske defines apocalyptic writing as activist literature and then proceeds to document why Lady Eleanor's gender prevents her from fully engaging the genre. The problem with Lady Eleanor's tracts, according to Matchinske, is that they "do not rally her readers to action" and "rarely involve much direct interaction with her identified audience." Matchinske contends that apocalyptic writing, such as Lady Eleanor's, which emphasizes interpretation over calls to action does not serve.[38] Her definition of apocalyptic writing overlooks what Bernard McGinn terms the essentially "'bookish' nature of the revealed message."[39] Books, after all, figure prominently in the two biblical texts—Daniel and Revelation—that underwrote the English apocalyptic tradition.[40] Further, apocalyptic is a mode that literally cries out for interpretation: "The visionary character of apocalypse as a genre guarantees that apocalypses make heavy use of symbols as a means of communicating their hidden message." As the title of one of the most important early modern interpretations of Revelation—Joseph Mede's *The Key of the Revelation* — suggests, apocalypses are like puzzles. Indeed, Mede described his book as "a clear Scheme presented to view; that it may be as a sure guide to those that are conversant in this holy Labyrinth, and a Touchstone for the finding out of the true interpretation and disproving of the false."[41] Because Lady Eleanor launches her career in 1625, she participates in the tradition of apocalyptic writing espoused by Napier, Brightman, and Mede that provides the foundation for the work of later, activist practitioners of the genre.[42]

The paradox of Lady Eleanor is that although she holds fast to traditional forms of apocalyptic writing and political authority, she emerges as one of the most truly visionary prophets of her generation. She begins her prophetic career in 1625 by mourning the death of a king and in so doing foregrounds the labor of separating from monarchy that consumes England throughout the seventeenth century. One way to account for Lady Eleanor's uncanny visionary sensibility is to consider her, in Claude Levi-Strauss's terms, as a "bricoleur." Like a "bricoleur," Lady Eleanor appeals to a limited set of materials to frame her response to her contemporary situation. In her case, the materials she uses consist of older ideas of apocalypticism and social hierarchy. The explanatory models she devises, like those of the bricoleur, represent the reordering of the materials in her "treasury": "He [the bricoleur] interrogates all the heterogeneous objects of which his treasury is composed to discover what each of them could 'signify' and so contribute to the definition of a set which has yet to materialize but which will ultimately differ from the instrumental set only in the internal disposition of its parts."[43] As someone who reworks old materials, Lady Eleanor can hardly be deemed an innovative thinker yet it is for precisely this reason that she so eloquently articulates the temper of her times. By speaking the language of Brightman and James I, whose legacies would be radically redefined in the Civil War era, she attempts to comprehend the vast changes sweeping English society in terms of the figures and ideas that underwrite them. Ultimately, it is her acute understanding of this older language that places her in the thick of things during the English Revolution.

IN THE NAME OF THE FATHER

After the publication of *Warning* in 1625, Lady Eleanor increasingly found herself at odds with its dedicatee, Charles. In 1628, she accurately predicted the month of the assassination of the King's most trusted advisor, George Villiers, Duke of Buckingham. As a result, she earned fame as "a Cunning Woman amongst the ignorant people" and the fear and disdain of Charles. Shortly after her successful prognostication, she moved to St. James to be near the Court so that she could proclaim the end of time or, as she puts it, "pressing Great *Britains* blow." Her move antagonized Charles, and he sent one of his servants to determine what she had "to do with his affairs" and to warn her that if she "desisted not, he would take another course."[44] For her part, Lady Eleanor had complained that Charles betrayed the class privilege of the aristocracy when, in 1631, he failed to spare the life of her brother, Mervin Touchet, the Earl of Castlehaven, who had been found guilty of ordering the rape of his wife and of sodomizing a male servant.[45] Indeed, in her 1633 broadside *Woe to the House*, she vilifies Charles as an Ahab who ruthlessly conspires to murder her brother, an innocent Naboth. The fact that she traveled to Amsterdam to find a printer willing to publish her broadside together with *All the kings of the earth shall prayse thee* and *Given to the Elector* further underscores the controversy surrounding her nascent vocation.[46]

Of the three texts she had printed in Amsterdam, *All the kings* is the only one to consider her prophetic identity. In *All the kings*, she responds to the censure she received in the years following the publication of *Warning* by aligning her prophetic authority with both the word of God and the word of the deceased monarch, James. She comes to denounce Charles's authority by representing her calling as filling the vacuum of power created by his father's death. Because she fails to find James's likeness in his son, she makes his daughter, Elizabeth, Queen of Bohemia, the dedicatee of her commentary on the visions of Daniel and the legatee of the dead king's theological agenda. Although certainly not the first woman writer to dedicate a text to Elizabeth, Lady Eleanor appeals to the Queen not because she is a paragon of virtue but because she is, quite literally, a descendant of James.[47] As a result of dedicating *All the kings* to Elizabeth, Lady Eleanor gains an identification with the Queen as the daughter of a powerful father that subsequently inspires her to appropriate her own aristocratic father's name as her prophetic signature.

In *All the kings*, Lady Eleanor briefly mentions the recent death, in November 1632, of Elizabeth's husband, Frederick, the Elector Palatine, but focuses most of her attention on the death eight years previous of James. The dedication to Elizabeth describes the Queen's father, James, as Lady Eleanor's fellow warrior in the struggle to suppress the "Beast," the Church of Rome: "Your Majesties [Elizabeth's] Throne, by degrees at length approaching humbly crave Royal patience, present the Man, greatly beloved, Daniel, intended to the King of chiefe memory your father, composed in a weeke (hastely) obtained not access, for with his fathers, the holy King was fallen asleepe, his soule beyond mortall sight, taken up to heaven, to partake immortall crownation; a good fight having fought MICHAEL against the Babylonian Dragon, so many Evangelicall combats and controversies with the Beast." In the one coded reference she makes to the Elector Palatine's death, Lady Eleanor identifies Elizabeth's widowed status as well as her royal father as sources of the Queen's unique authority. Through the anagram "ZAREP: VILAG." derived from one of the Elector Palatine's titles, the Palsgrave, or, as she spells it, "Palizgrave," she asserts that Elizabeth's widowhood grants her a place in prophetic history.[48] "ZAREP:VILAG." invokes the Phoenician town (village/VILAG?) of Zarephath where God directed Elijah with the promise that he would receive hospitality at the hands of a widow: "Arise get thee to Zarephath, which belongeth to Zidon, and dwell there: behold I have commended a widow woman there to sustain thee."[49] Lady Eleanor, through her anagram, transforms the literal remains of Elizabeth's dead husband into a means for asserting that as a widow Elizabeth can now follow in her father's footsteps by serving as a protector of prophets. In effect, Lady Eleanor seems to be telling the recently bereaved Queen that the only good husband is a dead husband, particularly when there is important prophetic work to be done.

No doubt, Lady Eleanor's disregard for Elizabeth's potential affective ties to her husband stems from her contention that her own husbands egregiously impeded her prophetic calling. Both of her husbands, Sir John Davies and Sir Archibald Douglas, burned her books. Although she does not specify Davies's motives, she notes that as a servant of Charles, Douglas feared his wife's writing would provoke royal displeasure.[50] As a result of his actions, each husband receives a curse from Lady Eleanor: she tells Davies "within three years to expect the mortal blow," and he dies shortly thereafter in 1626; and she cryptically predicts that *"worse then death should befal"* Douglas. By her account, this prediction is fulfilled when, during services at St. Martin's Church in 1631, Douglas is "strooken bereft of his sences, in stead of speech made a noice like a Brute creature." Following this episode, Lady Eleanor lived apart from Douglas who, until his death in 1644, was cared for by members of his family.[51] In Elizabeth, Lady Eleanor may well see an image of herself— a woman who has been relieved of wifely obligations and who can now undertake more serious labors. Her address to Elizabeth appears to enable Lady Eleanor to conceive of first Elizabeth and then herself as heirs to the prophetic legacy of James.

Beyond claiming that the death of the Elector Palatine grants the Queen of Bohemia a new political role, her dedicatory letter to Elizabeth positions mourning as the medium for her divine inspiration by juxtaposing the invocation of the dead king with two accounts of Lady Eleanor's calling. Her first narrative of the events of 28 July 1625 recalls *Warning* by describing an intellectual revelation that follows six months of study:

> In the first yeere of Charles King of Great-Brittaine twenty eight of the moneth of July, about six moneths after I began to understand the visions of the Prophet Daniel, which he saw in the first yeere of Bel[s]hacer, king of Babylon, a thing was revealed unto mee, and the word was true, but the time appointed long . . . is now to be accomplished shortly, I eate no pleasant bread, was mourning full three moneths to understand the visions.

Unlike *Warning, All the kings* denounces Charles and compares her role in his reign to that of Daniel under the sacrilegious and last Babylonian king, Belshazzar: "In the first yeere of Charles . . . I began to understand the visions of the Prophet Daniel, which he saw in the first yeere of Bel[s]hacer." While the allusion to Belshazzar refers to the opening of Daniel 7, her lament that she eats "no pleasant bread, was mourning three full moneths to understand the visions," almost exactly replicates the opening passages of the final vision of Daniel in Book 10: "In those days I Daniel was mourning three full weeks. I ate no pleasant bread." By making the "three full weeks" of mourning in Daniel into "full three moneths," Lady Eleanor could be referring to the time— almost exactly four months—between the death of James on 27 March and her calling on 28 July. (Lady Eleanor is often opportunistic in her calculations in order to assert correspondences between seventeenth-century and biblical events.) Regardless of whether this is the case, Lady Eleanor's allusion to the "mourning" of Daniel links the intellectual labor of exegesis with, in psychoanalytic terms, the "work" of mourning the dead—the slow process of disengaging the libido's attachment to the lost object.[52] Her use of "mourning" compares the suffering that accompanies the temporary inability to understand the divine will ("the visions of the Prophet Daniel") to the absoluteness of separation experienced in bereavement. Thus, by invoking the experience of mourning, Lady Eleanor tacitly links the feelings of loss that accompany her struggles both to comprehend Daniel and to come to terms with James's death. By 1633, the optimism about the new king's reign, that in *Warning* had found her celebrating her special knowledge of Daniel as one of the great achievements of her age, had been replaced by the suffering such knowledge brings.

When Lady Eleanor again describes the events of her calling in the very next paragraph, the theme of loss and ambiguity gives way to a vision of divine presence and clarity: "One thousand six hundred twenty five, July twenty eight, early in the morning, about dawning of the daye, I heard these words from heaven, as it were a musicall voyce, coming downe, saying, There is nineteene years & a halfe to the daye of judgement, hee that testifieth these things, sayth surely I come quickely."[53] While Lady Eleanor alludes directly to the closing lines of Revelation[54] rather than to Daniel, it appears that the "voyce" has helped her understand the riddle of Daniel with which she struggled previously: "dissolving within three dayes, former ambiguity." Doubtless, Lady Eleanor experiences the "musicall voyce" as a divine presence, but the emphasis on mourning throughout the text suggests that, in the manner of Isaiah, Lady Eleanor may have reconciled the loss of James by reconfiguring him as a divine voice. In the terms of Freud's "Mourning and Melancholia," such a substitution can be seen as symptomatic of an aberrant form of mourning in which the individual, refusing to relinquish the "loved object," turns "away from reality" and clings "to the object through the medium of a hallucinatory wishful psychosis."[55] As a tool for understanding prophecy, Freud's model can most usefully explain why prophets like Lady Eleanor might create an image of God that invokes the memory of a dead king. Clearly, since the publication of *Warning*, she had sought the sound of James's approval for her exegetical labours. She had hoped to hear the echoes of James's voice in his son but, as events after the publication of *Warning* attest, the son wanted her to disappear. So, Lady Eleanor turns to James's daughter Elizabeth for the protection that the widow at Zarephath gave Elijah and for the sort of patronage she believes James might have given her.

Much as Lady Eleanor had imagined, Elizabeth does indeed prove a better friend to prophets than Charles: she even lobbies her brother on Lady Eleanor's behalf.[56] Moreover, according to Lady Eleanor, the Queen of Bohemia's piety is such that it forestalls Britain's imminent destruction: "After which voyce the destroying Angell suddenly sheathed the sword, never so furiously drawne on that nation, for which blessing, and the happinesse to behold your face, and Royall progeny, walking in the trueth, honor, power and glory, be unto him that sitteth upon the Throne, even so come Lord JESUS." Lady Eleanor's suddenly merciful "destroying Angell" refers to the moment in Chronicles when David's sorrow for numbering the people ultimately results in God's intervening to preserve Jerusalem.[57] By observing that Elizabeth has similarly stayed God's wrath, Lady Eleanor implicitly links Elizabeth rather than her brother Charles with David's monarchical authority. Her admiration for Elizabeth notwithstanding, the close of the passage—"even so come Lord Jesus"—suggests Lady Eleanor's ardent desire to be in the presence of the "voyce." She had articulated comparable apocalyptic expectations in *Warning* but not nearly as feelingly. There, she portrays, through the imagery of Revelation, the second coming as deliverance from the devil in all of his various manifestations: "from which cursed triplicitie, three Monsters of the bottomlesse Pit, God deliver us, who will give us a Crowne of life: Come Lord Jesus, the grace of our Lord Jesus Christ be with you all" (55). Where previously she had sought Christ because he could rescue humankind from hell's monsters, in *All the kings* she desires union with Christ because he now bears the face of James whose image she sees in miniature in Elizabeth's virtues. In her role as the daughter of a powerful father, Elizabeth serves as a medium for bringing Lady Eleanor to James. Through Elizabeth, Lady Eleanor effectively expands James's paternity by merging it with divine fatherhood. As a result, James is no longer her colleague but the inspiration for her career.

With *All the kings*, Lady Eleanor moves from depicting James as the figure of Michael who wages war against Roman Catholicism to the image of God himself. Where her focus in *Warning* had been on Satan and the forces of evil, she now seeks to elaborate the image of God. Indeed the title of her text, *All the kings*, directly alludes to one of David's psalms that praises God: "All the kings of the earth shall prayse thee, O Lord, when they hear the words of thy mouth. Yea, they shall sing in the way of the Lord: for great *is* the glory of the Lord." In the dedicatory letter to Elizabeth, she illustrates her experience of hearing the divine "words" and later, in her text's exegetical section, she will introduce the figure of George Carr, a young boy possessed of prophetic knowledge: "Two saints, so called for gifts of the holy Ghost, precious in these dayes, the certain saint speaking, or wonderfull numberer of secrets, was a certaine childe about the age of 13 yeers in the yeere 1625 called Carr, of the nation of

Great-Brittain, that for certain mounths by signes . . . numbering foretold all things, beyond relation, but being terrified and provoked to speake lost the wonderfull gife [sic] for that time, after went beyond sea."[58] George Carr plays a prominent role in the account of her calling in her 1646 treatise, *The Lady Eleanor Her Appeal*, but here in a text which focuses on Lady Eleanor's experience of hearing the divine "voyce," Carr appears to be another physical means through which God communicates with Lady Eleanor.[59] In *Warning*, she had closed by describing her relationship to God in general terms: "And I thinke that I have also the Spirit of God" (56). By 1633, her understanding of divine inspiration and of divinity itself becomes focused. Now, God is a regal entity who speaks aloud to her just as he made his presence real in the figure of George Carr. Once Lady Eleanor ascribes James's image to God, she can begin to imagine her prophetic authority in political terms. Charles may have received the right to rule from his father, but Lady Eleanor acquires the right to prophesy from the amalgamation of a kingly and heavenly father. Although James may not have wanted a *female* prophet to authorize herself through him, he certainly would have appreciated Lady Eleanor for so strongly identifying his power with that of God. As he himself observed in the prefatory poem to his *Basilikon Doron*: "God gives not Kings the stile of *Gods* in vaine,/ For on his Throne his Scepter do they swey."[60]

By the time Lady Eleanor considers her prophetic identity for the third time in her 1641 *The Lady Eleanor, Her Appeale*, the political situation has altered dramatically, and she now finds herself watching the demise of Charles's reign. The opening dedication of *Her Appeale* "To the Honorable Assembly of the High Court of Parliament" indicates the changes that had taken place in her political fortunes as well as those of the English nation in the years between 1633 and 1641. The fact that she addresses *Her Appeale* to Parliament rather than to the members of the royal family, as she had her previous texts, underlines the increased power held by that governing body. The Long Parliament, which sat from 1640 to 1660, had begun to restrict Charles's prerogative powers through legislation such as the Triennial Act of 1641 which ensured that Parliament would meet every three years regardless of whether the King called for elections. *Her Appeale* recognizes this act as a sign that the time of "the blessed resurrection" approaches: "So passing or poasting to the time, at last of deliverance, the blessed resurrection. Heere unfolded that treble or threefold Coard, not easily broken nor altred: Sworne with a high hand, that meeting a *Triennial* &c." Beyond the official government channels, Charles's authority and that of William Laud, Archbishop of Canterbury, had been formally challenged by the 15,000 citizens of London who signed the Root and Branch Petition of December 1640 that called for the abolition of episcopacy. They realized one of their implicit goals when, in that very month, the House of Commons impeached Laud of treason and had him imprisoned.[61]

Lady Eleanor too bore grievances against Charles and Laud. When she compares *Her Appeale* to "JOSEPH . . . hated hetherto, for the *Evill-report* brought of his *Brethren*," she may be referring to the charges brought against her by Laud at the request of Charles for "presuming to Imprint the said Books [of 1633]." In 1633, the Commission for Ecclesiastical Causes responded to the texts, including *All the kings*, she had printed in Amsterdam and distributed in England by finding her guilty "of unlawful printing & publishing of books . . . to the great scandal of our Church and State." It was at this trial that Lady Eleanor was famously ridiculed for her use of anagrams. Laud's seventeenth-century biographer, Peter Heylin, records the notorious joke that the clerics trying her case enjoyed at her expense:

> *Lamb* then Dean of the *Arches* shot her through and through, with an arrow borrowed from her own Quiver; . . . he took a Pen into his hand, and at last hit upon this excellent *Anagram*, viz. DAME ELEANOR DAVIES, NEVER SO MAD A LADIE: Which having proved to be true by the Rules of Art, *Madam*, said he, *I see you build much on* Anagrams, *and I have found out one which I hope will fit you*; This said, and reading it aloud, he put it into her hands in Writing, which happy Phancy brought that grave Court into such a laughter, and the poor Woman thereupon into such a confusion.[62]

Mere humiliation did not prove satisfying enough for the Court, and they sentenced her to jail for an indefinite period of time. The "Notarium Publicum" at her trial, one Donaldson, observed the interest of the King in her case: "And she was further committed close Prisoner to the Gatehouse, and ordered there to remain during his Majesties pleasure, who had taken special notice of her and her Cause, and referred the Examination and Censuring thereof unto this Court." Upon the petition of her daughter, Lucy, Lady Hastings, she was released in 1635.[63] Her two years in prison did not deter her, and she was jailed again in late 1636 or early 1637 for banding together with a group of women to protest the "Romish" rituals practiced at the Cathedral of Lichfield. The spectacular nature of her defiance—she occupied the bishop's throne, declared herself "primate and metropolitan," and defaced the Cathedral's tapestries—only served to reenforce earlier accusations of her madness and resulted in her being committed to Bedlam.[64] As a woman who "violated social conventions and expressed religious . . . [and] political dissent," Lady Eleanor, according to Cope, was only too likely to have her contemporaries deem her insane.[65] In *Her Appeale*, Lady Eleanor effectively responds to the hardships she has experienced since 1625 by justifying her prophetic authority in political terms. She emerges as worldly wise and, as she herself puts it, a "Striplin grown up of 17. yeares."[66]

One sign of her heightened political self-consciousness is her response to those of her peers who challenge her legitimacy. Indeed, she explains that she writes to answer an old question about her right to publish her 1625 exegesis of Daniel, *Warning*: "And of whose making to justifie here, by whom Published; though hitherto by authority with-stood." Even though, she contends, *Warning* illuminated Daniel and signaled the end of the plague of 1625, it was repudiated by Charles. She proceeds "to justifie . . . by whom Published" in terms of her heavenly and earthly fathers' authority: "ELEANOR DAVIES, handmayden of the most high GOD of Heaven, this Booke brought forth by Her, fifth Daughter of GEORGE, Lord of CASTLEHAVEN, Lord AUDELEY, and Tuitchet. NO inferior PEERE of this Land, in Ireland the fifth EARLE."[67] According to Lady Eleanor, being the "fifth Daughter of GEORGE" grants her political legitimacy and strengthens her claim to being the "handmayden of the most high GOD of Heaven." Clearly, Lady Eleanor's earlier meditation in *All the kings* on the politics of father-daughter relationships inspires her move to identify her prophetic authority in terms of her father's name. While she had seen Elizabeth as particularly suited to perpetuating the legacy of her father the prophet-king, she felt certain that she too could act in her father's name.

Indeed, her father George Touchet may have unwittingly prompted her to deem herself his particular heir. Cope notes that at his death in 1617, Lady Eleanor, his youngest daughter, along with her first husband Davies became the administrators of his estate. As a result, they received "his personal estate in return for paying his debts." Although Touchet likely deeded this role to Lady Eleanor and her husband because of Davies's legal skill, and Lady Eleanor's older brothers and sisters did not contest her right to his property because his estate was not very valuable, his conferring this position upon his youngest daughter may have left her with a strong sense of entitlement.[68] So, when she urges Elizabeth to embrace her legacy as her father's heir, she may be referring to the role that her father has bequeathed to her. Only by delineating Elizabeth's relationship to political and spiritual authority, however, does Lady Eleanor gain a language for comprehending the potential political significance of the events of her own life.

Lady Eleanor's decision to predicate her authority in terms of her aristocratic father's name represents a deliberate attempt to justify her vocation in the terms of patriarchal politics. However, in a seemingly counterproductive act, she politicizes her prophetic authority in terms of aristocratic privilege in a text that denounces the king's legitimacy. Traditionally, the monarch and the aristocracy were seen as closely related links in the hierarchical chain of command. As one Elizabethan commentator put it, the aristocracy served as "brave half paces between a throne and a people." Early in her career, however, Lady Eleanor appears not to view the two as coterminous. Rather she simply argues that Charles must go: his reign, which she likens to the fourth monarchy described in Daniel, must collapse to make way for the predicted reign of Jesus, the fifth monarch.[69] After Charles's execution, however, Lady Eleanor does intimate an awareness that aristocratic and monarchical power are seen as interdependent. In *The Appearance or Presence of the Son of Man* of 1650, she insists that antiquity stabilizes the legitimacy of her family name while that of inherited political titles is subject to change: "*Item*, Daughter of *Audleigh*, or *Oldfield*, in the *Saxon* Tongue, no created Peership: a *Saxon* Baron afore the Conquest, As unto this day, preferring the act of time Antiquity, before Titles subject to be revers'd; and so far for the beginning and ending, of Kings and House of Lords." By distinguishing between aristocratic authority as birthright and regal power as birthright, she reveals her awareness that the two are conventionally linked and that her means of constituting her political identity and her opposition to monarchy might be seen as contradictory. She claims that while her inherited authority is essential ("no created Peership") that of kings is malleable ("Titles subject to be revers'd"). Moreover, by alluding to her Saxon blood, she establishes a kind of dichotomy between pre- and post-Conquest England. Kings, with their reversible titles, appear to be a Norman invention. By virtue of her lineage, Lady Eleanor deems

herself to be of the land and not a foreign creation. As Cope puts
it: "The baronage of Audeley . . . predated the Norman Conquest
and thus did not stand upon the 'yoke' of tyranny that her contemporaries believed the Normans had imposed."[70] By identifying herself as descended from an original Saxon family, Lady
Eleanor implies that her ancestors' role in the nation's founding
makes her a particularly authoritative prophet.

In as much as Lady Eleanor adopted the language of anti-
monarchicalism that would be employed in Charles's overthrow,
she remained fundamentally committed to the ideal of divine
right. She did not, like regicides such as John Goodwin, hope for
Charles's demise in order to realize a vision of justice. Rather
her objections to Charles's reign focused on two concerns: first,
his failure to live up to the high standard set by his father and
second, his (mis)fortune to rule at the dawn of apocalypse. For
Lady Eleanor, the latter concern emerges as a fact of apocalyptic
history that exceeds Charles's control. Even in *Warning*, prior to
her difficulties with Charles, she anticipates that his reign would
mark the age of deliverance: "And there shall be a time of trouble, such as never was since there was a Nation, even to that
same time, blessings and great felicities, being for the most part
accompanied with Corrections, and extraordinary Calamities;
Devotion and Religion of happinesse, in this life the Highest, not
exempt from superstition and heresie; And at that time thy People shall bee delivered; Every one whose name is found written
in the Booke, &c." (48). Because she is hopeful about Charles,
she may choose not to correlate his reign exclusively with "Calamities" and "Corrections" but imagines that these tremendous
changes will also be accompanied by "blessings and great felicities." In presenting a balanced vision of the apocalypse's torments and blessings, Lady Eleanor expresses optimism about
Charles's abilities. Moreover, Charles himself will assume the
heroic part, standing up as the Michael of Daniel "for the faithfull
Children of our Nation" (48). In *Her Appeale* of 1641, however,
Charles is imagined as playing a less savory role in the events of
the apocalypse. No longer the Michael of Daniel, his reign is now
likened to that of the great image of Nebuchadnezzar's dream
which represents the four kingdoms that will ultimately collapse
to make way for the coming of God's fifth kingdom. Lady Eleanor
finds in contemporary events a mirror of the chaos described in
Daniel: "Thus represented in this Mirror of former times, the
present age the visage thereof, &c. Also, no spare body unwildy
[sic, unwieldy] growne and great, every way dangerous division

therby unable to stand upon the feete: Not spared by Her [Lady Eleanor], whose song the Worlds farwell these."[71]

Although the level of personal invective toward Charles increases between the representation of apocalypse in *Warning* and that in *Her Appeale* and her later tracts, her discussion of apocalypse emphasizes the collapse of his reign as an historical fact. In 1647, for instance, she appeals to evidence in Revelation to predict the end of Charles's authority: "The Holy Ghost first knocks, so high extold, shews the end come, by New writ witnessed and Old; in whose Kalender the time set out, a week expired of Centuries thereabout: When as Twenty four from *Normand* Race sprung, cast their Crowns down, Times hourglasse (as 'twere) run." As she continues in her rhyming prose, she explains why there can only be "Twenty four from Normand Race sprung": "As Elders white arrayed so shine, Four and twenty first crownd of time: Seasons four, also with Feast days, crowns resign; aloud him praise, all proclaiming Eternity, away with tyrant Time they cry." Like the seasons, kings mark time; and at the second coming all such mortal indices will give way before an eternal song of praise to the Almighty. Since the time of the Norman Conquest, England has had twenty-four monarchs, types of the twenty-four Elders who surround God's throne in Revelation. Over time, in other words, England has acquired the requisite number of kings or elders to surround the Lamb's throne so that now the nation can enter into a blessed state.[72]

For Lady Eleanor, Charles's reign must end in order that Christ's reign might begin. While she does indeed offer reasons for Charles's overthrow that transcend the facts of apocalyptic history, she does not present the sustained critique of monarchical absolutism that appears in John Goodwin's *The Obstructors of Justice* (1649). Goodwin did not oppose monarchy *per se*, but he did object to absolutism. Kings, he argued, are created by the people and so are obliged to them: "although it shall be supposed, that the king simply and absolutely is Superiour to his people, yet having entered into a civil, yea and sacred covenant and bond with them, the breach hereof on his part giveth unto them a Lawfullnesse of right and power to compel him to the terms of his argument; or to make satisfaction for his violation of them." Like Goodwin and many of the polemicists who advocated Charles's execution, Lady Eleanor questioned Charles's stewardship: "The careless *Stuart* by name, *justly turned out of Stewardship, what Trust to be repos'd in such a ONE? unto this day not weighing the many Caveats entered, and sacred Stat-*

utes, Matt. 24."[73] The allusion to Christ's parable in which watchful and careless servants illustrate the fates, at the Second Coming, of the saved and the damned, respectively, nevertheless, places Lady Eleanor's remarks on Charles's poor "stewardship"/ "Stuartship" in an apocalyptic context. Clearly, like the "evil" servant in Matthew, Charles had doubted his lord's imminent return and therefore permitted himself to "smite his fellow-servants, and to eat and drink with the drunken."[74] Lady Eleanor does not with Goodwin insist that Charles derives his power from the people, but she does believe that God requires him to serve his fellow servants. Less interested in critiquing tyrannical authority than Goodwin, Lady Eleanor translates Charles's carelessness into yet another feature of apocalyptic history.

Lady Eleanor's belief that history was driven by the imminent return of Christ was most famously articulated by John Archer in his *The Personal Reign of Christ Upon Earth*. Published in 1641, the year that Lady Eleanor had described Charles as the monarch whose reign precedes that of Christ, *The Personal Reign* details the features of Christ's anticipated earthly government: "But I call this last state of his [Christ] *Monarchicall*, because in this, when he entreth upon it, he wil govern as earthly Monarchies have done, that is, universally over the world, (in those daies known and esteemed) and in a worldly visible earthly glory; not by Tyranny, oppression, and sensually, but with honour, peace, riches, and whatsoever in and of the world is not sinfull; having all Nations and kingdoms doing homage to him, as the great Monarchs of the world." Archer predicted that Christ would begin his thousand year reign in 1700. As compared with Lady Eleanor, Archer provides a much more fully elaborated and political vision of millennium. After Christ completes his reign, Archer prognosticates, he will entrust the Saints to govern: "he will withdraw to heaven again, and leave the Government to the dead Saints raised up, among whom the Apostles shal be chief."[75] Archer's vision of the rule of the Saints would powerfully influence radical sectarian thought and would, in particular, become a mainstay of Fifth Monarchist ideology. The most militant of the sects, the Fifth Monarchists believed that they were called to usher in the millennium (using force if necessary) and to govern the unregenerate.

While Lady Eleanor shares with radical sectarians the view that all traditional earthly institutions, including the monarchy, will ultimately fall at the Second Coming, she also remains a firm believer in the divine right of kings. Her understanding of the nature of kingship itself emerges most fully in her meditations on James and can best be summarized in his words: the king is "Gods lieutenant in earth." Even Charles, despite her prediction that his reign would be punctuated by the apocalypse, could have remained God's lieutenant on earth. In *Warning*, she had imagined him as a type of the angel Michael who, in a period of chaos, serves the people. Of course, Charles's father James had, in her eyes, successfully fulfilled this requirement of monarchy. It is in his role as intermediary between heaven and earth that Lady Eleanor in her later tracts continues to memorialize the dead king. In *Sign*, first printed in 1644 and then reissued in 1649, Lady Eleanor likens James to Hezekiah. As she had previously, she portrays James as an excellent king, but she now details some faults: he permitted the Spanish ambassador Gondomar too much influence, and he pursued a Spanish match for his son Charles. Still, Lady Eleanor essentially admires him and, in a richly suggestive passage, portrays him as the image of Jacob's ladder: "Of which days come about again, this great Revolution ushering the day of Judgement, his coming in the Clouds; whereof as follows, of *Jacobs* ladder reaching to heaven gate, then, The express Epitomy of King *James's* life of *Great Britain*."[76] This dense passage involves a great deal of "unfolding." The sequence appears to be as follows: the English Revolution is a sign of the imminent apocalypse. Meditating on Christ coming in the clouds leads her to consider Jacob's ladder and the angels who use it to travel between heaven and earth. Finally, the one mortal who similarly straddled these two worlds was James. Through the image of Jacob's ladder, the passage draws an unbroken line between God and James. (Moreover, that the name "James" is the English form of the Latin "Jacobus" sutures the tie even more firmly.) James is literally the most well-connected of kings, and it is this feature of his reign that, according to Lady Eleanor, made him so successful.

Ironically, Lady Eleanor's depiction of James as linked to God via Jacob's ladder sets up a visual image akin to that of Charles in the frontispiece of *Eikon Basilike* (1649). The Royal Martyr appears linked to heaven by two beams of light simultaneously descending from and ascending to the clouds. The first comes from heaven and enters Charles's head bringing "*Clarior e tenebris*" [light from darkness]. The second proceeds from Charles's eye heavenward. The beam of light is identified as "*Coeli Specto*" [heavenly sight], and it resolves in the image of a crown marked with the words "*Beatam et Aeternam*" and "*Gloria*" [blessed and eternal, glory].[77] Meditating on the famous frontispiece, Henry King would translate the image to fit a Charles now ensconced in heaven:

> And when Thy darted Beam from the moist Sky
> Nightly salutes Thy grieving Peoples Eye,
> Thou like some Warning Light rais'd by our fears,
> Shalt both provoke and still supply our Tears.

Like Lady Eleanor's James, Henry King's Charles continues to influence his people from his heavenly throne. Although she had as early as 1633 prophesied Charles's doom, her attitude toward James participates in the same understanding of monarchical authority that conditions the Royalist panegyric produced after Charles's death. She shared Archbishop Ussher's sentiments on the essential nature of monarchical authority: "The King is not only Glorious, but Glory; Not only Powerfull but Power."[78] After James's death, she insisted that his "Glory" and "Power" perdured, and she personified this belief by making his the heavenly voice which called her to prophesy.

Lady Eleanor, however, could not extend the royal prerogatives of essential "Glory" and "Power" to Charles because she did not believe that he possessed divine right. Early in her career, she began to look around for other worthy heirs to James's power. She settled first on Elizabeth who, although not James's son still, as a daughter, retained a claim to the essence of her father's person and power. Next, she insisted that she herself, as a prophet, could be an heir to her father's essential authority. Her own noble patronymic, she contended, gave her access to an essential "Glory" and "Power." As time passed, she never quite abandoned the vision of absolute power promulgated by Ussher and his fellow Royalists, but she did intimate that it was not restricted to kings or even to those of noble birth.

Indeed, in *The Lady Eleanor Her Appeal* of 1646, she suggests that she finds a substitute for James in George Carr, an apparently deaf and mute boy possessed of prophetic powers. She first encounters Carr, significantly, just prior to James's death: "Shewing withall about a few dayes before the former kings departure this life, how first of all there came a Scotish Lad to this City, about the age of Thirteen, one *George Carr* by Name, otherwise cald the dumb Boy or Fortuneteller." In a pregnant juxtaposition, the visionary Scottish boy appears on the scene just as the visionary Scottish king breathes his last. Moreover, as she writes in the spring of 1646, Charles appears to be the most ineffectual and untrustworthy of leaders; having recently suffered defeat in the second of two civil wars, he flees to the Scots' army in the hopes that they will restore his authority. Thus, Carr seems a more eligible substitute for James than his own son. At any rate, Carr emerges as a kind of heir to James's legacy because he, like the dead king, plays an active role in spurring her vocation. She recounts how she invites Carr to stay with her at her home in Englesfield. Once there, he proceeds to entertain the local clergy and magistrates with feats of prediction: "Sometimes who would take the Bible or a Chronicle, and open it, and close it again, then cause the aforesaid Youth to shew by signs and such like dumb demonstrations, what was contain'd therein; which things he so to the life exprest and acted, as were it a Psalm or Verse then feign'd to sing, though saw not a letter of the Book." After about three months time, he appears to overcome his deafness and even acquires a "whistling voice." He continues to entertain the locals but they turn against him, outraged, it appears, by his ambiguous identity: "whilest others of that calling [ministers] as liberal of their slanderous tongues; that no longer might be harbored in our house, likened to Friar Rush, Servants had so incensed their Masters, setting all on fire, with Justices of the Peace and Church-men, giving out he was a Vagrant, a Counterfeit, or a Witch." Amazingly, as her neighbors' rage reaches a fever pitch, Lady Eleanor discovers her own prophetic calling: "Immediately upon which the Spirit of Prophesie falling likewise upon me, then were all vext worse then ever, ready to turn the house upside down, lay this to his charge too."[79]

The George Carr narrative appears fully elaborated only in *The Lady Eleanor* of 1646 and constitutes one of the most symbolically significant episodes of her canon. In terms of her attitudes toward authority, it marks a moment of extreme uncertainty. George Carr clearly possesses prophetic gifts yet the people of Englesfield detest him. By 1646, Lady Eleanor could readily identify with his plight, for she had suffered all manner of humiliation at the hands of outraged officials. At the same time that she recounts the skeptical reception of Carr's, and implicitly her own, prophetic gifts, she finds herself, along with her fellow countrywomen and men, watching the crowned king, God's lieutenant on earth, battling his subjects to retain his authority. Although she does not mention Charles's travails explicitly in the context of the George Carr episode, they provide a subtext for the distrust of conventional sources of authority (such as the magistrates and ministers of Englesfield) that underwrites the narrative. Old certainties about the essential nature of authority have broken down. At the same time that her text dramatizes this collapse, it presents a new authority, Carr, whom she perceives to be a legitimate visionary, as linked to James. Her text suggests that in a world turned upside down, James remains the source and origin of all that is true and real. While her contemporaries may not recognize Carr's special skills and her own, both are valid because both derive from James. He is her semiotic anchor; "the former kings departure this life" does not merely set the context for her narrative but provides its focal point.

VIRGIN DAUGHTERS

While Lady Eleanor attributes divine authority to Carr, she insists that his special powers derive from his kinship with a dead king. The Scottish boy is to some degree an extension of the Scottish king. Indeed, he uncannily bears the identical surname "Carr" of one of James's favorites and another Scot, Robert Carr.[80] As for her own prophetic authority, it comes from a voice whose power she shares by virtue of her family name. With the publication of *Her Appeale* in 1641, she makes the voice a permanent feature of her vocation narrative. (Even in 1646, she would follow her narrative of Carr's role in her calling with a separate account of the voice.) In addition to establishing the voice, *Her Appeale* relates what would become another signature feature of her vocation narrative, the voice's injunction to virgin meekness.[81] Previously, in *All the kings*, she observed that the voice delivered a "Propheticall admonition unto humility and meeknesse." By 1641, the voice echoes her claims for the primacy of the father-daughter bond as it personifies "humility and meeknesse" by commanding this twice-married mother of three to be "as the meek Virgin":

> but so came to Passe in the yeare aforesaid, 1625. Shee [Lady Eleanor] awakened *by a voyce from* HEAEVN, in the Fifth moneth, the 28. of *July*, early in the Morning, the Heavenly voice uttering these words.
> "There is Ninteene yeares and a halfe to the day of *Judgement*, and you as the meek Virgin. These sealed with Virgins state in the Resurrection, when they not giving in Marriage."

The "Heavenly voice" glosses its definition of virginity with an allusion to Revelation. "'These sealed with Virgins state in the Resurrection, when they not giving in Marriage'" refers to the following vision of God's elect: "And I looked, and lo, a Lamb stood on the mount Sion, and with him an hundred fourty and four thousand, having his Father's name written in their foreheads . . . These are they which were not defiled with women; for they are virgins. These are they which follow the Lamb withersoever he goeth. These were redeemed from among men, being the first fruits unto God and to the Lamb."[82] The "having his Father's name written in their foreheads" of Revelation becomes the "'sealed with Virgins state in the Resurrection'" of *Her Appeale*. While Revelation 14 limits this "state" to men who are "not defiled with women," Lady Eleanor extends membership in the chosen 144,000 to women by transforming the text of Revelation 14 into a repudiation of marriage: "'when they not giving in Marriage.'"

Lady Eleanor's anti-matrimony stance marks a radical departure from orthodox Protestant readings of Revelation 14. According to Thomas Brightman, the passage does not denounce marriage but rather attributes membership in the chosen to men who possess spiritual rather than physical virginity.[83] Indeed, Brightman had warned that an anti-matrimony reading of this passage could lead to the "Sodomitry" characteristic of the Roman Catholic clergy: "*Aretas* saith well, that these words are not spoken in the dispraise of Marriage . . . What was this a band of Bachelors, and of Priests onely? . . . Certainly, Christian Preists did not want wives, till *Hildebrand* opened a window to *Sodomitry*, least that his *Clergy* should be defiled with a chast Marriage."[84] Lady Eleanor's account of her call flies in the face of orthodox Protestantism first by creating a space for women among Revelation's chosen and second by denouncing the virtues of matrimony. For Lady Eleanor, the absence of matrimony means that women too can possess "his Father's name written in their foreheads." Again and again, Lady Eleanor appeals to essences and origins because she views female power as residing in woman's essential and originary bond to the father.

In one of her later works, *From the Lady Eleanor, Her Blessing to her Beloved Daughter* (1644), she develops the political implications of virginity and makes it the point of departure for a model of prophetic authority that applies, usefully, to married and unmarried women alike. Surprisingly, she invokes the battered body of the Jezebel of Kings to prove that women retain a claim to the paternal signifier: "But because the *Daughter of a King* as JEHU speake, *Here forborne the Remainder, buryed in silence*, for so births PREROGATIVE *surmounts* or *goes* before *that gain'd* by Marrage *as descent* and *blood,* a Character not to be blotted out, wherewith follows the state of VIRGINITY, the presidence theirs, *Not in subjection as others.*"[85] Virginity remains a permanent feature of a woman's identity and so she can avoid the "subjection" commanded in Paul's first letter to Timothy that Lady Eleanor interprets as applying only to married women.[86] In order to bolster her claim, however, Lady Eleanor overlooks the cruel irony, in the account of Jezebel's death, that forms Jehu's command to "bury her: for she is a King's daughter." When Jehu encounters Jezebel he is in the early stages of a mission to eliminate Baal worship which she and her father, the aptly named Ethbaal (Hebrew for "with Baal"), had promoted. Thus in ordering Jezebel's burial, he appears to act not out of homage to Ethbaal but out of contempt: "And he said, Throw her down. So they threw her down: and *some* of her blood was sprinkled on the wall, and on the horses: and he trode her under foot. And when he was come in, he did eat and drink, and said, Go, see now this cursed *woman,* and bury her: for she *is* a king's daughter."[87] Jehu has her killed, steps on her, eats a meal, and then orders her remains to be buried out of a professed respect for her father. After the dogs have finished with her corpse, Jehu's soldiers can bury only her skull, feet, and the palms of her hands; and so Jehu effectively slanders the name of Ethbaal into eternity by claiming to bury Jezebel's brutally dismembered body out of respect for him. From a biblical account that describes violence against the daughter of a powerful father, Lady Eleanor finds positive evidence for the eternal kinship, undisturbed by marriage, of fathers and daughters. While the narrative of Jezebel's burial hardly seems a likely proof text for female authority, Lady Eleanor, as befits an ardent proponent of anagrams, makes it so by focusing on the letter and not the spirit of Jehu's law to make "births PREROGATIVE" available to all women.

Through the Jezebel narrative, Lady Eleanor constitutes virginity as a figure for female authority. Women need not be virgins but only fathers' daughters in order to lay claim to "births PREROGATIVE." In addition, her radical understanding of virginity illuminates the significance of the simile that figures in the voice's message: "and you as the meek Virgin." By 1641, when she first recorded this command, Lady Eleanor was no longer a virgin but she was fully capable of being "as the meek Virgin." As a virgin, she can be numbered among the 144,000 "sealed with Virgins state in the Resurrection." Within the context of the divine command, virginity emerges as a trope through which women can lay claim to the sacred authority inherent in the "Father's name written in their foreheads."

Lady Eleanor produces a notion of virgin power that paradoxically couches hostility toward male authority in patriarchal terms.[88] By identifying herself as her father's daughter, she appears to be paying a kind of homage to George Touchet. Yet her antipathy toward her first husband Davies's authority over her articulates an unwillingness to obey the man her father has selected to govern her. As Cope notes, Lady Eleanor's marriage to Davies was arranged by her father: "Davies's connections at court presumably enabled him to gain social benefits from marrying the daughter of a peer, while [Lord] Audeley bargained that he would be able to obtain far more in Irish lands through Davies than he granted to conclude the match . . . Whether either considered Lady Eleanor's feelings about the arrangements we do not know." In their introduction to Davies's poems, Robert Krueger and Ruby Nemser suggest that the ability to "acquire" Eleanor Davies was a sign of Sir John's economic and social success. In essence, at least in her first marriage, Lady Eleanor was reduced to the status of an object whose exchange between Davies and Touchet resulted in the bettering of each man's personal interests.[89] She effectively became a participant in what Gayle Rubin has famously termed the "exchange of women": " 'Exchange of women' is a shorthand for expressing that the social relations of a kinship system specify that men have certain rights in their female kin, and that women do not have the same rights either to themselves or to their male kin. In this sense, the exchange of women is a profound perception of system in which women do not have full rights to themselves."[90] By identifying herself through the trope of virgin daughterhood, Lady Eleanor attempts to choose her subjectivity to patriarchal power. She repudiates her status as an object to be exchanged between two men, opting instead to view herself as one who can inherit power and property. Ultimately, she celebrates her father's name and her virgin daughterhood in order to resist the ways patriarchy, through marriage, subjects women.

Lady Eleanor's particular understanding of divine right finds her idealizing James and denouncing Charles, and spurs her to develop a model of female authority that privileges the father-daughter bond. Although marriage, in her view, frequently obfuscates women's essential connection to their fathers' authority, she insists that women retain, if only figuratively, their virginity. Moreover, Lady Eleanor's trope of virgin daughterhood implies women's access to power as an *essential* component of the father-daughter tie. Because they remain as virgins in their relationships to their fathers, they can always acquire authority through that bond. Fathers and kings anchor Lady Eleanor's metaphor of virgin daughterhood and enable her to develop a model, if only a derivative one, of women's essential authority.

"KINGLY POWER"

Given Lady Eleanor's privileged social status, we might be inclined to define her monarch-centered approach to female power as inspired by her membership in England's aristocracy. To do so, however, would be to underestimate the prestige of the monarchy across all strata of English society. The case of Elizabeth Poole, one of Lady Eleanor's contemporaries and a prophet, illustrates the broad appeal of monarchy. Poole can best be described as a member of the middling sort. She was a single woman and a seamstress who, according to her friend T. P., made her living exclusively through her own labor: "she hath no livelihood amongst men, but what she earns by her hands."[91] Moreover, as distinct from Lady Eleanor, Poole was a member of a religious sect, the Baptists. While Poole and Lady Eleanor certainly came from different worlds, both put the king at the center of their models of female authority. Poole, however, would not ascribe power to women as virgin daughters but as wives.

Poole rose to prominence in the months preceding Charles's execution. In late December of 1648 and again in early January of 1649, she appeared before the Council of Officers of the New Model Army to advise them how to treat the king whom they then held as their prisoner. She asserted that although the Army Officers now possessed the right to wield the king's power, they must not execute the king because he embodied the origin of their authority.[92] Her most striking way of describing the relationship between the king and the Army was in terms of a marriage in which a husband had failed in his obligations toward his wife thereby giving her the right to usurp his authority but not to harm his person. For Poole, the model of righteous and just wifehood provided a means for articulating female authority in a milieu that was rapidly disavowing the notion of hereditary power. Nevertheless, her desire to preserve the person of Charles reveals her lingering attachment to the ideal of divine right monarchy. Poole, like many of her peers, and not least of all Lady Eleanor, was not ready to see the political order in terms of law and contract but persisted in comprehending the social order as structured by the person of the king.

The published account of the oral and written messages Poole delivered to the Council of Officers, *A Vision: Wherein is manifested the disease and cure of the kingdome* (1648), shares Lady Eleanor's attempts to make sense of a society in transition in terms of traditional forms of authority.[93] Even Poole's forays into what we might term contract theory are held in suspension by her faith in divine right. She, for instance, advises the Army that they now possess the king's power because Charles, who received his authority from God, failed to wield it according to the divine command: "The Kingly power is undoubtedly fallen into your hands; therefore my advise [sic] is, that you take heed to improve it for the Lord. You have justly blamed those who have gone before you, for betraying their trust therein." The King's failure to govern according to the divine will means that his power, "the spirit of Judgement and Justice," now appears "most lively" in the Army. Moreover, when asked if the Army should share this power with Parliament and people, she replies in the negative. The power has been entrusted to the Army which is "in the place of watchmen." Although Poole insists that the Army and not Charles rightfully possesses the king's power, her understanding of political authority itself echoes that of the Royalist Archbishop Ussher: "There can be no Dominion in the World, unlesse there be an Eminency of power in some one or other. If a man be wronged in any Court, he may lawfully appeale higher, but then, Appeales must not be Infinite, there must be a supremacy of power somewhere to rest in."[94] Poole's justification of the Army's authority evokes Ussher's "supremacy of power" only to insist on the transferable nature of such power.

Still, she maintains that while the Army may possess "the supremacy of power," it cannot embody "the supremacy of power" in the same way that Charles can. For Poole, the chain of command is clear: God commits his trust to the king and then, when the king fails him, to the Army. Yet the Army cannot completely supplant the king because he is the author of their "bodyes": "You have all that you have and are, and also in Subordination you owe him [Charles] all that you have and are, and although hee would not bee your Father and husband, Subordinate [to God], but absolute, yet know that you are for the Lords sake to honour his person. For he is the Father and Husband of your bodyes, as unto men, and therefore your right cannot bee without him, as unto men."[95] The king, in other words, provides the secular, political mold of the Army's authority which itself is derived from God. The king, as any Royalist would agree, is the ultimate source for the language of power.

At the same time that the king is the earthly source of power, he is also bound by a contract with his subjects to punish evildoers and praise those who do well. His power comes from God but includes obligations to his subjects that Charles has failed to observe: "Forget not your pitty towards him [Charles], for you were given him an helper in the body of the people: Which people are they that agreed with him to subject unto the punishment of evill doers, and the praise of them that doe well: which law is the spirit of your Union." The king embodies authority, but he is brought into "Union" with his people through the "law." Although Poole insists on the "law" or "agreement" as the standard by which the king's right to continue to reign may be determined, she also maintains that even when the king breaks the bond of the "Union" with his people, he should not therefore be simply separated from them. Rather, their "Union" possesses mystical overtones and binds king and people as husband and wife: "And although this bond be broken on his part; You never heard that a wife might put away her husband, as he is the head of her body; but for the Lords sake suffereth his terrour to her flesh, though she be free in the spirit to the Lord; and he being uncapable to act as her husband, she acteth in his stead; and having the spirit of Union abiding in her, shee considereth him in his temptations, as tempted with him."[96] While the people, like a wife, are initially subject to a higher earthly authority, both are entitled by the very fact of their union with their "head" to expect their superiors to fulfill the terms of their union. Should their superiors betray their trust, the people may act in their superiors' stead, yet possessed of the "spirit of Union," they should forego eliminating their overlords altogether.

Although Poole does not explicitly set out to establish a model of female political authority, her use of matrimony as a figure for the relations between king and subjects implies that the "husbandly power" can fall into the hands of women. Her figurative marriage, like Lady Eleanor's figurative virginity, enables her to imagine female authority as contingent to patriarchy—the source, as both women would agree, of all power. Yet while women in Lady Eleanor's vision possess rights to power through their blood ties to their fathers, Poole's model grants women access to patriarchal authority through their roles as wives: "the King is your Father and husband, which you were and are to obey in the Lord, and no other way, for when he forgot his Subordination to divine Father-hood & headship, thinking he had begotten you a generation to his own pleasure, and taking you a wife for his own lusts, thereby is the yoak taken from your necks."[97] Should a woman find herself married to a man who uses her exclusively to satisfy his own lusts, then she is no longer required to obey him. Even as she intones a theory of individual rights, she does so in terms of a hierarchical chain of command. Women have rights, but they accede to power only when husbands forget their "Subordination to divine Father-hood & headship." Power, for both Poole and Lady Eleanor, comes from above, and women can only acquire it under the aegis of a father or a husband.

In a world in which patriarchy and monarchy formed the terms of political discourse, Poole and Lady Eleanor attempted to extend this language to embrace political roles for women as women. Lady Eleanor would remain truer to the hierarchical matrix of descent and lineage in creating a model of virgin daughterhood. While, for her part, Poole would modernize monarchical and patriarchal authority. According to Poole, being king or being a husband did not absolutely determine a man's right to continue to wield power. By her lights, he still had to fulfill his obligations to his subjects in order to retain his authority. In comparing monarchy to matrimony, Poole implied that women could, in limited circumstances, seize their husbands' power. The husband remains in place as the source and origin of authority in the household, yet Poole's emphasis on the agreement binding husband and wife begins to concede power to the dictates of an impersonal law. Nevertheless, Poole's model, as much as that of Lady Eleanor, depends upon the authority of a central patriarchal figure. For both women, the breadth and scope of the father's power spur metaphors of female authority that focus on women's relationships to men. Ironically, these two prophets appeal to women's roles as men's social subordinates—as wives and daughters—in order to imagine ideals of female political authority and self-determination that suggest, even if only tentatively, theories of women's rights.

2

Sodomy and Female Authority: The Castlehaven Scandal and Lady Eleanor's *The Restitution of Prophecy* (1651)

I<small>N</small> 1651, <small>WHILE IMPRISONED IN THE FLEET, LADY ELEANOR PRODUCED</small> one of her most densely allusive texts, *The Restitution of Prophecy*. Her express purpose in writing *Restitution* was to urge watchfulness in the face of Christ's imminent return. Toward this end, its fifty-two pages[1] address a sprawling array of cosmic and mundane, and public and private concerns, including: Queen Henrietta-Maria's Catholicism; Queen Mary's bloody and Queen Elizabeth's glorious reigns; the trial and execution of Lady Eleanor's brother, Mervin, Earl of Castlehaven; Castlehaven's wife Anne Stanley as a type of the Whore of Babylon; undue prominence of the theater; pathetic state of publishing; Sir Kenelm Digby's poisoning of his wife Venetia Stanley; execution of the Earl of Strafford; General Fairfax's response to one of her tracts; the crimes and executions of Archbishop Laud and Charles I; wool as a good defense against cold weather; and calculations of the end of time. She claims to organize this jumble of topics according to the three apocalyptic parables in Matthew 25, and her text falls into three sections loosely headed by the rubrics: ten virgins, talents, and separation of sheep from goats.

In addition to this broad framework, Lady Eleanor provides a more useful key to understanding her burgeoning text. She likens it to a map that simultaneously provides direction and requires her readers to interpret various signposts in order to gain direction. While preeminently topical rather than allegorical, *Restitution* demands the same sort of reading practices as Bunyan's *Pilgrim's Progress*. For instance, Lady Eleanor insists that an account of Sir Kenelm Digby's murder of his wife Venetia

Stanley must be included in any map of London: "Requisit as any in our Cities Map to be displayed."[2] The narrative of Digby's crime both contributes to the literal, visual image of mid-century London and should, she suggests, prompt her readers to meditate on the city's sad state. As long as she supplies the salient details, her readers can, her text implies, piece together the significance of events themselves. In one of her earlier tracts, *From the Lady Eleanor, Her Blessing* of 1644, she characterizes her prophecies as written in a kind of shorthand: "being like the hony: and like the hony gathered out of so many parts, I shall the lesse need to excuse it unto such as have a ful knowledge of the Scriptures, That should it be written at large a Chronicle or a booke as ample as those tables, of the Mapps of the World could I suppose not contain it." Hers is a prophetic vision of extraordinary magnitude, so expansive that "a Chronicle or a booke as ample as the tables, of the Mapps of the World . . . could not contain it." She explains further that she does not write "at large" because the imminence of the Second Coming means that there is not enough time for "voluminous" books: "Not sutable to the little book, being but an *Epittomie* as it were, and so much for being not voluminous especially when the time so short too."[3] She recognizes that the breadth of her topic makes it "Not sutable to the little book," but the shortness of time leaves her little choice.

Her *Restitution* is a prime example of a text teeming with images not fully elaborated. Its profuse catalogue of people and events illustrates the chaos that characterizes a society particularly ripe, because so dissolute, for the Second Coming. Like Pope in *The Dunciad*, Lady Eleanor enumerates the decay that permeates every aspect of her culture. In Lady Eleanor's case, her wide-ranging yet interconnected images simultaneously affirm her explicit argument about the imminence of the end of time and constitute new meanings based on relationships that emerge from the matter of her text. *Restitution* is a map that shows the way but also presents opportunities for divining new connections between its many and varied signposts.

One of the major landmarks on the map of *Restitution* and one that ultimately points to a new vision of female authority is Lady Eleanor's extensive meditation on the fate of her brother, the Earl of Castlehaven. In 1631, Castlehaven had been convicted and executed for raping his wife and committing sodomy with a servant. His trial marked the first successful prosecution for homosexual acts involving adults since sodomy had been made a felony in 1533.[4] The outrageous nature of his supposed crimes scandalized his contemporaries and disgraced his relatives. Indeed, Barbara Breasted has argued that the emphasis on chastity in Milton's *Comus* is meant to distance the Earl of Bridgewater and his family from their sordid kinsman. The possible tie between *Comus* and the "Castlehaven Scandal" comes not from Castlehaven's crimes *per se* but from allegations that he coerced his twelve-year-old daughter-in-law and Bridgewater's niece, Lady Elizabeth Audeley, into having sexual intercourse with one of his servants. Once the scandal became public, Lady Audeley was deemed a whore. Breasted contends that Milton created the character of the heroically chaste "Lady" specifically for Bridgewater's fifteen-year-old daughter Lady Alice Egerton, who played the part in the masque's original production, in order to distinguish her from her cousin.[5]

For Castlehaven's sister, his conviction on charges of sexual misconduct did not arouse feelings of shame but rather provoked her to denounce the ruling authorities who found him guilty. Between 1633 and 1651, Lady Eleanor published four treatises protesting Castlehaven's innocence —*Woe to the House* (1633), *The Word of God to the City of London* (1644), *The Crying Charge* (1649), and the aformentioned *Restitution*. For the most part, her tracts represent Castlehaven's execution as an instance of failed justice symptomatic of both Charles I's impotence as king and the approach of the last days. *Restitution*, however, incorporates the details of Castlehaven's trial and execution into a lengthy meditation on why she has been appointed to revive the "Buried Talent" of prophecy (343). She insists that her brother's execution and her own imprisonment are symptomatic of a society deeply in need of reform. In *Restitution*, she aligns her plight with that of her deceased brother and in so doing constitutes the ghost of Castlehaven as the perfect double of an incarcerated agent of God's will.

For Lady Eleanor, the sensational nature of her brother's supposed crimes prompts her not merely to identify with his social alienation but to consider the relationship between so-called "sexual deviance" and the workings of political power. In *Restitution*, she tacitly recognizes that her society has condemned her and Castlehaven because as female prophet and supposed sodomite both interrogate the structure of political power by assuming renegade sexualities. Their challenge to political authority rests in their capacity to translate "perverse" sexualities into the idiom of political authority. Jonathan Dollimore terms this ironic reversal "transgressive reinscription": "a mode of transgression which seeks not to escape from existing structures but rather a subversive reinscription within them, and in the process their dislocation or displacement." For Castlehaven's part, "transgressive reinscription" surfaces in the text of his trial in his alleged efforts to locate homosexual desire within homosociality. The witnesses' accounts of his actions show him using his wife and his daughter-in-law to articulate his feelings for his male lovers. Castlehaven deeds these women to his male sexual partners and in so doing parodies the way that "male heterosexual desire," in Eve Kosofsky Sedgwick's terms, conventionally consolidates "partnership with authoritative males in and through the bodies of females."[6] Further, in his defense, Castlehaven urges his fellow peers to recognize not him but his accusers as subverters of patriarchal authority. Lady Eleanor concurs with his conspiracy theory and insists that her prophetic career vindicates Castlehaven: God punishes a nation guilty of executing a man falsely charged with the "sin against nature" with the ministrations of a truly grotesque figure, a female prophet. While "natural" ties of blood link Lady Eleanor and Castlehaven as sister and brother, a shared belief that a corrupt political order has engendered them as deviants binds them together as convicted sodomite and female prophet.

More than a means for critiquing a decadent age, Lady Eleanor's ruminations on Castlehaven become the fulcrum through which *Restitution* develops a new model of female authority. While in her earliest tracts, Lady Eleanor embraced the father's name as a source of female authority, in *Restitution* she focuses on the failure of patriarchy as enabling female power. The old structures of monarchy and patriarchy have declined to the point that a thoroughly emasculated group of peers accepts the word of (in Lady Eleanor's view) the sluttish Lady Castlehaven against that of her husband, the Earl himself. For Lady Eleanor, the diminished authority of masculine culture means that another force—aggressive female sexuality—gains sway. Ironically, in as much as Lady Eleanor professes to despise viragoes such as Lady Castlehaven, she comes to predicate her own authority as a prophet on the demise of the homosocial ties that have empowered her sister-in-law. In the scope of Lady Eleanor's career then, *Restitution* represents a new approach to the question of female prophetic authority: no longer exclusively tied to the father's name, her legitimacy as a visionary emerges from the ashes of patriarchy. Central to Lady Eleanor's new justification of female authority is her brother's role in the eponymous Castle-haven Scandal.

"Spurious Seed"

Although Castlehaven was convicted of sodomy, his trial has very little to do with the sexual act we know as sodomy. In early modern England, sodomy had yet to be specified as anal penetration but instead could encompass "any sexual act" that did not "promote the aim of married procreative sex." Thus, sodomy could signify "acts that men might perform with men, women with women . . . men and women with each other, and anyone with a goat, a pig, or a horse." In Castlehaven's trial itself, the definition of sodomy became a topic for debate. The testimony detailing his acts of sodomy does not depict the Earl penetrating the bodies of his male servants but only using them to ejaculate. For instance, Castlehaven's servant Lawrence Fitzpatrick asserts that the "Lord made him lye with him at Fountaine, and Salisbury, and once in the bed, & *semen consumpsit* [spent seed], but did not penetrate his body." Another servant, Giles Broadway, claims that Castlehaven "used his body like a woman, *sed numquam penetravit, quamvis inter femine, semen suum consumpsit* [but at no time did Castlehaven penetrate him, although he spent his seed between his thighs]."[7] Because neither of the men who claim to have engaged in sexual acts with him assert that he penetrated their bodies, Castlehaven asks the judges to determine whether or not the charge of "buggery" applies: "That supposing it were true which they [Fitzpatrick and Broadway] deposed (which he hoped would not so prove) he urged to be cleared, whether the Statute did intend that all kind of pollution (man with man) were *Buggery* or not, seeing by their Confession, there was no Penetration." Unfortunately for Castlehaven, the judges argue for a broader reading of sodomy: "they answered it was *Buggery* by the Law, and that the Law of this Land made no distinction of *Buggery*, if there be *Emissio Seminis* [emission of seed]."[8]

But *"Emissio Seminis"* was not the sole reason Castlehaven's case was brought to trial. Indeed, as Jonathan Goldberg claims, early modern sodomy had to be coupled with another transgression before it became a matter of public censure: acts of sodomy "emerge into visibility only when those who are said to have done them also can be called traitors, heretics, or the like, at the very least, disturbers of the social order that alliance—marriage arrangements—maintained." Similarly, Cynthia Herrup observes that Castlehaven was convicted for a complex of sinful actions that constituted him as a lewd character in a general sense: "Castlehaven's behavior was seen as a unity; the case was not about any one crime, but about a style of living that made believable his complicity in a variety of moral crimes. The threat he exposed was not in isolated actions, but in the way that sin compounded sin."[9] One of Castlehaven's kindred "moral crimes" consisted of his reputedly being Catholic. Prior to his marriage to the Countess, he had flirted with Catholicism, but, according to Herrup, he appears ultimately to have conformed to the Church of England. Nevertheless, old allegations die hard, particularly for an Earl with strong ties to Ireland, and he proved unable to shake the stigma of Catholic leanings. Historians B. R. Burg and H. Montgomery Hyde have noted that the Attorney-General, Sir Robert Heath, who prosecuted the "papistical" Earl was a "bitter anti-Catholic." Moreover, Heath had the support of "zealous English Puritans" who saw in Castlehaven's transgressions an opportunity "to bring a Catholic nobleman to trial under circumstances where the Romish Charles I and his Catholic queen could not exert influence."[10]

The question of Charles's involvement in Castlehaven's trial and conviction is the subject of some historical debate. Lawrence Stone asserts that Charles could have but chose not to intervene on Castlehaven's behalf. He maintains that Charles's decision to let justice run its course represented a futile attempt to shore up the "moral authority" of the aristocracy: "Throughout the whole of this period archidiaconal courts and town magistrates had been treating the sexual peccadilloes of the lower orders with extreme severity, and the discrepancy between the generally enforced moral code and the licence of the Court became an established part of public belief. Impinging upon the puritan conscience, this was a powerful factor in undermining the moral authority of both the peerage and the Court." Ultimately, Charles's failure to pardon Castlehaven underscored the decline not only in the moral authority but also in the political authority of the "peerage and the Court." The form of power they embodied, says Stone, began to give way to that articulated by the "urban bourgeoisie and the puritan divines." These two groups initiated "the shift away from paternal authority" in favor of extending "the power of the central government." Unlike Stone, Herrup contends that Charles actively sought to bring Castlehaven to trial because the Earl had offended the King's deeply held beliefs in virtuous fatherhood. In her view, Charles was the least likely English king to be sympathetic to Castlehaven.[11]

Charles's extraordinary decorousness notwithstanding, the jury of peers may also have found Castlehaven's sexual behavior particularly threatening to their authority as fathers and heads of households. Herrup asserts that the "Earl's alleged profligacy and lewdness made him the enemy rather than the protector of his house and so by implication the enemy of every household." One crime that the peers appear to have decided was particularly "unfatherly" was Castlehaven's alleged role in contriving his wife's rape. In an act that was certainly much more transgressive than raping her himself, Castlehaven apparently urged and enabled his servant, Broadway, to violate the body of an aristocratic woman, Anne, Countess of Castlehaven. Broadway testifies that Castlehaven commanded him to have sexual intercourse with his wife: "He lay at the beds feet, and in the night he [Castlehaven] called for Tobacco, and as he brought it, caught him, and bid him come to bed to him and his wife, and held one of his wives legs, and both her hands, and at last he [Broadway] lay with her, notwithstanding her resistance."[12] The Countess adds, in her deposition, that the rape drove her to attempt suicide: "she would have killed her selfe afterwards with a knife, but that hee [Castlehaven] took it from her." In making his case against Castlehaven, however, Heath does not invoke the Countess's pain and humiliation but rather focuses on the rape as a violation of matrimonial order: "for I find his intentions bent to have his wife naught, which the wickedest man that ever I heard of before would have vertuous, and godly, how bad soever himself be."[13] What Heath deems troubling is not Castlehaven's violence against his wife but his conscious effort to corrupt her virtue. The fact that the peers found him more guilty of rape than of sodomy suggests their unwillingness to tolerate his flagrant assault on conventional ideals of family order.[14] After all, in sodomizing his servant, Castlehaven had merely reproduced the relationships of power that structured the early modern social hierarchy. (As Alan Bray observes, homosexual relationships were "common between masters and servants.")[15] But by employing his servant to rape the Countess, he had deliberately conspired against aristocratic values by corrupting his wife's chastity.

While the peers recognized and responded to the charges of rape and sodomy as distinct entities, the text of Castlehaven's trial suggests that the Earl employs the system of marriage alliances as a vehicle for expressing his homosexual desire. According to the trial testimony, Castlehaven had threatened the authority of his family name not only by exhorting Broadway to rape his wife but also by engineering a sexual relationship between another servant, Henry Skipwith, and his daughter-in-law, Lady Elizabeth Audeley. The twelve-year-old Lady Audeley was the daughter of the Countess by a previous marriage and the wife of Castlehaven's son, also by a former marriage, James Touchet. In her deposition, Lady Audeley claims that Castlehaven blackmailed her into having intercourse with Skipwith: "When the Earl solicited her first, he said, that upon his knowledge her husband loved her not; and threatened, that he [Castlehaven] would turn her out of doors, if she did not lie with Skipwith; and that if she did not, he would tell her husband she did." After the Earl coerced her into assenting to his scheme, Skipwith claims that Castlehaven helped him penetrate her body: "she was but twelve years of age when he first lay with her, and that he could not enter her body without art; and that the lord Audley fetched oil to open her body."[16] While Castlehaven organized this liaison, in part, to satisfy his voyeuristic desires, he also hoped, according to Skipwith, that it would produce a son: "my Lord said that hee would rather have a boy of his getting than any other."[17] Much more cogently even than in the case of his wife's rape, Castlehaven, in encouraging Skipwith to father a son and illegitimate heir with Lady Audeley, deliberately attempts to subvert patriarchal authority. The editor of the 1679 version of the trial elaborates the, to him, horrifying implications of Castlehaven's "bastard" intentions: "to betray the Chastity of an Innocent Lady of 12 years, his own Daughter-in-Law, whose Children (if any had been) should have been Peers of this Realm." As Herrup puts it: "To encourage the very thing that so much law and custom was intended to avoid was almost unthinkable."[18]

The sexual relationship between Skipwith and Lady Audeley not only threatens patriarchy's claims to authenticity but also serves as a vehicle through which Castlehaven articulates his desire for Skipwith. Among the three servants who are named as Castlehaven's bedfellows, Henry Skipwith appears, as Fitzpatrick asserts, to have been "the speciall favourite of the Lord." Fitzpatrick is not alone in documenting the special relationship between Skipwith and Castlehaven: all of the witnesses refer to him as either the Earl's primary sexual partner or the chief actor in his scenes of debauchery. According to another servant, Walter Bigges, Castlehaven presented his "speciall favourite" with gifts of money and land including an annual salary of five hundred pounds and a one-time gift of one thousand pounds. In light of all that is suggested about his alliance with Castlehaven, Skipwith is remarkably vague about the nature of his sexual relationship with his master. His deposition states simply that: "He spent five hundred pounds *per annum* of the Lords purse. He lay for the most part in bed with the Earle: hee gave him his house in Salisbury, and a Mannour of a hundred and threescore pound *per annum*; and that he usually lay with the young Lady, and there was love before and afterwards."[19] While Skipwith's testimony is ambiguous enough to save him from formal charges of sodomy, it does, for all practical purposes, suggest a sex-for-money relationship.[20] By incorporating his sexual liaison with Lady Audeley into the network of sodomy and money, Skipwith tacitly recognizes that her body participates in the exchange of goods and passion between himself and Castlehaven. Unlike gifts of money and land, however, Lady Audeley's body serves as a site through which the Earl can circulate his affection for his "speciall favourite" in terms of patriarchal authority. Through her body, Castlehaven attempts to express the "love that dared not speak its name" by proposing that his own family name refer not to the paternity of his son but to that of his beloved Skipwith.

The legal authorities present at Castlehaven's trial do not, of course, explicitly recognize that he reverses the structure of patriarchal authority to articulate his illicit desire. As Goldberg notices, the "homosocial imaginary" "depends upon the unavailability or unavowability . . . of its relationship to homosexuality." However, patriarchy's unspoken affiliation with homosexual desire emerges in the closing statement of the trial's master of ceremonies, Sir Thomas Coventry: "O thinke upon your offences, which a Christian ought scarce to name, and which the depraved nature of man, which carries us to all vice, yet hates this unnatural sin; and you have not onely offended against the nature, but the rage of a man [James Touchet?], jealousie; and though you dye not for it, yet you have abused your daughter, and having honour and fortune to leave behind, you would have had the spurious seed of a varlet to inherit both."[21] What is immediately striking about Coventry's outrage is that he does not focus his remarks on the legal charges of rape and sodomy but on sodomy and the "abuse" of Castlehaven's "daughter." Discoursing on the "unnatural sin" leads Coventry to deem Castlehaven an unnatural father who violates his son Touchet's power over his wife's body by handing his "daughter" over to a "varlet." The fact that

Castlehaven has displaced the authority of his own son appears to be less worrisome to Coventry than the broader affront to aristocratic patriarchy of transferring property to a trading partner who is presumably incapable of returning the favor: Skipwith, after all, cannot confer "honour and fortune" on anyone. Because Coventry links sodomy with a disadvantageous alliance forged by two men through the body of a woman, he tacitly recognizes that Castlehaven uses a homosocial structure to effect a potentially subversive exchange between two men. Coventry's "spurious seed" realizes the possibility that Castlehaven deeds Lady Audeley to Skipwith not only to disrupt lines of inheritance but also to represent the *"Emissio Seminis"* that can pass between two men in another kind of illicit union.

While the text of Castlehaven's trial demonstrates how he undoes the homosocial to express his homosexual desire, his own defense invokes the homosocial in order to assert that the charges brought against him are part of a conspiracy organized by the subjects of patriarchy—his wife, his son, his servants. Just before the jury begins its deliberations, Castlehaven urges the peers to consider how quickly his plight could become theirs:

1. Woe to that man, whose Wife should be a Witness against him!
2. Woe to that man, whose Son should persecute him, and conspire his death![22]
3. Woe to that man, whose Servants should be allowed Witnesses to take away his life!

And he willed the Lords to take this into their consideration; for it might be some of their cases, or the case of any gentleman of worth, that keeps a footman or other, whose wife is weary of her husband, or his son arrived to full age, that would draw his servants to conspire his father's death.

Castlehaven's tale of woe attempts to terrorize his fellow peers by presenting him as a father whose social subordinates have engaged the legal justice system to upend his rightful authority. Despite his efforts to persuade his peers that his and their interests intersect, his appeal for clemency falls on deaf ears. Herrup suggests that the peers deny his plea precisely because his understanding of patriarchy violates their sense of themselves as fathers: "Castlehaven's actions threatened the establishment so deeply because his alleged behaviour and his defence followed so closely, if scurrilously, ordinary expectations about the behaviour and rights of every patriarch within his home. His was a perversion of a ubiquitous ideal, and like any good caricature, it had the power to make people see the original with fresh eyes."[23] As Castlehaven had hoped, the peers may well have noted their kinship with him, but, unfortunately for him, they did not like what they saw.

By appealing to the absolute authority of paternity, Castlehaven attempts to stimulate a form of homosocial bonding that his peers refuse to grant him. Perhaps because he perceives himself to have been betrayed by his fellow noblemen, Castlehaven writes a letter to his sister, Lady Eleanor, just before his execution in which he identifies himself with Jonah, the prophet of broken promises: *"Reveale O Daniel, I send thee 1631. farewells with thankes for thy letter and advice. But I am bound for* Nineveh: *And having bidden Tarshish farewell. Not fearing death, I doe not desire life."*[24] Imitating his sister's appropriation of the prophetic persona of Daniel, he takes on the burden of Jonah. While Daniel's prophecies consist of astonishing predictions and complex visions, those of the reluctant Jonah are ultimately emptied of meaning by a God who fails to obliterate Nineveh. Because God had commissioned Jonah to preach the destruction of Nineveh, the subsequent salvation of the city "greatly displeased" the prophet. Jonah claims that by rescuing the city God has broken his word to him and has, consequently, undermined his prophetic authority. Angered by God's betrayal, Jonah insists that he would be better off dead: *"It is* better for me to die than to live."* As he welcomes death, Castlehaven too finds himself traduced, if not by God *per se*, by a vision of patriarchal authority in which he had placed his faith. To some degree, he may be right to claim betrayal. As Herrup notes, the peers needed to repudiate Castlehaven because he made them look bad: "By corrupting the ideal of patriarchy, the Earl revealed too starkly an abusive power that all patriarchs sought to cloak over with talk of responsibility and benevolence."[25] Because he revealed the dark side of patriarchy, he had to be silenced.

On the other hand, Castlehaven himself can be said to have deliberately distorted patriarchy. In the pleasure he allegedly derives from watching Broadway rape his wife and Skipwith have sexual intercourse with his daughter-in-law, Castlehaven resembles the Marquis de Sade's libertines who, according to Roland Barthes, revel in the various scenes of debauchery they create: "Libertine morality consists not in destroying but in diverting; it diverts the object, the word, the organ from its endoxal usage; however, for this theft to occur, for the libertine system to prevaricate at the expense of common morality, the meaning must persist."[26] Even at his most unfatherly, Castlehaven, like Sade's libertines, remains constrained by "endoxal usage." Ultimately, Castlehaven emerges from the accounts of his trial as having used the language of patriarchy to reveal its affinities with violence and "transgressive" sexual desire. Rather than assessing him in moral or legal terms, we may do well to remember Castlehaven as a kind of visionary.

"HERMOPHRODITE ACTING MANKINDE"

Although Castlehaven's tale of woe fails to persuade the jury of his innocence, it becomes the vehicle through which Lady Eleanor defends her brother's memory. In her *Crying Charge* of 1649, she concurs with his assessment that he is a patriarch wronged and characterizes him as a martyr for household reform: "And this mans house utterly ruined, chiefly, because had declined Popery, before his untimely death ever suspected; endeavoring to reform his Family, by which means cast himself upon the merciless times. Mervin, Earl of Castlehaven, that faithful Martyr."[27] Lady Eleanor insists that, despite countervailing claims, Castlehaven stands not for Roman Catholicism but for Protestantism, and not for sexual depravity but for the family. Her first three responses to her brother's death lay the blame for it on the "false" testimony of the Countess, the perjured testimony of his servant Broadway, and the diffidence of Charles. In *Restitution*, however, these themes coalesce to place Castlehaven's execution at the center of a battle of the sexes in which voracious female sexuality triumphs over lapsed masculine solidarity. Castlehaven himself had seemingly cued his sister's interpretation of events when he warned his peers about scheming wives: "Woe to that man, whose Wife should be a Witness against him!" It would be for his sister to elaborate the deleterious consequences of his woe.

In her aptly titled 1633 broadside *Woe to the House*, Lady Eleanor introduces the evil character, the Countess of Castlehaven, who populates all of her responses to her brother's execution. She imagines the Countess together with her sister, Elizabeth Stanley, Countess of Huntingdon, as part of a depraved duo that has, respectively, deprived Castlehaven of his life and Lady Eleanor of her property. As the mother-in-law of Lady Eleanor's daughter Lucy, the Countess of Huntingdon participated in a legal action that challenged Lady Eleanor's right to inherit the property bequeathed her by her first husband Sir John Davies. The Countess of Huntingdon and other members of her family sought to have the property transferred to Lucy and her husband Ferdinando Hastings so that it could add to the family's holdings. From 1627 to 1633, Lady Eleanor and her second husband Sir Archibald Douglas engaged in a legal tug-of-war with the Hastings family. Lady Eleanor was briefly awarded the property just around the time of the printing of *Woe to the House*. However, because she was subsequently arrested and imprisoned for distributing *Woe* and her other 1633 treatises, she lost her right to the property and would not regain it for another decade. In the *dramatis personae* of *Woe*, Lady Eleanor expresses her contempt for the Countess of Huntingdon's efforts to seize her property with the anagram: "Elizabeth Stanley. That Jezebel Slain." She pairs the Countess of Huntingdon with a second Stanley sister, the Countess of Castlehaven, whom she denounces with another suitably rancorous anagram: "Ana Stanley. A Lye Satann."[28]

Woe portrays both Stanley sisters as types of Jezebel. Not surprisingly, Lady Eleanor focuses on Jezebel's role in Naboth's assasination to illustrate how both the Countess of Castlehaven has conspired against her husband and the Countess of Huntingdon has sought to subvert the terms of Davies's will:[29] "So she wrote letters in Ahabs name, and sealed them with this seale, and sent letters unto the El-ders, and to the Nobles that were in the city. She wrote in the letters &c. Set two men sonns of Belial before him, to beare witnesse against, saying, &c. And the men of the city, the Elders, and the Nobles who were the inhabitants of the city, did as Jezebel had sent unto them. And there came two men, children of Belial, and the men of Belial witnessed."[30] Her transcription of Kings suggests that as types of Jezebel both Stanley sisters lay claim to power that is not rightfully theirs: "she wrote letters in Ahabs name." For Lady Eleanor, who believed so strongly in the authority of family names, assuming a false name becomes the most egregious and threatening of transgressions. Indeed, when the Countess of Castlehaven is seen as a type of Jezebel, her false claims of truthfulness find the "El-ders" and "Nobles" ceding power to her and executing Castlehaven. While Lady Eleanor's appropriation of Kings emphasizes Jezebel's duplicity, it subtly insinuates the unwitting collusion of the "Nobles" as ratifying that woman's evil plots. More than on Castlehaven's innocence, the passage meditates on the fatal results that follow the Countess's duping of the "Nobles."

Although Lady Eleanor in *Woe* identifies the Countess of Castlehaven and the Countess of Huntingdon as types of Jezebel and Castlehaven as a type of Naboth, she does not specify a seventeenth-century type of Ahab. Some of her later writings, however, suggest that with respect to her brother's situation Charles might be a likely candidate to fill Ahab's role. For instance, in her 1644 *Word of God*, she portrays Charles in Ahab-like fashion standing idly by as her brother is sent to his death. She rather sneeringly depicts Charles attempting to elevate the manner of her brother's death by offering him the opportunity to be beheaded rather than hanged. According to Lady Eleanor, Charles's belated effort to recognize Castlehaven's noble status meets with scorn from her brother: "And so what the prisoner answered to them: *when his Majesties Chaplins came and told him the king had a gracious purpose to alter the manner of his death. And that he should be beheaded like a Noble man: Replyed he should esteeme that Haulter which should draw HIM to Heaven before a collor* [sic] *of pearle or the like.*" In her 1649 *Crying Charge*, Lady Eleanor also insisted that Charles failed to act on her brother's behalf, and she urged the Army Officers trying Charles's case to add this to the list of his crimes against the nation. Moreover, as an extension of his political impotence, Lady Eleanor views Charles, like Ahab, as unduly uxurious. In her 1644 *From the Lady Eleanor, Her Blessing*, Lady Eleanor directly likens Henrietta-Maria to Jezebel. The latter promoted Baal worship while the former advances the equally heathenish, in her view, Roman Catholic faith: "This blood-thirsty Mistress of *Charmes* and *Spells* like Satans falling those aspiring Spirits." Echoing both her 1633 *Woe* and the Ahab-Jezebel story, Lady Eleanor even goes so far as to attribute all of England's problems to the new Jezebel, Henrietta-Maria: "The occasion of this LANDS *deep* CONSUMPTION *SHE*, And wast made *thereof: Woe to the House of God*, and the House of PARLIAMENT both, the nursing mother of *DRAGONS*, those *Sonns* of *BELIALL* in armes, for as her name is, so is she MARRAH: *The GALL of bitternesse.*"[31] While her Jezebels of 1633 and 1644 do seize power from male rulers, her meditations on the Book of Kings and its seventeenth-century types do not portray an inverted world order in which grasping female desire triumphs over weakened institutions of male power. That will come later in *Restitution*. But already she has begun to lay the framework for a reading of Castlehaven's trial that emphasizes the betrayal of her early modern Naboth at the hands of the king and the peers.

From the outset, *Restitution* signals its focus on female authority with its catalogue of powerful female figures. None of Lady Eleanor's previous texts open with such a plethora of women. This is not to say, however, that her catalogue is a pro-woman showcase. Rather, her review of the political impact of these women is mixed. She begins by comparing her own relationship to her prophetic tracts to Mary's relationship to Christ. Then she moves to consider the first of the three apocalyptic parables in Matthew 25 that structure *Restitution*—the account of the bridegroom and the five foolish and five wise virgins who await his arrival.[32] Talk of weddings leads her to consider Charles's unfortunate match with the Catholic Henrietta-Maria. One Catholic queen suggests another, and she takes up the topic of the bloody reign of Mary Tudor. The memory of Queen Mary inspires the happier memory of her half-sister Queen Elizabeth's reign. Turning to the second apocalyptic parable in Matthew 25—that of the talents—she introduces Castlehaven's execution. This prompts her to denounce his wife whom she compares, in short order, to the Whore of Babylon. Meditating on the Countess's whorish treachery against her brother inspires her to imagine the Whore as ruling over London. In perhaps her most stunning satirical excursus, Lady Eleanor presents the Whore governing Dulness-like over a city given to all manner of dissolute behavior. Like Pope, Lady Eleanor takes particular umbrage at the state of contemporary publishing: "that *mother* of *Witchcrafts*, branded for a Baud, whose *Babel-Pyramid* fired. Fictions of fresh *edition, University Excrements* daily, whereby *oppressing Shops* and *Presses* with them: overflowing too shameful, whilest *Close-Stools* set to sale, lined through with *Scriptures old* and *new*" (354). Lady Eleanor's Whore oversees a publishing milieu in which "University Excrements" predominate in book shops while Scripture is relegated to the linings of chamber pots.

Her catalogue portrays both women whose power bodes ill for mankind and women whose authority is consistent with patriarchal values. In particular, her discussion of Elizabeth I focuses on the Queen's virginity as a sign of her patriarchal legitimacy. She identifies Elizabeth simply as an excellent ruler who was buried on the feast of the Annunciation: Mary Tudor was "By her *Virgin Sister* succeeded, in the Five and fortieth of whose unmatchable Reign was Interred at the *Virgins Annunciation*" (348). Lady Eleanor emphasizes Elizabeth's kinship not with her half-sister Mary Tudor but with Virgin Mary. And because Elizabeth's death occurs on the feast of the Annunciation, Lady Eleanor implies that the Queen, like Virgin Mary, has been called by her heavenly father to bear his word. In this respect, Elizabeth shares with Lady Eleanor a right to claim political authority predicated upon the "Heavenly voyce" of the father.

Two of Lady Eleanor's earlier references to Elizabeth corroborate, by explicitly commenting on the Queen's gender, the sense in *Restitution* that she embodies the proper form of female authority. First, in *Great Brittains Visitation* produced at the height of the Civil War in 1645, she compares the magnificent, manly reign of Elizabeth with the effeminacy of contemporary Royalists: "whose [the Royalist soldiers'] Image with deformed haire, Hermophradite Locks, none of that mayden Queens doubtlesse with Breast plates all, &c. such tormenting doings and Dolers unknowne in her dayes." Elizabeth ruled like a man and order prevailed, whereas contemporary Royalists behave as women and so chaos predominates. While she does not paint a particularly flattering portrait of femininity, Lady Eleanor indicates that women can participate in power's masculine nature. Shortly after Charles's execution, she returns to the topic of Elizabeth's reign in *The New Jerusalem at Hand* to assert that, despite opinion to the contrary, men do not necessarily make better rulers: "in making him [Charles] King of *Great Brittain*, evident the Lord repenting himself much more, well served for their Repining, whom *Nothing but a king would serve*, who blest were above all kingdoms; so in a virgin *Queens* renowned Reign."[33] Although she does not identify this Elizabeth as ruling like a man, she certainly does not indicate that she rules like a woman. Rather her virginity, a link in so many of Lady Eleanor's texts between women and paternal power, appears to be the reason for her "renowned Reign."

While, on the one hand, Lady Eleanor's catalogue of powerful women suggests that women can effectively govern in accordance with her version of patriarchal values, her catalogue also indicates that women can gain power independent of traditional structures of authority. This is evident not only in the individual wicked women who have risen to the fore, but also in the structure of *Restitution* itself. While the first half of *Restitution* is laden with figures of female authority, the second half describes the executions of some of the period's most prominent men: Castlehaven, Strafford, Laud, and Charles.[34] The massing of male and female authorities at each end of *Restitution* suggests that, to some degree, the text concerns a power struggle between two opposing forces. While a kind of battle between the sexes does contribute to the tone, the text also indicates that women have only gained power through the decline of masculine authorities. Rather than a direct confrontation, *Restitution* emphasizes the negative consequences that derive from the collapse of traditional patriarchal rule.

Much of *Restitution* and particularly its response to Castlehaven's execution explores the more destructive face of female power. In taking up the subject of her old nemesis, the Countess, she deems her a type of the Whore of Babylon whose successful testimony against Castlehaven signals the approach of the end times. She predicates the Countess's resemblance to the Whore in terms of the imagery that adorns the Stanley family crest: "I will shew thee the *Mystery* of the *Woman*. [Castlehaven][35] And the Beast that *beareth* or *carrieth her*, &c. Expresly *Herals* their *Mystery* which *demonstrates*: And present *Century* the seventeenth. *As behold whose Arms? And they shall eat her Flesh and burn her with Fire*, besides hers some four-footed rather . . . What *Bruit* or *Flesh* of Beast in most request, *Eaten*, &c. Points to so many *Stags Heads* born in a *Bend*, or their *Skulls*, &c. Touching whose *Arms* suffices so much refer'd to *Sign Posts*" (350). The three stags' heads emblazoned on the Stanley coat of arms suggest, for Lady Eleanor, the passage in Revelation in which the seven angels predict that the minions of the Beast and the Whore will turn against her and "eat her flesh."[36] Because the Stanley crest symbolizes the "Flesh of the Beast in most request" on the eve of the day of judgement, Lady Eleanor not only identifies the Countess as a type of the Whore but also indicates that her wicked reign fast approaches its conclusion. By making the Countess into an arbiter of apocalypse, Lady Eleanor can reconcile her brother's death as symptomatic of a political order nearing the end of its tenure.

As further evidence of the depravity of the era, Lady Eleanor identifies the Countess's marital infidelity as the specific act that makes her both a type of the Whore and a leading political figure. For Lady Eleanor, the Countess's betrayal of her husband is consistent with the treachery of the Church of England: "when she no ordinary *Whore*, charged with a *Husband, Blood*: worthy of no other *Cup, Naked* and *Burnt*. Credible *Witness* of the *Churches Apostacy, Figures* in her later *Days* what a faithful *Spouse*; sealed with *Sabbatical Heads* of the Scarlet coloured *Beast* (*Cruelties Character*) with *Oxford* and *Cambridge*, no mean *Strumpets*, whose Denomination interrested [sic] in the *Ten Horns*" (352). Like the "Sabbatical Heads" of the Church of England, the

Countess has been an unfaithful "Spouse" and is "charged with a Husband, Blood." While Lady Eleanor employs an image common to early modern apocalyptic writing when she represents the Whore of Babylon as a type of the apostate church, her contention that a historical woman, the Countess, serves as a referent for the Whore marks a significant departure from the mainstream of apocalyptic literature. According to Christopher Hill, the seventeenth-century figures commonly identified as types of the Whore were also generally acknowledged political entities. Over the course of the revolutionary era, those linked to the Whore included: bishops, Charles I, Charles's armed supporters, and the Fifth Monarchists.[37] By giving the Whore of Babylon the name of a woman who would not have been recognized by most as a political player, Lady Eleanor invokes a misogynous image in order to lend cosmic significance to the Countess's deeds. For Lady Eleanor, the idea that a woman driven by unbridled lust could gain a position of authority becomes not merely a fiction of the Book of Revelation nor a figure of speech for describing a corrupt ecclesiastical government but a reality borne out in the person of the Countess.

Precisely by employing a derogatory figure of female sexuality can Lady Eleanor elaborate the deleterious effects of the failure of the Peers to bond as brothers to rescue the Earl. With Castlehaven's conviction, they have, in Lady Eleanor's mind, handed a brother over into the clutches of a sexually voracious woman: "Cast by a *Jury* of Peers: His unnatural *Jury* of *Brethren*, as sold him, *figure* of the *Lamb*, called the *Dreamer*: *scorned* and *stript* of his *Garment*. Also between those two, through her lust" (356). Like the brothers in the Genesis account of Joseph, Castlehaven's peers have sold him into bondage in Israel.[38] While "between those two, through her lust" explicitly refers to the lust of the Countess that causes the Earl, like Christ crucified between two thieves, to be killed between Broadway and Fitzpatrick, it also resonates the Joseph story.[39] When Joseph was sold into slavery, the wife of his first Egyptian master, Potiphar, accused him of attempting to rape her. Her false charge came after Joseph had literally fled her efforts to seduce him.[40] By invoking the Joseph account, Lady Eleanor effectively correlates brotherly duplicity with overweening female sensuousness. Like Joseph's brothers, the peers have sold Castlehaven into the bondage of female caprice. The failure of aristocratic homosociality ushers in a new form of sexual deviance: instead of exchanging women between men, Castlehaven's jury takes on a female trading partner and sacrifices a man on her behalf. In the eyes of his sister, Castlehaven's jury rather than her brother is guilty of "unnatural" acts.

By critiquing the failure of aristocratic male solidarity, Lady Eleanor recalls Castlehaven's "three woes" defense. And like Castlehaven himself, Lady Eleanor's text contends that by declaring him a sexual pervert the jury has granted power to a wicked woman. Lady Eleanor effectively "inverts" the decision of the jury of peers by asserting that they, in convicting her brother, have undermined their own political authority. In his discussion of Renaissance theatricality, Dollimore identifies the sort of "inversion" Lady Eleanor's text invokes as a trope of insubordination: "Inversion becomes a kind of transgressive mimesis: the subculture, even as it imitates, reproducing itself in terms of its exclusion, also demystifies, producing a knowledge of the dominant which excludes it, this being a knowledge which the dominant has to suppress in order to rule."[41] By convicting Castlehaven of sodomy, the forces of the "dominant" have engendered the Countess as a phallic woman and have thus rendered themselves impotent. In other words, Lady Eleanor counters the legal injunctions against her brother's purported acts of sodomy with the threat of a castrating figure of gender abomination. Much more harrowing than the possibility of male-male sexual contact is the reversal of male-female sexual roles that the jury of peers has inaugurated. Although the "dominant" typically "suppresses" the "knowledge" that the exchange of women and "spurious seed" between men may be psychically interchangeable, Lady Eleanor's text suggests that, in convicting her brother of sodomy and validating the Countess's testimony, the peers elevate her brother's wife above her naturally subject position and tacitly reveal the "unnatural" ties binding them together as brothers. If not linked through the subordination of women, then another medium—spurious seed, perhaps—joins Castlehaven's "unnatural Jury of Brethren."

Lady Eleanor finds further evidence of deviant behavior on the part of Castlehaven's persecutors when she compares her brother's treatment before the law with that of his contemporary Sir Kenelm Digby. According to Cope, Digby, "despite his popish religion, associations with the Queen, and alleged responsibility for his wife's sudden death in May 1633 by forcing her to drink 'viper wine,' had escaped the fate of Mervin, earl of Castlehaven."[42] Lady Eleanor's brooding and complex meditation on her brother's unjust punishment opens by framing the Countess's "supposed" rape and Digby's wife, Venetia Stanley's "real" victimization in terms of the story of the rape of Europa: "What *Strumpet, Baud,* &c. As *points* to that *fiction*: of ravished *Europia,* carried on the *Bull* into the *Sea*: true as the others [the Countess's] *Rape* . . . so to another [Venetia Stanley's story] not long since no *fiction* on this *River* . . . And *Knight* Errand [Digby], no small *Bull*: supported by his Hand; laid upon her . . . With his Venetian, she free of the aforesaid three *Stags Heads*; the *Horns* his too &c. with her *Cup* of *Viper Wine,* that never awakened" (354–55). Like the Countess, Venetia Stanley belongs to the Stanley family, but she has been "freed" from the insignia of the "three Stags Heads" by death. Digby is not punished for his deeds but rather, as Henrietta-Maria's servant, participates in the raucous goings-on of the Queen's court.

Lady Eleanor describes Henrietta-Maria's court as a type of the regal gathering presided over by Herodias that features the execution of John the Baptist as an entertainment:

> All which copied out by that *Piece,* when his [Herod's] *butcherly birth-day* kept, bound himself, &c. Instructed by her *Mother Baud,* dancing her lacivious *Jigs* and *Tricks*: beheaded the *Baptist*; late by her, and her Ladies not onely Hermophrodite acting *mankinde*; but sworn by his *precious,* &c. And *wounds* by their base *Players. Let us eat and drink, to morrow is our last*: More true then aware of, notwithstanding a Mote in anothers Eye perceive, so returning to his last account, made *even,* or confession on *Tower-hill,* arrived the *Haven* above, *This day be thou with me,* &c. *Enter thou into thy Lord and Masters joy. Easter* Term, *An. Dom.* 31.(355)

What makes this passage so rich is that the main characters in the biblical account of John the Baptist's execution suggest a number of seventeenth-century types. As the Queen's servant, Digby could be a type of Herod matched with her Herodias. Charles, because a ruler, could easily fill Herod's role. Both the Bible's Herod and Lady Eleanor's Charles are men who are dominated by their conniving wives. Charles may not have wanted to execute Castlehaven but, like Herod, feels constrained by his promise: "but sworn by his precious." While Henrietta-Maria is clearly a type of Herodias, the Countess is another candidate for the part. Perhaps as "Mother Baud," she instructs her daughter Elizabeth, a potential type of Salome, to testify against Castlehaven. As for Castlehaven, he is a type of the passage's John the Baptist and Christ. In his role as John the Baptist, he suffers at the hands of a domineering woman, the lusty Countess. Worst of all a group of effeminate men—"Hermophrodite acting man-

kinde"—aids her muderous plot. With biting sarcasm, Lady Eleanor indicates that "Hermophrodite acting mankinde" must share
credit for "beheading the Baptist" with the Countess and her
"Ladies." In defining the impotence of Charles and the peers,
Lady Eleanor raises the specter of gender confusion.[43] As her-
maphrodites, the men of her generation have a pronounced femininity. In other words, the impotence of the hermaphroditic
aristocracy may underscore a latent desire to be penetrated, to
have their bodies used as those of women. As Lady Eleanor
might have it, the failure of homosociality is not simply "unnatural" but conducive of homosexuality.

While "wicked" women such as the "lusty" Countess and the
idol worshipping Henrietta-Maria have achieved political prominence, they have done so because the men of Lady Eleanor's
generation have not behaved like real men. As much as she professes to despise these women, her text portrays her prophetic
authority as similarly derived from the breakdown of traditional
male institutions. Of course, Lady Eleanor does not represent
herself as a grasping, ambitious woman; indeed she identifies
herself with Virgin Mary and thereby implicitly offers her prophetic career as an antidote to the reign of the Whore. Nevertheless, Lady Eleanor's focus on the phallic aspect of the Mary
myth—the Virgin's ability to become pregnant without a human
father—parallels the Whore's characteristic displacement of
male authority. She likens the publication of her text to the birth
of Christ because both enter the world without conventional
fathers: "This *Babe*, object to their scorn, for speaking the *truth*,
informing of things future, notwithstanding thus difficult to be *fathered* or *licensed*. That *incision* to the *quick*, hath under gone;
without their *Benediction*, in these plain *Swathe-bands*, though
commended unto thy hands" (344). She translates her career-
long "difficulty" with official censorship into a figure of parthen-
ogesis. And while the myth of the virgin birth suggests divine *inflatus*, Lady Eleanor obfuscates the possible agency of a
supernatural being by concentrating on the mundane legal requirements for publication. Her text cannot be "fathered" or "licensed," so it must be printed outside of official channels,
undergoing an "incision to the quick." Such an "incision," her
text and career intimate, was rendered by Lady Eleanor's willingness to surmount the legal obstacles posed by official "father-
hood" and not by the active intervention of God. With the
publication of *Restitution*, Lady Eleanor implies that she reluctantly but necessarily usurps paternal authority.

While her representation of herself as a type of Mary only tacitly disparages her gender, her later claim that her prophetic
commission is due to the contemptuousness of her male contemporaries offers a strategically negative assessment of woman-
kind: "The present *Age* sent to School to the *Ox, Ass*, and *Camel*;
In their *Litter* knows its owner, better observes the time, and for
times Mystery and *Seasons*. The weaker *Sex* preferred more
proper for them, requisit for former days neither" (365). As Cope
notes, the "Ox, Ass, and Camel" are "proverbially stubborn animals." Moreover, the passage obliquely alludes to the story, in
Daniel, of King Nebuchadnezzar's ejection from his palace for
not acknowledging God's almighty power: "the most High ruleth
in the kingdom of men, and giveth it to whomsoever he will."
Once driven from human society, Nebuchadnezzar was forced to
dwell among animals as an animal. Lady Eleanor had presented
the story of Nebuchadnezzar in *Given to the Elector* as an admonition against vanity and pride:

> Hardened in pride, unheard of such,
>   the wilde Ass with did dwell:
> Sent to the Ox it owner knows,
>   undreamt of this his doom . . .
> Whose Heart made equal with the Beast,
>   driven out with those that Bray;
> The Diadem as well fits thee,
>   Ass, go as much to say.[44]

In *Restitution*, she suggests that because the men of her generation have affected the stubbornness of stupid animals, God has
decided to break with historical tradition and address these pathetic men through the voice of a member of the "weaker Sex."
Her existence as a prophet then serves as a form of divine punishment. Once again, she appeals to male ineffectuality as the
form of social deviance that requires her to publicize her visions.
Her simultaneous assertion of the dreadful circumstances that
enable her vocation and the legitimacy of her prophetic authority
circles the corpse of her brother and the failure of aristocratic
homosociality that kills him.
　　The final irony of Lady Eleanor's self-representation is that by
identifying herself as a woman driven to wield political power because the men of her generation have become hopelessly incapable of leadership, she inadvertently allies herself with the Whore
of Babylon and, by extension, with Anne, Countess of Castle-

haven. In a certain sense, this is not terribly surprising since both women appear indifferent to the virtues of wifely submission. As a woman who predicted the death of her first husband Sir John Davies (after he burned her prophetic writings), Lady Eleanor can hardly condemn her sister-in-law for turning against her husband: "she a common Whore her husbands accuser." Perhaps Lady Eleanor continues to denounce the Countess's role in the Earl's trial long after his death because she envies her power to occasion her husband's execution. For Lady Eleanor's part, after each of her husbands destroys her literary offspring, she can only predict rather than cause the evil that befalls Davies and Douglas.[45] Regardless of whether Lady Eleanor secretly admires the Countess's greater authority over her husband's demise, the structure of female power in *Restitution* makes her sister-in-law into a sister who achieves authority through the failure of male homosocial power. As the Countess's double, Lady Eleanor not only defends her brother's memory but also transforms his conviction on charges of sexual deviance into the source of her prophetic authority. Ultimately, *Restitution* translates the sister's love for her brother into a bond between two unlikely sisters. And, in so doing, it anticipates the rise of a new form of female power unmoored from the authorizing structure of patriarchy.

Engendering Conspiracy

The kinship that *Restitution* forges between Lady Eleanor and the Countess, the prophet and the whore, anticipates a favorite caricature of texts that denounced the women prophets who wrote and spoke during the revolutionary period.[46] Perhaps the most hysterical and most violently misogynous of the treatises to oppose women's visionary authority is the Restoration diatribe, *The holy Sisters Conspiracy against their Husbands* (1661). An anonymous satire on sectarian and, specifically, Fifth Monarchist ideology, *The holy Sisters* portrays a fictional meeting of women engaged in conspiring to resist the new regime's proposed ban on their religious gatherings. The sisters plan to subvert Charles II's government by burning the City of London and slaughtering their husbands. Many of their sectarian brothers have already been jailed for attempting to overthrow the government and the "holy sisters" lament the loss of the sweet embraces of these men. Unlike their husbands, who withhold that "due benevolence, which . . . is owing from the Male to the Female," the brothers, it appears, are eager to embrace them in the arms of their "fervent affection" and to share their "breathings and pantings" with them.[47]

By emphasizing the sexual meanings latent in the language of spiritual inspiration, *The holy Sisters* undoes the rhetorical figures that Lady Eleanor and her sister prophets employed. While Lady Eleanor claims that her book's lack of an earthly father affirms her prophetic authority, *The holy Sisters* suggests that the sexual promiscuity of the sectarians comparably displaces earthly paternity. According to one of the sisters, Charity, she and her sectarian sisters cannot identify the fathers of their children because they have had sexual intercourse with so many men: "but what they doe to us, they do it with sobriety and discretion, and in pure love and affection, that they may raise up an holy Generation of young Saints; who may only know their Fathers after the spirit and not after the flesh; (as the children of the world do) though there were twenty of the Brethren contributing to the begetting of one little Saint."[48] Thanks to the number of the "Brethren" who participate in "the begetting of one little Saint," the holy sisters' children understand the paternal role in strictly spiritual terms. While Lady Eleanor appropriates the myth of the virgin birth to assert that her text lacks an earthly father, the author of *The holy Sisters* suggests that when female prophets deny the secular origins of their offspring they in fact use the language of spirituality to conceal their sexual licentiousness.

At the end of the text, the sisters' husbands intone their own counter-conspiracy for the purpose of preventing the spiritually inspired liaisons of their wives. In response to the question: "what, shall we doe with our Wives,/ That fisk up and down the Town?," the husbands imagine a number of ways to contain their "fisking" wives. Sylas and Sam, for instance, suggest an "Italian Lock," while Nat and Wat advise their fellow husbands to "lay 'um" and "splay 'um" in order to "make 'um safe." All assembled agree, however, that these measures are not enough: "The Sisters have such a Trick!/ No Instrument will/ Seclude 'um from ill." Finally, Dan and Mystical Sphinx contrive a definitive solution:

> Let's doe 'um like men, quoth *Dan*,
> Let's fill up their Chincks.
> Say's Mystical *Sphinx*,
> Quoth *Tassie*, then I'm your man![49]

In "doing" their wives "like men," the disgruntled husbands propose a social order in which all potential sexual relationships involve men and (wo)men with their distinctive "Chincks" filled in. Unlike the homosociality invoked by Castlehaven, that of the husbands does not function by exchanging women between men but by making the holy sisters' bodies like those of men. Nevertheless, both Castlehaven and the husbands speak through the bodies of women to articulate an "unspeakable" desire. And, in both cases, the dynamic relationship between sexual repression and political oppression that underwrites homosociality results in real or imagined acts of violence against women. Positioned between Castlehaven's trial and *The holy Sisters'* diatribe, Lady Eleanor's *Restitution* translates the terms of homosocial desire into a vehicle for female prophetic authority.

While women in the accounts of Castlehaven's trial and the unholy brothers' counterconspiracy suffer at the hands of excessive masculine authority, Lady Eleanor escapes the deleterious effects of male homosociality by lamenting its demise. Evoking her brother's tale of woe, she insists that his execution has undermined patriarchal authority. As a result, domineering women have taken center stage, representing not the rise of some new Amazonian tribe but the consequences of male ineffectuality. Lady Eleanor portrays a significant rupture in the cosmic order that finds women of all stripes, ranging from lascivious sirens to virginal prophets, stepping into the gap left by a generation of weak-willed men. The author of *The holy Sisters* sees the world much differently. Masculine impotence appears less the culprit than overweening female sensuousness. Women, according to this author, are different from men, and this sexual difference must be mastered so that order might prevail. Men, as they had for Lady Eleanor, no longer establish the ontological standard from which the meaning of woman derives but rather must impose their will on the very different bodies of the weaker sex. Although Lady Eleanor does not see women as distinct from men, she does suggest that female sexuality can be a source of female power and so anticipates both *The holy Sisters'* unflattering portraits of female prophets and actual female visionaries, such as Anna Trapnel and Margaret Fell, who directly situate their legitimacy in terms of their bodies.

3

The Semiotics of Fasting in Anna Trapnel's
The Cry of a Stone (1654)

FOR ELEVEN DAYS AND TWELVE NIGHTS IN JANUARY OF 1654, THE
Fifth Monarchist prophet, Anna Trapnel, uttered "Revelations"
on topics ranging from God's promise that the saints would rule
the nation to the, in her mind, misguided policies of Oliver Cromwell. During this time, she lay at Whitehall "in a Trance, without
taking any sustenance, except a cup of small beer once in 24
hours."[1] Her prophecies were recorded by an amanuensis and
were published as *The Cry of a Stone* (1654). Because the content of Trapnel's prophecies corroborated the political views of
the numerous Fifth Monarchists and their sympathizers who attended her bedside, the spectacle of her body, apparently closed
to earthly and open only to heavenly nourishment, served to enhance the authority of her prophetic message and, by extension,
her sect's political agenda. That Trapnel's body signified mightily
for her fellow sectarians is evident in the hagiographical tones of
the closing lines of *Cry*. There, the "Relator" (the title given to
her unnamed amanuensis) describes her restored body as nothing short of miraculous: "after she had kept her bed 11. dayes
together without any sustenance at all for the first five dayes, and
with onely a little toste in small beer once in 24 hours for the rest
of the time, she rose up in the morning, and the same day trav-
elled on foot from *White-Hall* to *Hackny*, and back to *Mark-Lane*
in *London*, in health and strength."[2] Clearly, the Relator intends
for his reader to see Trapnel's instantaneous and complete recovery as further evidence that her physical "symptoms" were
the effects of divine inspiration rather than of illness.

In addition to persuading her fellow sectarians that her words
were divinely inspired, Trapnel's miraculous body figured cen-
trally in her message itself. Although she repeatedly refused
regular nourishment as she prophesied at Whitehall, she incor-

porated food imagery into many of her prophecies. For instance, she directs merchants to prefer heavenly to earthly food:

> You have your Canded Ginger, and
> Your Preserved Nutmegs too:
> That so you may delight therein,
> And your mouthes overflow.
>
> But! oh there's canded things indeed,
> Which is covered with Gold,
> There is not such preserves as they
> Which shall be turned to mould.

(30)

More valuable than the "canded" food that they traverse the seas to find is the "Gold" of heavenly nourishment. Trapnel typically deploys food imagery, as she does here, to exhort her auditors to pursue ascetic practices. Of course, exhortations to otherworldliness are a common feature of seventeenth-century religious discourse, but what makes their appearance in Trapnel's texts so striking is that they are frequently cast in terms of food and thereby implicate the body and that they serve to advance a sectarian identity politics. In her *Report and Plea*, also written and published in 1654, she insists that abstemious food practices are integral to Fifth Monarchist identity: the saints are those who do not desire "Kitchin-belly-chear, nor Lardery-dainties, nor Banquet-sweet-meats."[3] Because Trapnel's fasting graphically illustrates her own repudiation of luxurious foods, her body becomes an example, if an extraordinary one, of the behavior that the chosen naturally emulate. In effect, Trapnel attempts to rationalize her body's extraordinary capacities as the model for Fifth Monarchist political and religious identity. Ultimately, she encourages her audience to recognize her prophecies as politically authoritative not because her body articulates the marks of divine possession but because her body articulates the marks of divine possession shared by all of the saints. Trapnel becomes political precisely by making the extraordinary exemplary.

Trapnel's attempt to generalize her own bodily experiences as a model for Fifth Monarchist identity complicates feminist claims that early modern women who sought to make their words public recognized their bodies as liabilities. Margaret Ferguson describes the problem of the female body for women writers in terms of an ideology of chastity that "made silence an equivalent of bodily purity." Similarly, Diane Purkiss contends that women's bodies were conventionally read as signs of "chaos and disorder." And, in regard to female visionaries such as Trapnel, she further argues that they used fasting to manifest a stable female body: "By representing their bodies not as open and uncontrolled but as closed to everything except God, they presented those bodies as sealed containers for the meanings instilled into them from outside, producing not a multiplicity of monstrous texts but a single unitary text whose origin was not in doubt."[4] Consistent with Ferguson's and Purkiss's claims about cultural attitudes toward the female body, Trapnel's self-representation does, in part, recognize the concern with boundaries, with openings and closings, that fuels early modern anxieties about women's bodies. Indeed, Trapnel appears to speak to these anxieties when she recounts how, during a previous fast, she had the sensation of satiety although she did not eat: "I found a continual fulness in my stomack, and the taste of divers sweet meats and delicious food therein, which satisfied me"(5). Closed to secular food, her body is implicitly open only to divine nourishment. Trapnel, however, does not exclusively comprehend her body as a female body; and in turning from autobiography to politics, she projects her capacity for physical self-denial as a feature of being chosen. In essence, Trapnel embraces her culture's anxieties about the female body only to transcend them by making her own body into a model for political and religious authority.

By representing her body as a model for the body politic, Trapnel invokes the "gender neutral" language of political theory to make her body into the standard measure of political authority. Such a standardizing gesture is, of course, common among canonical, male political theorists of the Western tradition. And Trapnel's vision of religio-political authority, with its emphasis on fasting and the body, can be seen to follow suit. After all, anyone, male or female, can be redeemed by God's saving grace; and anyone can, as a consequence of receiving grace, forego luxurious foods. Being a woman is not an essential prerequisite for fasting. Historically, however, the vast majority of extraordinary fasters in medieval and early modern Europe were women. Moreover, Trapnel's immediate contemporaries who fasted for lengthy periods of time were women. Throughout history and even up until the present, women "have used control of appetite, food, and the body as a focus of their symbolic language."[5] In the medieval and early modern periods, in particular, women used their bodies to illustrate their relationships with God. Thus, when Trapnel articulates her body as a vessel of divine grace, she implicitly locates herself in a female tradition that includes medieval saints and mystics, early modern "miraculous" fasters, and, in her case, her mother. At the same time, she presents her body as a model for Fifth Monarchist identity; and in so doing, she tacitly universalizes a female tradition of speaking about God through the body. By endowing women's history with broad political meaning, Trapnel's *Cry* emerges as a singular discourse in the literary history of both female inedia and political theory. Her text charts a radical movement from practice to theory, from numerous women's narratives about their bodies to a new vision of the body politic.

THE "SWEETNESSE OF MANNA"

One key to understanding how Trapnel transforms her gendered body into the model for a Fifth Monarchist body politic is her relationship to her contemporary, Sarah Wight. In 1647, at the age of fifteen, Wight began to prophesy when, after four years of "despairing fits," she received assurances of divine grace: "He hath dispossessed the strong man, and hath taken possession of my soule, and will dwell with me for ever, for ever, for ever."[6] This experience of redemptive grace forms the core of her prophetic message as recorded by an unnamed amanuensis and published by the prominent Baptist minister (and later Fifth Monarchist) Henry Jessey as *The Exceeding Riches of Grace* (1647).[7] While Wight's message lacks the political edge[8] of Trapnel's, she delivers it in a similar manner.[9] She proclaims God's redemptive power as she lies in bed and foregoes eating for some seventy-six days. She insists that although she appears not to eat, she in fact eats heavenly food: "No eye of man sees it, but the eye of God. None could taste the sweetness of the Manna by looking on it, none but they that eat of it" (*ER*, 33).

Amazed by the confluence of Wight's visions and her extraordinary fasting, many of the faithful, including Anna Trapnel, gathered at her bedside. Indeed, *Exceeding Riches* includes Trapnel (identified as "Hanna Trapnel") in a list of those who "have been with this Handmaid [Wight]" and who were "of esteeme amongst many that feare the *Lord* in *London*" (*ER*, "To the Christian Reader"). In her three remaining appearances in *Exceeding Riches*, Trapnel is portrayed as prophesying in a manner akin to Wight's. The text glosses one of Wight's many assertions of God's loving kindness toward her "vile" self with the observation that Trapnel spoke similarly: "The like expressions were by *H. T.* [Anna Trapnel] another in London, that in sicknesse lately was in such a frame" (*ER*, 43). Although the text does not specify the time when Trapnel speaks, we later learn that she prophesies in June 1647 just as Wight's period of prophesying is winding down. And although Trapnel does not fast nearly as long as Wight does, Jessey implies that both women share related experiences of divine *inflatus*: "About the same time of *June* beforesaid, the *Relator* heard of one H. T. [Anna Trapnel] that then had great enjoyments of God, could not take in a crumme or sip of the creatures for full six dayes together, yet being in bodily health" (*ER*, 139). Jessey further underscores the connection between Trapnel and Wight when he recounts how the Relator appeals to Foxe's Book of Martyrs to explain the simultaneous existence of these two gathered church prophets: "That Mr. *Fox* in the *Book of Martyrs*, cites many *Miracles* wrought, and *Prophecies* uttered both in the *first hundred* of yeers after the Apostles, and in the *second, third, fourth, fifth*, and so on to this time. . . . Mr. *Fox* cites *Prophecies* of late times, revealed to *John Hus*, to *Martin Luther*, yea and to *himselfe*" (*ER*, 140). In the eyes of Jessey and Wight's Relator, these two seventeenth-century women prophets participate in a tradition that dates back to the beginnings of Christianity.

Beyond their similar prophetic styles, Jessey undoubtedly saw Trapnel and Wight as related because both belonged to London's gathered church milieu. The gathered church or Independent movement of the 1640s established the groundwork for institutionalized nonconformity by emphasizing voluntary church membership. In so doing, the Independents under the leadership of Jessey, among others, undermined the Presbyterian quest for a parish-based, national church: "By insisting that there was a first-class church available to saints in the gathered church, the Independents destroyed the integrity of the parish community and thereby ruined the Presbyterian reformation which was to secure a godly discipline upon fallen mankind in an inclusive church." Although the Independents were interested in creating a corporate identity for the visible saints, they nevertheless practiced a policy of religious toleration that called for "the acceptance of the separate church alongside the parish."[10]

While Wight's precise role within the gathered church movement is unclear, we do know that Jessey came into contact with her through her mother: Wight is "The Daughter of a gracious

Matrone, of mine acquaintance in the *Parish* where I weekly preach in *London*" (*ER*, "To His Christian Friends"). Trapnel's church affiliations are much more clearly defined. From 1642, she is closely identified with the Baptist "teacher" (and later, Fifth Monarchist) John Simpson. According to the brief autobiography that precedes *Cry*, she appears around 1649 to have joined the church at All-hallows the Great where Simpson had been established as a teacher: "I have walked in fellowship with the Church meeting at *All-hallows*, (whereof Mr. *John Simpson* is a Member) for the space of about four years" (3). Moreover, she attempts to authorize herself in terms of the broader gathered church movement of the 1650s: "I am well known to . . . Mr. *Greenhil* Preacher at *Stepney*, and most of that society, to Mr. *Henry Jesse*, and most of his society, to Mr. *Venning* Preacher at *Olaves* in *Southwark*, and most of his society, to Mr. *Knollis*, and most of his society, who have knowledge of me, and of my conversation; If any desire to be satisfied of it; they can give testimony of me, and of my walking in times past" (3). At the time of the publication of *Cry* in 1654, all of the churches she mentions were, to varying degrees, affiliated with the Fifth Monarchists. Simpson, Greenhill, Jessey, and Knollys had all signed the 1651 *Declaration of Divers Elders and Brethren of Congregationall Societies* that had launched the Fifth Monarchy movement.

Because the Fifth Monarchists drew their members largely from Congregationalists and Baptists, their religious beliefs did not differ significantly from those groups. B. S. Capp claims that the distinctiveness of the Fifth Monarchists arose from their millenarianism: "the Fifth Monarchists were unique, amongst the major groups, in that millenarianism formed the basic core of their doctrines, and was indeed the *raison d'être* of the movement. It was unique, too, in claiming the right and indeed the duty of taking arms to overthrow existing regimes and establish the millennium, and also in its detailed formulation of the political, social and economic structure of the promised kingdom." In many ways, the political agenda that defined the Fifth Monarchists of the 1650s was the product of the Independents' advocacy in the 1640s of voluntary church membership. Where the Independents insisted that God sanctioned the new churches they founded, the Fifth Monarchists maintained such churches could form the nation's ruling elite. The Independent belief in religious toleration had given way to the "hardening of denominational lines"[11] that found the Fifth Monarchists promising to "establish a godly discipline over the unregenerate masses" in the "imminent Kingdom of Christ on earth."[12]

Just as the strongly millenarian and exclusive agenda of the Fifth Monarchists succeeded the religious toleration of the Independents, so too has Trapnel's career been seen as succeeding that of Wight. Nigel Smith claims as much when he observes that "Anna Trapnel could be said to have modelled herself on Sarah Wight. The initial events in her prophesying career are remarkably similar to her predecessor, as if Sarah Wight had established the required behavior and rhetoric for a gathered church prophetess." As Trapnel's career developed, however, "She took Sarah Wight's mode of prophetic behaviour into another, more sensitive political arena."[13] Trapnel herself attests that she launched her career by consoling individuals in spiritual crisis and then moved onto delivering politically inflected messages to a broader audience. She distinguishes her early career as characterized by her despair of receiving grace, followed by her subsequent experience of grace, and finally by her efforts to comfort "afflicted and tempted ones" (3).

This sequence of despair, redemption, and guidance to the "afflicted" comprises the entire scope of Wight's career. Indeed, one of the longest sections of *Exceeding Riches* focuses on Wight's conversations with "despairing" women who attend her bedside in the hopes of receiving spiritual counsel. The typical interview involves a "Maid being in deep despair" who approaches Wight with the fear of being damned: "I am darkened in understanding, and I am tempted to believe there is no God, nor no Creation from God" (*ER*, 44). Wight responds with empathy by reminding her visitor that although she now experiences grace, she too was once similarly tempted: "So was it with me, I was so tempted: The very Creation shews there is a God, and yet I could not beleeve it"(*ER*, 45). While Trapnel acknowledges her own role as a comforter of the afflicted, she insists that her new position as the conduit for God's political will is much more important: "And when that time was ended; I being in my Chamber, desired of the Lord to tell me whether I had done that which was of and from himself. Reply was, thou shalt approve thy heart to God, and in that thou hast been faithfull in a little, I will make thee an Instrument of much more; for particular souls shall not only have benefit by thee, but the universality of Saints shall have discoveries of God through thee"(3). As an "Instrument of much more," she will benefit "the universality of Saints" rather than "particular souls." Clearly, she recognizes the broadening of her audience as an advance over her early vocation and perhaps, quite literally, over the career of Wight itself. Regardless of whether Trapnel saw herself in some kind of competition with Wight, reading *Cry* through the lens of *Exceeding Riches* reveals a woman self-consciously exploring what it means to present God's will for the English nation to the "universality of saints."

Anna Trapnel does not surpass Sarah Wight, however, in the length of her fasts, but this too appears to be related to the political content of her prophetic message. While Jessey claims that Wight does "not eat a crumme of bread, or other meat, in 76 dayes," Trapnel's fast lasts only some eleven days (*ER*, 138). Trapnel's fast may well be more pointed because it is occasioned by a specific political event. Trapnel found herself at Whitehall in January of 1654 because the Council of State had called a prominent Fifth Monarchist preacher, Vavasor Powell, to "come thither to give an account before them of some things by him delivered in his publique Exercises in *London*" (1). According to Capp, Powell was one of the Fifth Monarchist preachers who had reacted "violently" in December of 1653 to the dissolution of the Barebones Parliament (one comprised of a significant number of Fifth Monarchists) and the creation of the Protectorate. Capp reports that on December 19, Powell, together with another Fifth Monarchist preacher, Christopher Feake, publicly denounced Cromwell as "'the dissemblingest perjured villaine in the world.'"[14] Statements such as this one accounted for Powell's being interrogated in early January. In responding to Powell's arrest by fasting and prophesying, Trapnel replicates a pattern that her text suggests had been in place since the spring of 1647. At that time, when the Army was approaching the City of London, her fasting gave rise to a "Vision" about future political events: "And having fasted nine days, nothing coming within my lips, I had upon the ninth day this Vision of horns; first I saw in the Vision the Army coming in *Southwark*-way, marching through the City with a great deal of silence and quietness, and that there should be little or no bloud spilt; this was some weeks before their coming in" (5). While this earlier period of prophecy appears to have been more private than her prophesying at Whitehall, it too responds to a specific event with a pointed message about the course of the nation.

In their relative brevity and in the specificity of the political messages linked to them, Anna Trapnel's fasts resemble her contemporaries' use of public fasts to invoke divine aid in times of national crisis. *A Directory for the Publique Worship of God,* the devotional manual issued by Parliament in 1644 to replace the Book of Common Prayer, defines the purpose of public fasts: "When some great and notable Judgements are either inflicted upon a People, or apparently imminent, or by some extraordinary provocations notoriously deserved; as also, when some speciall blessing is to bee sought and obtained, Publique solemne Fasting (which is to continue the whole Day) is a Duty that God expecteth from that Nation, or people." In 1642, Parliament instituted a monthly program of fasts that was officially intended as a response to the rebellion in Ireland but was practically inspired by England's domestic crisis. This program of fasts and sermons continued through the execution of Charles I and became, in H. R. Trevor-Roper's words, a powerful "means of co-ordination and propaganda" for the parliamentary cause.[15] Although Trevor-Roper contends that the parliamentary order for public fasts to be held on the last Wednesday of each month did not significantly penetrate the countryside, it played an important role in shaping parliamentary politics during the Civil War years. There, abstinence from food was accompanied by sermons that unabashedly concentrated on current political crises. According to Trevor-Roper, these sermons served to spur the members of Parliament onto increasingly more radical acts. For instance, the October fast day sermon of 1644 exhorted a reluctant Parliament to pursue the execution, desired by its leaders and an angry mob, of William Laud, Archbishop of Canterbury: " 'When your gins and snares catch any of the bloody birds', cried the Rev. Henry Scudder, 'dally not with them: blood will have blood; contract not their bloodguiltiness upon your own souls by an unwarranted clemency and mildness.' "[16] Similarly, the December fast day sermon of 1648, preached by Thomas Brookes, urged regicide: "Parliament, he declared, should ignore the 'ignorant, sottish people who think that the doing of justice will undo a land', and recognize that, on the contrary, neglect of justice will provoke God 'to throw all your religious services as dung in your faces.' He therefore recommended to them the classic examples of holy murder and impious clemency: Phinehas who did not wait for judgment; Saul and Ahab who spared the kings whom God had commanded them to kill."[17]

In 1649, Parliament abolished the monthly program of fasts and sermons because they were no longer necessary: "The real purpose of the monthly fast had been to provide a constant sounding board of parliamentary policy, a regular means of contact with, and propaganda to, the people. By the spring of 1649 none of these purposes could be fulfilled." In its time, as John Wilson notes, the program of monthly fasts had served as "a means for displaying the unity of the parliamentary cause and as a vehicle for rendering the cause coherent through symbolic political ceremonies which, theoretically at any rate, engaged the entire realm."[18] The voluntary refusal to eat stood at the center of a public ritual that sought to give birth to a new political order.

Although Parliament abolished the regular program of fasts in 1649, it continued to hold public fasts on special occasions until its dissolution in 1653. During this period, the preachers were increasingly drawn from the more radical sects and several prominent Fifth Monarchists—Vavasor Powell (1650), John Simpson (1651), and Christopher Feake (1652)—were invited to address Parliament. While the fast day sermons of Feake and Simpson appear not to have been published (as was the case with many of the later fast-day sermons), that of Powell appeared in 1651 as *Christ Exalted above all Creatures By God His Father*.[19] Powell's sermon delivered in February of 1650 urged the members of Parliament to make their policies consistent with the political and theological agenda of the saints. He praises Parliament for a government that has thus far incurred divine favor: "The heavens smile, and the earth laughs and rejoyces at the execution of Justice, yea, some do observe that the Lord hath shewed himselfe more gracious to this land in externals, since you have appeared and acted for him of late." He insists that Parliament can continue to receive God's blessing by following the saints' lead: "God wil deale well or ill with you, as you favor them [the saints], or frown upon them, therefore look upon the Saints next Christ, as your safest and strongest sanctuaries." As if the sermon had not been threatening enough, Powell closes on a thoroughly menacing note: "you that are in Authority blesse the name of the Lord, that he hath not suffered you to be broken in peeces, praise him."[20] Once Powell had been imprisoned, in part, for objecting to the dissolution of the very Parliament he had once addressed, Trapnel would assume the mantle of his fiery rhetoric and direct it to Cromwell and his supporters. Moreover, the fact that her first group of published texts should appear the year after Parliament (and its fast-day sermons) had indeed been "broken in peeces" suggests them as a substitute for the official literature of hunger and abstinence.

While Trapnel appears to pattern her food abstinence after the public fasts that the entire nation, theoretically, embraced, both Trapnel and Wight deploy inedia in a way that links them to fasting women in the medieval and early modern periods. In her landmark study, *Holy Feast and Holy Fast*, Carolyn Walker Bynum documents how some medieval Catholic women practiced food abstinence as a means of resisting traditional structures of familial and clerical authority and of attaining greater self-realization.[21] Food played such a powerful role in these women's piety, she contends, because "food is not merely *a* resource that women control; it is *the* resource that women control—both for themselves and for others. In the long course of Western history, economic resources were controlled by husbands, fathers, uncles, or brothers. Yet human beings can renounce, or deny, themselves, only that which they control." For these women abstinence from food produced the mortified flesh that enabled them to identify with Christ suffering on the cross. In essence, they embraced the conventional association of carnality with women in order to identify with the crucified humanity of Christ: "It was from age-old notions that God, mind, and power are male whereas soul, flesh and weakness are female that women drew inspiration for a spirituality in which their own suffering humanity had cosmic significance."[22]

Like her medieval forebears, Trapnel draws on the traditional terms of female sexuality to explain that her weakness comes from being filled, quite literally, with the Lord's spirit: "they say these are Convulsion-fits, and Sickness, and diseases that make thy handmaid to be in weakness; But oh they know not the pouring forth of thy Spirit, for that makes the body to crumble, and weakens nature" (29). As the handmaid of the Lord, she is the perfect, passive vessel of the Word. Wight takes the idea of female passivity one step further and insists that she cannot eat because her body's desires have been satisfied by her beloved, Christ: *"I have what I did desire; I have a crucified Christ: I am so full of the Creator, that I can take in none of the Creature. I am fild with heavenly Manna: I am sore, from the crown of the head, to the sole of the foot. But let the Lord doe what he will with me: let him take me to his eternall rest, I am content: or leave me in this vaile of misery, I am content. Thou art a free agent: Thou workest when thou wilt, and where thou wilt"* (ER, 31). Wight's repeated assertions of desire for Christ strongly evoke the passionate spirituality that, according to Bynum, the abstinence of medieval women saints and mystics also produced: "abstinence [was seen] as preparatory to and simultaneous with true feeding by Christ. It was identification with Christ's suffering; it was affective, even erotic, union with Christ's adorable self."[23]

While Wight and Trapnel could resemble their medieval fore-bears, they also participated in the early modern and female tra-dition of miraculous fasting. From the late sixteenth century through the Restoration, a significant number of accounts ap-peared of fasting maids in both England and Continental Europe. As distinct from the accounts of medieval saints and mystics, those of early modern fasting women tended to view abstinence not as a component of a woman's spirituality but as a self-con-tained event that offered "ocular proof" of God's existence. In her review of the hagiographies and spiritual autobiographies of medieval women fasters, Bynum repeatedly notices that their food abstinence is linked to eucharistic devotion and identifica-tion with Christ's suffering humanity. Hence, this distinctly reli-gious literature does not describe women who exclusively starve themselves but whose abstinence finds them eating miraculous hosts provided by angels, consuming the pus emitted by the sores of the infirm, and feeding others with precious oils pro-duced by their breasts. Miracles permeate the medieval litera-ture of extraordinary fasting, and while they do not end with the Reformation, their emphasis shifts dramatically. No longer para-gons of suffering and service to others, fasting maids of the early modern period served to prove God's continuing presence in the world. As one early modern account described the significance of the Dutchwoman Eve of Fleigen's fourteen-year fast: "The Omnipotent Creator of the world, hath not in times past onely expressed the glory of his power, in his wonderfull composition, framing and presenting to the eye of Man all sorts of creatures, both in heaven, earth and the waters: But even now at this day, is the same his miraculous hand working still."[24] Because accounts such as this one viewed extraordinary fasting women as sites of religious revelation rather than as purveyors of a Christ-like spirituality, they pointed to an emerging modern and secular consciousness in which the self becomes "the historical and cul-tural medium for redemption."[25] To recognize the bodies of ex-traordinary fasters as sites of divinity is to verge on recognizing ordinary men and women as revelatory vessels.

Perhaps the best example of how early modern miraculous fasting merged sacred and secular meanings is the story of Eve of Fleigen. While the lives of medieval women ascetics were most frequently recorded in hagiographies and spiritual autobiogra-phies, her story appears in genres not exclusively dedicated to religious subjects—news accounts and histories, a ballad, and secular dramatic works. From these sources we learn that Eve,

the daughter of "meane and very poore parents," experienced
fasting as God's answer to her prayers for liberation from the trials of poverty: "Living in this extremity of misery, she often . . .
made earnest prayers to God, that he would take pity of her
wretchednes, and relieve her, from that daily hunger, by which
her body was tormented & consumed: her prayers were heard,
according to her request: And such compassion tooke the Almighty of her miseries that in the yeare 1594, her desire of feeding, which in former times she had, grew to be faint, & very
small." Unlike the daughters of affluence who comprised the
medieval fasters Bynum describes, Eve of Fleigen does not use
control over food to express her spirituality but rather she invokes divine aid to gain control over food.[26] Her fast is not motivated by a desire to conquer worldly appetites but to master her
impoverished material circumstances. Although Eve of Fleigen's
poverty makes her an atypical example of an early modern fasting maid—most were the daughters of tradesmen and bureau-
crats—her story illustrates how fasting could serve to fashion a
public identity for a young, typically unmarried woman.

Like Trapnel and Wight, Eve of Fleigen was visited by many
prominent people. The woman who "in her younger dayes . . .
[had been] compelled to keepe swine for the country people" became the object of the attentions of Queen Elizabeth of Bohemia,
the Countess of Meurs, as well as of "a thousand persons (both
honourable and of other conditions)." Of all of the texts documenting Eve's fast, the ballad "You gallant maidens of the world"
most strongly asserts the secular benefits of her asceticism. Cast
as a first-person account delivered in the voice of Eve herself,
the ballad admonishes young maids to notice how her fasting has
elevated her above the rank and file of "damsels." When she recounts the visit of Elizabeth of Bohemia, she literally identifies
the life-sustaining fragrance of her famous flowers as a form of
currency:

> And, therewithall, I gave the prince [Elizabeth]
> a nosegay of sweete flowers,
> For by the vertue of such like
>   I take my breathing power[s].
> The which the gentle lady tooke,
>   in kinde and humble wise,
> As if they had been Jemmes of worth
>   and Jewells of great prize;
> And, for the same, returnd me backe
>   a guift of good red gold,

> An hundreth Dollers presently,
> the which my keeper told,
>
> With charge that I should be maintaind,
> accordinge to my will.[27]

While initially attributing her fasting to a desire to avoid losing her soul to "wanton sin," the ballad's Eve of Fleigen ultimately realizes inedia as a means of social and economic advancement. Not just an ordinary damsel anymore, she has become a real lady with an income of her own.

Although Eve's fasting could be seen as making her an enterprising member of the lower class, playwrights such as William Beaumont and John Fletcher, William Davenant, and Jasper Mayne saw her abstinence as promulgating a disturbing sexual impenetrability.[28] For instance, Eve figures in Beaumont and Fletcher's *Love's Cure, or, The Martial Maid* (1605?/1626?), a comedy dedicated to righting the "monstrous metamorphoses" that have confused the sexual identities of the mannish Clara and the effeminate Lucio. While the respective upbringings of Clara and Lucio have temporarily distorted their "natural" identities, Eve of Fleigen's fasting has, according to the servant Lazarillo, permanently distorted her feminine form: "they say her guts shrunk all into Lute-strings, and her neather-parts cling'd together like a Serpents Taile; so that though she continued a woman still above the girdle, beneath that she was monster."[29] Although Lazarillo has just bemoaned the demise of female chastity in his age, he makes Eve's abstinence from food and, presumably, from all bodily pleasures into a metaphor for a Duessa-like duplicity. Because Eve does not permit her body to be penetrated by food and, implicitly, by the male penis, she must be both duplicitous and physically monstrous.[30] Like Fletcher's Lazarillo, Shakespeare's *Measure for Measure* also recognizes female asceticism as a problem. The play invokes the broad tradition of "fasting maids" when the Poor Clare novice, Isabella, pleads with Angelo for her brother's life and offers to bribe him "with true prayers/ That shall be up at heaven and enter there/ Ere sunrise, prayers from preserved souls,/ From fasting maids whose minds are dedicate/ To nothing temporal." Isabella's identification with the asceticism of fasting maids is completely in keeping with her character: at the beginning of the play, she tells another nun that she desires "a more strict restraint/ Upon the sisterhood, the votarists of Saint Clare." Against her express

wishes, however, the pressure of the play seeks to pull her away
from the convent and away from asceticism until finally the Duke
insists that they marry: "Give me your hand, and say you will be
mine."³¹ Ultimately, both plays recognize female fasting as en-
gendering an intolerable autonomy.

While popular ballads and dramatic works viewed fasting
maids as either class heroines or duplicitous virgins, the emerging scientific discourse understood their bodies' marvelous capacities as offering important insights into the workings of both
the human body and the divine plan. The developing early modern interest in careful and methodical observation appears most
noticeably in the accounts of miraculous fasters in the emphasis
on authenticating vigils. The literature repeatedly features vigils
like those established by the Earl of Devonshire to verify Martha
Taylor's fifty-three-week fast. According to Thomas Robins's
Wonder of the World (1669), the Earl, together with members of
the local gentry, on two separate occasions organized between
fourteen and twenty "maids" to "wake and watch with her."
Passing both tests with flying colors, Taylor persuaded her ex-
aminers that her feats of inedia were authentic: the maids "certi-
fied that she did receive no mortal food, but onely the wetting of
her lips with Spring water in a spoon: and as it is very credably
reported, this hath given him [Devonshire] very good satisfaction, and he doth believe it to be true." Described by the text's
title page as a "Well-wisher to the Gospel of Jesus Christ," Robins deems the Earl's vigil as providing further evidence for Taylor's being "one of the Lord's chosen vessels." Yet, for himself,
he finds the combination of her miraculous body and her "discoursing of the Scriptures" to be the most compelling reason to
believe that she is divinely inspired.³²

Even in accounts that are more heavily weighted toward scientific discourse, the alliance between religious and scientific
meanings remains in place. For instance, the account of Jane
Balan's three-year fast draws upon anatomical observation,
early modern medical theory, and Christian theology.³³ *A true
and admirable Historie, of a Mayden of Consolans* (1603) (translated by Anthony Munday from Lescarbot's French popularization of a medical treatise by Francois Citois) provides a striking
description of the effects of Jane Balan's fast on her young body:
"the inferiour part of the belly, by little & little is in such maner
grown leane, and dried up in her, as downe from her sides, as so
along to her navill, there remaineth nothing of the belly which
shee had before. There is only in this place . . . a Cartilage or

gristle, hanging pointed down from *thorax*, or *sternum*, after the maner of an eaves or penthouse, which throwes off from the building, all the water that falls on the top or coverture." Appealing to both his observation of Balan's emaciated body and the authority of Aristotle, Galen, and "the consent of all Phisitians," Citois determines that Balan's inedia is the result of a breakdown in her "naturall heate." Although Citois produces an explanation that does not depend upon theology, he nevertheless insists that, in some cases, extraordinary fasting can be miraculous: "But as for persons of such rare sanctitie, we thinke not their fast to have bin by any sicknesse: but only by the special will of God, and that natural appetite then returned, at the time limitted by his providence."[34] Maintaining, however tenuously, a belief in theological explanations, *A true and Admirable Historie* also underscores the increasing tendency to comprehend extraordinary fasting as the result of illness.

While Wight's and Trapnel's texts emphasize their fasting as divinely inspired, even they attest to the power of the emerging medical discourse. In Wight's case, her bedside was literally attended by four doctors, all of whom, Barbara Ritter Dailey observes, would become or were already members of one of two prominent scientific institutions—the College of Physicians and the Invisible College (the forerunner of the Royal Society). Dailey argues that *Exceeding Riches* articulates both the tension between spiritual and medical understandings of fasting and an attempt to reconcile this tension. In Doctor Thomas Coxe's question to Wight: "Some say of your *Comfort*, that it is but a *Delusion*. How do you know tis no *Delusion*?," Dailey sees evidence of rationalist skepticism (*ER*, 114). At the same time, she maintains, it was possible for a man like Jessey, who himself had studied medicine, to believe "that experimental religion and experimental science were allied profoundly."[35] Although Trapnel is never questioned by any doctors, she rejects the rumour that her extraordinary fasting can be explained away as an illness: "they say these are Convulsion-fits, and Sickness, and diseases that make thy handmaid to be in weakness; But oh they know not the pouring forth of thy Spirit, for that makes the body to crumble, and weakens nature" (29). The influence of scientific inquiry notwithstanding, Trapnel and Wight prophesied in an era in which substantial and politically significant audiences regarded them with wonder comparable to that of the hagiographers of medieval women saints and mystics.

SCRIPTURAL ENTRAILS

As women had since the thirteenth century, both Wight and Trapnel experienced their bodies as conduits of divine revelation. Of the two Interregnum prophets, however, Wight emerges as more mystically inclined. Her fasting bespeaks a spirituality focused on intense and intimate union with Christ. At times, seemingly overcome by Christ's redemptive power, she gives herself over to ecstatic and repeated expressions of joy: "Now I have my desire; I desired nothing but a crucified Christ, and I have him. I desired nothing but a crucified Christ, and I have him; a crucified Christ, a naked Christ; I have him, and nothing els. I am sore all over; I can neither hear, nor see; I desired him so, and I have him so, and I have nothing els" (*ER*, 22). While Wight's language of passionate love for Christ would have been familiar to the medieval mystic Margery Kempe and the sixteenth-century saint Teresa of Avila, it apparently disturbed her seventeenth-century Baptist editor Henry Jessey. Throughout *Exceeding Riches* he, together with Wight's unnamed amanuensis, strives to document how Wight's words accord with scriptural truth.[36] For her part, Trapnel has a less heavy-handed editor and amanuensis, but, as Jessey himself might argue, she does not need one. Trapnel herself assumes the role of scriptural annotator and incorporates many of Jessey's framing devices into her own self-presentation. This is not to say that Trapnel does not give herself over to ecstasies as vivid as Wight's. Indeed, she does have visionary raptures, but she insists that they are consistent with the Word: "The Life of vision here is excellent and precious, and glorious, when it is according to the Scripture, and comes from thy Spirit . . . Vision! the body crumbles before it, and becomes weak" (74).[37] Her body may "crumble" before her "Vision!" but anchored to Scripture as she is, she does not surrender to her body's will. While Wight focuses on the immediacy of her visionary experience, Trapnel seeks to make hers legible by making it consistent with the text of the Bible. Ultimately, Trapnel's rationalizing zeal serves to make her a Jessey-like agent of her own subjection. It is only through this textual subjection, however, that she can universalize and thus politicize her bodily experiences.

For Jessey as well as, presumably, for Wight's amanuensis, what makes her bodiliness potentially heretical is that the audience of *Exceeding Riches* will misinterpret her as a unique phenomenon. They fear, in effect, that she may be read as some sort of independent operative who has no connection to scriptural truth. Thus, in one of his opening remarks, Jessey admonishes his readers against celebrating the person of Sarah Wight: "As you reade, *Consider; Admire* the Lord in his *surpassing Grace* to ungodly *ones.* Do not so commend the party, that is but an *Earthen vessel, born in sin,* as you are: but still all along exalt and commend *the LORD*" (*ER*, "To the Christian Reader"). Just as Wight's visionary experiences and her body's extraordinary capacities are the product of divine inspiration, so too are her words. According to Jessey, she speaks *"in such sweet Streines of* Scripture-*phrases, so* opening, *and* descanting *upon severall places, so drawing out the Gospel*-Marrow" as though she were an "experienced Minister *of the Gospel*" ("The Epistle Dedicatory"). The text of *Exceeding Riches* reenforces his claim by providing a substantial index to the scriptural passages to which Wight purportedly alludes entitled, "A Table of the Places of holy Scripture, that in this Book are opened, illustrated, and applied." Moreover, throughout the text, Wight's publishers directly gloss her words with corresponding scriptural citations. Typically, they simply provide the biblical citation, but when, it seems, they want to ensure that the reader recognizes a given correspondence, they reproduce the scriptural passage in full. For instance, when she describes herself as "drunk with the spirit," Jessey and her amanuensis respond with the following biblical passages: "[Alluding, it seems to . . . Eph. 2. 18. *Be not drunk with wine, but be fil'd with the Spirit*: or to *Act.* 2.15.–17. *These are not drunk-but the Spirit is poured out upon them.]*"(*ER*, 50). If she were simply "drunk with the spirit" of her own accord, she might be subject to unknown influences of questionable origins. So, for Jessey, it may well "seem" more legitimate to suggest that she "seems" to be alluding to moments when Scripture sanctions a certain kind of spiritual bacchanalia.

The feature of Wight's speech that appears to trouble Jessey most is her frequent use of repetition. In describing the process of transcribing and editing *Exceeding Riches*, Jessey notes that some of her repetitious speeches were condensed: "*and once or twice, matters of the same verse, opened two or three severall dayes, are put together, as if all had been spoken on one day; to prevent often Repetitions: though some* repetitions remain *as she uttered them: All* repetitions *are not vaine; some are very* Emphaticall, *and very* usefull: *as* Returne, Returne, O Shulamite, Returne, returne" (*ER*, "The Epistle Dedicatory"). In specifying Wight's repeated exposition of "matters of the same verse" over the course of days as receiving the editor's knife, he indicates that the text does not fully represent occasions when she repeats words and phrases. Moreover, he insists that her use of repetition, like that in the love poetry of the Song of Songs, is not "vaine" but serves the proper, "usefull" function of emphasis. While Wight's repetitions certainly do serve to emphasize certain ideas, they also appear to give her great pleasure, as she speaks of her ("vaine"?) desire for her beloved. The Relator himself tacitly suggests that she achieves an ecstatic state while repeating the words "Love him" over and over again: "Then speaking somewhat louder, shee said; *Love him, Love him*, &c. These words shee repeated nine or ten times in ardency of affection" (*ER*, 20). Her "ardency of affection" notwithstanding, the margin of the text notes that she evokes a pattern of repetition found in the Greek text of the Book of Revelation: "As . . . (Holy, holy) is repeated 9. times in the Greek of Platins Edition (which is cou[n]ted the best) Rev.4.8." (*ER*, 20). Clearly, Wight was not familiar with this text, but the editorial point in alerting readers to this correspondence appears to be to assert once more Wight's absolute receptiveness to the same divine inspiration that underwrites the Bible and to insist that her use of repetition does not satisfy her own vain fancies.[38]

Jessey's concern is, perhaps, well-founded because Wight's use of repetition does suggest that she takes real pleasure in words themselves. Her Relator records how after her repeated expressions of awe over Christ's sacrificing himself for sinners, she appears to be pleased with her speech: "Doe you not see an excellency in him? . . . Who came he to dye for? for sinners; aye for the greatest sinners, the chiefest sinners, the chiefest sinners. A dying Christ, for a denying *Peter*; a dying Christ, for a denying *Peter*; a dying Christ, for a denying *Peter*. *Peter* denied him, and yet he died for him. Goe tell *Peter*! Goe tell *Peter*! Ah *Peter*! *And then she paused a while as admiring it*" (*ER*, 16–17). Of course she may be simply "admiring" Christ's willingness to die for sinners such as herself and Peter. Throughout her period of prophesying, she appeals to biblical figures who repudiated the Father and the Son in order to demonstrate that Christ comes to redeem the "chiefest sinners." Still, the symmetry of the thrice-repeated "A dying Christ, for a denying Peter" suggests the rhythms of a mantra, spoken for the purpose of both communicating and producing feeling. For Wight, language appears to possess a material existence of its own, and she delights in its rhythms and cadences. Her apparent interest in the sounds and forms of words undercuts Jessey's efforts to portray her as a *tabula rasa* that God writes upon. "Earthen vessel" that she is, she does not absolutely subject her own desires in conveying God's word but pleasures herself in transmitting her experiences of divine presence.

Nowhere is the authorizing power of the body more apparent than in her account of the temptations and despair that preceded her experience of redemption and of the "comforts" that followed. Like most conversion narratives, hers describes a progress from spiritual death to spiritual rebirth, but it also marks a journey from physical longing to physical fulfillment. Given the fact that the onset of her *"Afflictions in Spirit"* occurs when she is twelve, simultaneous with the onset of puberty, and that her "time of love" occurs when she is fifteen, it is not wholly surprising that sexual awakening should be a subtext for her conversion narrative. Moreover, Wight was not the only seventeenth-century woman to structure her conversion narrative around "the ordinary materials of her woman's existence." According to Patricia Caldwell, events such as marriage and childbirth mark significant turning points in Elizabeth White's *Experiences of God's Gracious Dealing* (1669).[39] But what is so striking about Wight is that she experiences her climactic moment of divine illumination exclusively through her body: Her assurance of grace comes as her body metamorphoses into a sealed container.

> She further said; *That the same day wherein she was forced to lie down (viz. April 6) she was taken in all her body: All was shaken, and she trembled: exceedingly. That her hands were clinch'd up together, and so were her feet, as if it were by the Cramp; and her mouth was drawn up as a purse; and her eyes were with the ey-lids folded up and closed; and her hearing was taken from her; and she had no motion nor desire of any good. Mine own eyes* (said she) *pitied not my self; and just then was the time of love.* (ER, 60–61)

Unlike Wight, Elizabeth White's moment of redemption focuses, quite conventionally, on her "heart knowledge" of a scriptural passage, although it too coincides with a bodily event—that of childbirth: "But whilst I was considering of these Things, I had this Scripture set home with abundance of Sweetness, Psal. 53. 15. *Call upon me in the Day of Trouble, and I will deliver thee, and thou shalt glorify me*: And in the Time of Extremity this Word was set home upon my Heart again, and my good GOD made me to Experience the Truth of it in a wonderful Manner, for I had speedy Deliverance beyond my Expectation, which filled my Heart and Mouth with Praises to the LORD."[40] While God makes her "Experience the Truth" of the Word through her "speedy Deliverance," he does not appear to have brought on labor but only to have shortened its length. Moreover, in Elizabeth White's case, the Word frames her experience of God's comforts, whereas Sarah Wight receives divine comfort through a vision of Christ crucified: *"I never had rest, till I saw myself crucified with Christ, and that my sins pierced him: and there came out of his side, a fountaine of bloud, for the guilt of sin, and not onely so, but a fountain of water to wash away the filth of sin, to wash away all my sin"* (ER, 53). As with the "tremblings" that mark God's presence in her body, Wight's knowledge of God's redemptive power is shaped not by a text but by her vision of Christ's pierced body.

The Word is, however, not completely absent in her conversion narrative, but her ability to derive comfort from it appears to be contingent upon either the yearning or sated condition of her body. Before she receives God's comforts, she cannot find solace in reading the Bible. She agonizes over her inability to find biblical accounts of individuals as fallen as she deemed herself to be who were ultimately saved: *"If all the sins of the world were in one party, I thought it was all nothing to mine. I could not find any in all the Scriptures that obtain'd mercy, that was in my case. Yet he hath shew'd mercy to mee, the chiefest of sinners"* (ER, 37). She not only fails to find comfort in reading but it adds to her torments. In the midst of desperately rifling through Scripture in search of consolation, she also literally attempts to kill herself: "Shee oft attempted wickedly to destroy her selfe, as by drowning, strangling, stabbing, seeking to beat out her braines, wretchedly bruising and wounding her self. The chiefe cause of *such* weaknes since" (ER, 7–8).[41] As painful as her self-destructive acts may sound, she insists that she could not feel them until after she receives grace: *"in my Terrors . . . I abus'd my body; but I never felt it till now, I beat my head oft against the wall; and took my flesh in my teeth: and the more and ofter I did it, the lesse I felt it . . . And that I did so then, is the cause why I lie here now. For now that he hath brought me to my selfe, now I feel it"* (ER, 115–16). At the same time as she feels the pain that her wilfulness has inflicted upon her body, she also feels refreshed by the presence of Christ in her body: "I have Manna to eat of, he feeds me with hidden Manna. It was pleasant to the eye: but they felt no sweetnesse, by looking on it, but by tasting of it" (ER, 38). It is only in conjunction with the pain and pleasure which accompanies her intensely sensuous experience of self-knowledge that she can find comfort in reading the Scriptures. For instance, she gradually rises from her bed, following her seventy-six days of fasting and weakness, with the guidance of particular scriptural passages: "Besides those three or foure places of *ministring* to others, there were *six places* more brought to her, of such as *Jesus Christ raised up* by his power: and they were set on with power on her soule . . . shee desired, if shee might have a place to her more particular. Then was given in that in *Luk.* 8. end; where *Christ* said; *Maid, arise*" (*ER*, 136). Once she has received grace, the text of the Bible can serve to frame the miraculous recovery of her body.

Like other mystic thinkers of the period, Wight "cannot but take" her "points of reference from the Bible" even as she privileges the authority of divine inspiration over that of the Letter.[42] While Paul distinguishes between letter and spirit, in part, as a way of urging the Corinthians to forego the Mosaic dispensation in favor of the "new testament . . . of the Spirit," Wight focuses on this distinction as one between the word printed on the page and that, after Paul, "written . . . with the Spirit of the living God . . . in fleshy tables of the heart."[43] Clearly, these are the words or epistles that matter in her own experience of redemption, although she publicly affirms the authority of the Bible. For Wight, knowledge of God in the "fleshy tables of the heart" clearly precedes knowledge of God in the Word. The best efforts of her scripturally-minded editors notwithstanding, Wight's point in *Exceeding Riches* is that reading the Bible requires self-knowledge, and, for her, self-knowledge comes through a body "exceedingly" transformed and made peculiarly sensitive through God's love.

Unlike those of Sarah Wight, Anna Trapnel's narratives of receiving God's grace and her special prophetic powers emphasize the role of sermons and scriptural texts.[44] In *Cry*, she describes how, suffering from an apparently fatal illness, she gains the faith to believe that the Book of Hosea prophesies her recovery: "Seven years ago I being visited with a feaver, given over by all for dead, the Lord then gave me faith to believe from that Scripture. After two days I will revive thee, the third day I will raise thee up, and thou shalt live in my sight: which two days were two weeks that I should lye in that feaver, and that very time that it took me, that very hour it should leave me, and I should rise and walk, which was accordingly" (3).[45] Her narrative of her spiritual and physical redemption invokes the Word in a way that closely resembles Elizabeth White's description of her deliverance from the pain of childbirth. Sick with a "feaver," God comes to Trapnel through "Scripture" to predict the end of her physical sufferings. In her spiritual autobiography, *A Legacy for Saints* (1654), Trapnel presents a much more detailed account of her physical and emotional state before and during this two-week period in July 1646. Again, she foregrounds the way that Scripture frames her visionary experience: "and in the midst of this and many other requests to God, this Scripture was presented, *Hosea* 6.2. which voice was from God . . . it came thus, after two daies I will revive thee, and the third day I will raise thee up, and thou shalt live in my sight, and with a full perswasion that I should recover." She again invokes Scripture when she indicates, also in the *Legacy*, that her first experience of grace in 1642 occurred during John Simpson's sermon on Romans: "when this Sermon . . . upon that 8. of the *Romans* was almost ended, I said, Lord I have the Spirit, in this confused manner as I found a witness within me that I had the Spirit in those particulars that were declared, but my spirit strongly run out to the Lord for a clear manifestation of his love in Christ, and suddenly my soul was filled with joy unspeakable."[46] Although, like Wight, Trapnel experiences divine presence as pleasurable—she is "filled with joy unspeakable"—she consistently represents her experience as contingent to and inspired by a scriptural text.

Scripture plays such a formidable role in constructing Trapnel's prophetic identity, *Cry* insists, because it authorizes every legitimate prophetic utterance. In the autobiographical section of her text, she repeatedly glosses some of her more pointed political prophecies with their scriptural analogs. For instance, after a vision in which a group of "proud Oaks," representing the forces that oppress the Fifth Monarchists, crumble and thereby enable the formerly persecuted "little shrubs" (the Fifth Monarchists) to grow and thrive, Trapnel tells us that she "desired Scripture to this Vision." Subsequently, she is told—"Reply was"—to examine the "first of Isaiah" (12).[47] For Trapnel, Scripture becomes the standard against which the veracity of a given prophecy can be determined. Thus, when her imagined detractors attribute her prophecies to the spirit of madness and distraction, not to mention "immodesty," she counters by affirming that her prophecies are consistent with the teachings of Scripture: "it is the Lord that comes, and enlarges, and fils with his Spirit, and lays his foundation with precious stones and sparkling colours . . . Oh thy servant knows it is from thy Spirit; let them know that is so too, by the language of it, by the Rule through which it comes: how is the written Word carried forth in it! thy Spirit takes the Scripture all along, and sets the soul a swimming therein" (67). While, like Wight, her visions are the product of her direct experience of the divine, they also always represent "the soul a swimming" in Scripture.

Trapnel further emphasizes the resemblance between the text produced from her words and the biblical text when, in her opening song, she assumes the voice of God speaking to the prophet John and commands her Relator to "write":

> Write how that Protectors shall go,
>   And into graves there lye:
> Let pens make known what is said, that,
>   They shall expire and die.
>
> (19–20)

In stanza after stanza of this her opening song, she calls upon someone (whether she directly addresses the Relator is unclear) to write down her prediction about the decline of England's current political authorities. Her call to "write" evokes the opening of Revelation in which God commands John to direct his prophecies about the future to the angels of each of the seven churches.[48] Trapnel's appropriation of the divine command to write provides a literary context for the literal scene that produces her text. While Wight preeminently gains self-knowledge through her body, Trapnel acquires it both through the Bible and through the process of her words being made textual: she knows herself to be speaking on God's behalf because another transcribes her words. Whereas Trapnel appears to be quite conscious of the fact that her words are being transcribed, Wight, according to Jessey, "knew not that others listened, and heard her, (and wrote it downe)" (ER, "Epistle Dedicatory"). Whether this was in fact the case is irrelevant, but this detail emphasizes Wight's characteristic privileging of presence and immediacy. Trapnel's self-knowledge, on the other hand, depends upon the text of the Bible and the textuality of her own words. Just as John transcribes God's words, so too does her Relator copy out the words she utters.

While Trapnel, Jessey, and Wight's amanuensis emphasize the correspondences between Scripture and the divine revelation that coincides with extraordinary fasting, Sarah Wight appears to celebrate her body as a self-contained site of divine knowledge.

Wight's amanuensis practically admits this when he describes the virtual untranslatability of Wight's affect: "This she speaks, as all that follows, with a low voyce, in a humble, modest, melting manner, her teares sometimes stopping her speech. He [Jessey] and the rest, listened, and were greatly affected in hearing her. It cannot affect so much in hearing it at second hand, as if you had heard her selfe, with such brokenness of heart uttering it" (*ER*, 35). Words alone cannot convey the full significance of her experience of divinity but only her physical presence can. Although Trapnel's text does recognize the affective qualities of the body, it also attempts to portray a legible body. The distinction between the representational strategies of Wight and Trapnel evokes Michel Foucault's narrative of the early modern shift away from the body as a site that can manifest power. Like the bodies of the proto-bourgeois subjects of torture Foucault describes, Wight's body is a medium for displaying extraordinary power. As Foucault assesses the spectacle of torture, it "made the body of the condemned man the place where the vengeance of the sovereign was applied, the anchoring point for a manifestation of power, an opportunity of affirming the dissymmetry of forces."[49] For her part, Trapnel represents her body as more than a medium for showcasing power. She makes her body into a text that, like the law in Foucault's *Discipline and Punish*, articulates both the power and the reason of divine authority. By rationalizing her body according to Scripture, Trapnel is able to theorize her body as a set of political practices in a way that the excesses of Wight's prophetic self-presentation do not permit. Still, in sharp contrast to the kind of subjectivity that Foucault describes, Trapnel attempts to preserve the body's claims to authority. Rather than privileging the word/Word over the body, she seeks to reconcile the distinct claims to authority of both.

In the very ways that they comprehend their bodies as spectacles, Wight and Trapnel mark a shift in emphasis from a dramatic to a legible body. As much as Jessey might want to celebrate Wight's childlike innocence, her text suggests that she possesses a fairly well-developed theatrical sensibility. In addition to fasting, Wight's prophesying is characterized by a period of blindness and deafness that is intermittently "cured" by visits from two central figures in her life—her mother and her half-brother, Jonathan Vaughan. Her encounter with her mother is particularly dramatic because it comes when "many were present" and after she tearfully laments her disobedience toward her mother: *"If any did know, what it is to murmure against a God, and against a Parent, and felt for it what I have felt; they would never doe it. Nothing more burdens me, then my murmurings and disobedience against my Mother"* (ER, 24). Once she has publicly proclaimed her rebelliousness, she asks that "her mother might come to her" and "Mistriss Dupper her neighbour in Lawrence Pountney-lane, held open her eyes, and shee saw and knew her mother: and then immediately her ears also were opened, that she might heare her mother speak to her, and she testified to her, that shee had pardond her, and lov'd her as her own soule. And then, her heart was at rest, shee was satisfied: Her hearing then continued about halfe an houre" (ER, 25). More than three hundred years later, one can readily imagine the hushed tones and sense of awe that must have pervaded the room when Wight so extravagantly received her mother's pardon. In rendering her guilt through a highly charged performance of her body's special powers, Wight may also be dramatizing the ambivalence and aggression that characterized her relationship with her mother.[50] Wight's insistence that she see and hear her mother may well indicate an inverted power play in which she deploys her miraculous body to upstage her mother's gracious pardon. In dramatizing the private tensions of the mother-daughter relationship, Wight makes herself a spectacle of divine power before both her mother and the broader public.

For her part, Trapnel clearly discourages members of her audience from gazing upon her with dumb wonder. Rather, she expressly calls upon the spectators gathered around her bedside to extract meaning from observing her body's special powers: "That a poor Creature should subsist without sustenance, what a gazing is there at this poor thing, while you forget the glory that is in it, go into the Marrow, what matters it for the bone, let them have the Spirits, it is no matter for any thing else" (38). Trapnel urges her audience not to "gaze" upon her stupidly but to read into the "marrow" of her body's meaning. She likens her body to a text that articulates a central point. Further, she maintains that texts can just as readily be likened to bodies as bodies can to texts. For instance, she illustrates that the godliness of Fifth Monarchist revelatory speech derives from its embodied quality: The Fifth Monarchists are "not as those deluded spirits, that go running about the streets, and say, we have such Visions and Revelations, who come out with their great speeches of vengeance, and judgement and plagues: Oh, but thine that come from thee, thou givest them Humility, Meekness, Bowels, and Tears" (22). Fifth Monarchist speech does not merely come from the realm of feelings but quite literally comes from the gut. Trapnel's focus on the authority of the digestive tract clearly generalizes her own ability to "subsist without sustenance" as a kind of Fifth Monarchist moniker. While she insists that the special capacities of her body alone should not have the power to astonish, she focuses our attention on the conjunction of word and body as the site of a new kind of power in which the concordance between a speaker's body and words becomes a sign of authority, distinguishing one as the member of a political elite. For Trapnel, the Fifth Monarchists are "chosen" not because they claim to embody God's promise but because the relationship between their words and bodies *proves* that they possess divine sanction.

In addition to encouraging the faithful chosen, Trapnel frequently exhorts the "backslidden" Oliver Cromwell and the New Model Army to mend their ways and to take up the "generation-work" of ushering in the millennium that so preoccupied the Fifth Monarchists.[51] Her song to Cromwell is particularly interesting because in it she attempts to liken her own role as a divine instrument to that which her ideal Cromwell would enact. Although she denounces as self-aggrandizing his establishing himself as Protector, she still holds out hope that he will redeem himself in God's eyes. Therefore, she opens her song by identifying him with Gideon, the Israelite war hero who humbly refuses to exercise political power on his own behalf: "And Gideon said unto them, I will not rule over you, neither shall my son rule over you: the Lord shall rule over you."[52] Sadly, she reports, she can no longer count Cromwell among "Gods diadems" because he has neglected his "vows and promises" to "the most blessed Son" (53, 55). She represents her fallen Gideon as corrupted by carnal pleasures and blames London's civil leaders for seducing him with extravagant food:

> O Aldermen, O, that you had
>   considered he was flesh,
> You would not have so nourisht him
>   and brought forth your relish,
> Which was a relish to proud flesh,
>   which shall crumble to dust,
> For truly it hath in him and you,
>   raised up fleshly lust:
> Oh tremble yee therefore, for you
>   have roasted meat so dry;
> His Wines you did mingle, whereby
>   you have blinded his eyes.

(55)

Her song strengthens the connection between food and fleshly lust of a venereal kind by comparing Cromwell to Samson, the Israelite deliverer who was ultimately "blinded" as a result of submitting to Delilah's wiles:

> *Oh desire rather a dish of herbs,*
>   *than this thy stalled ox*
> *With those rather desire t' sit down*
>   *that strength may be in thy Locks:*
> *That no Delilahs so great and strange*
>   *with speeches fair and sweet,*
> *May take thee from that which is true,*
>   *and exceeding compleat.*

(54)

Like the Samson of Judges, Cromwell, according to Trapnel, might still be redeemed and might ultimately play his annointed role as an agent of providential history if only he would "desire" to do so. The only way back for Cromwell, however, is literally through the body of Christ. Trapnel insists that she pleads "for him on his sick-bed,/ that he might see the breast,/ Where he should be restor'd to life" (55). Although these lines indicate that the ailing Cromwell must look upon "the breast" in order to be redeemed, the illness metaphor suggests that he must also suck from the breast as a way of regaining his health. Moreover, some twelve lines later, Trapnel appears to specify whose breast—Christ's—Cromwell needs to "see" as she exhorts Christ to aid in the Protector's rebirth by nursing him with "Cordials":

> *Thy servant* [Trapnel] *said, oh Lord give him*
>   *Cordials from thy dear self,*
> *That he may come and drink of thee*
>   *who art his saving health.*

(55)

In providing even the barest lineaments of the figure of Christ as nursing mother, Trapnel invokes an image more fully elaborated in the mystical writings of some medieval and early modern women. Carolyn Walker Bynum's work indicates that the image of Christ as nursing mother appears frequently in writings by and about medieval women mystics. For instance, she notes that Catherine of Siena's hagiographer "recounts her ecstasies, trances, frenzies, bleedings, and tears at the eucharist, and he associates her craving for Christ's blood, like her drinking of pus, with a nursing Christ."[53] Catherine's own writings emphasize this correlation between Christ's bleeding breast and a mother's lactating breast: "we must do as a little child does who wants milk. It takes the breast of its mother, applies its mouth, and by means of the flesh it draws milk . . . We must attach ourselves to the breast of Christ crucified, which is the source of charity, and by means of that flesh we draw milk. The means is Christ's humanity which suffered pain, and we cannot without pain get the milk that comes from charity."[54] Trapnel's contemporary, Martha Hatfield similarly calls upon her auditors to nurse at Christ's breast: "Oh let us suck sweetnes from Jesus Christ, as the childe sucks milk from the mothers breast; the harder we draw, the more we shall get; the childe wrangles and wrangles till the mother give it the pap in the mouth, and then it's quiet and satisfied . . . a poor soul seeks, and knows not what it wants, and wrangles, and wrangles till it get Christ; all the world will not satisfie it, but . . . when it gets Christ then it is satisfied."[55] While Catherine of Siena insists that we must participate in Christ's pain in order to "get the milk that comes from charity," Martha Hatfield urges her listeners to "draw hard" in order to be satisfied by Christ. In either case, the reward for sucking at Christ's breast can only come from adopting a childlike pose of absolute dependence on Christ for nourishment. And as inexact as Trapnel's image of Christ as nursing mother may be, she employs it in order to exhort Cromwell to the same kind of dependence on Christ that a child has on its mother. Ultimately, *Cry* maintains, Cromwell can exercise righteous political power only by assuming a Trapnel-like posture of helpless infancy before his Lord.

For Trapnel proper and improper eating relates not only to righteous political power but also to authoritative speech. In essence, the mouth that consumes proper foods also emits the right words. She initially suggests, for instance, that Cromwell has the makings of a man of grace. He is hampered, however, by a mouth full of scriptures not adequately digested:

> *Let him not imitate those Kings,*
> *which knew nothing of God,*
> *They did not regard what they saw*
> *or read within thy word,*
> *But he hath a great tone thereof,*
> *he hath his tongue there tipt,*

Oh he hath many Scriptures which
come thorow his lips.

(54)

Neither condemning nor celebrating Cromwell's use of scripture-talk, she seems to indicate that he could be a seventeenth-century Gideon, but that he has yet to realize fully his abilities. While her tone throughout her hymn to Cromwell remains hopeful, her later prose addresses to the Protector predict his demise in terms of food and speech. She warns Cromwell that his vainglory will deprive him of clear speech and delightful nourishment: "I tell you the Lord God will Ecclipse your Glory, he will put a stammering speech into you, you shall not suck from Gods Wine-cellars, the Lord will not bring so much as a taste of his Wine to you" (68). Trapnel not only suggests a correlation between clear speech and modest eating habits but further indicates that food and words are interchangeable objects. Someday, she admonishes, Cromwell and his followers will have to eat their words: "The Lord would have your Protestations, Vows, Covenants and Narrations brought into your Pallace against you, this shall be bitterness in your dishes; You shall have plenty and fulness, but without comfort" (70). Like corrupt food, corrupt words poison both body and soul.

Trapnel's identification of pure words with pure bodies curiously serves to instantiate the very fleshliness she appears to denounce. When, for instance, she praises the saints for spreading the Word and for foregoing bodily desires, she implicitly makes their bodies into icons of godliness: "There are a great many whose God is their bellie, and they are willing to be silent; oh but you Saints, do you go and speak to such as would shut this open door, as is open to the sheep" (64). The pure bodies of the saints enable them, unlike the silent slaves to physical desire, to pursue a fulsome kind of speech. Moreover, she argues that those who worship the loathsome "belly god," constitutionally lack the capacity to speak truly of God: "Oh! thou [God] wilt say, what have you to do to take the name of God in your mouth, when you act for your bellies?" (62). Her text wonders how they can take God's name in their mouths when they are busy filling their mouths with food in order to satisfy their bellies. Indeed, by identifying those mouths that both consume excess food and "take the name of God" as sacrosanct, she implicitly sacralizes those mouths, such as her own, that open only to speak of God. An orifice that grants access to the sealed container of the body, the mouth be-

comes for Trapnel the privileged site of the drama of belief, signifying the simultaneity of the victory over fleshly desire and the
complete accession to God's will. It is precisely because the
mouth is so susceptible to corruption that it can become the vessel of purity.

Trapnel's representation of herself and the members of her
sect as icons of godliness did not contradict a religious ideology
that both denounced the role of sacred icons in Catholicism
and argued for redemption by faith alone. Rather, the work of
historian Ann Kibbey and sociologist Max Weber suggests that
materialism such as Trapnel's was central to radical English
Protestantism. Kibbey argues that Puritan iconoclasm negated
the distinction between people and objects, ultimately investing
sacred icons with human powers and celebrating living human
beings as material signs of God's saving grace.[56] Kibbey maintains that because Puritans "invested spiritual power in the material shapes of religious ritual, the *figurae* of Catholic religion
could be rendered powerless to captivate the Protestant only if
the material shape itself was recognizably destroyed and represented as such." Hence, she notes that when radical Protestant
iconoclasts attacked Catholic images they would adopt an "execution style," literally lopping statues' heads off as though they
were human beings. In denying sacred status to specific objects—vestments, relics, paintings—radical Protestants portrayed all matter both living and inert as potentially possessed of
special powers. One could obtain these special powers only by
subordinating "one's own social subjectivity" to the will of a
Christ who can inspire material shapes with sacred essence. As
a result, the "elect" gathered in communities that readily asserted their "privileged sacramental subjectivity with respect to
people who . . . [were] not members of the mystical body."[57] The
Fifth Monarchists exemplify this particular form of radical Protestant elitism when they claim that they will rule the world in
the millennial age, and Trapnel corroborates this view of Fifth
Monarchist authority by portraying her body and those of the
saints as icons of being chosen.

In addition to distinguishing the saved from the damned, radical Protestant materialism, Weber argues, contributes to the rise
of capitalism. Weber, like Kibbey, views radical Protestantism as
sacralizing everyday life, his particular focus being on the role of
labor. He contends that early modern radical Protestants understood secular labor as a kind of religious calling: "The only way
of living acceptably to God was not to surpass worldly morality

in monastic asceticism, but solely through the fulfillment of the obligations imposed upon the individual by his position in the world. That was his calling." Because one's calling was a way of glorifying God, radical Protestantism did not employ injunctions against growing wealthy but rather saw success in worldly affairs as a sign of being chosen. Excess wealth could, however, become a problem if the believer embraced the idleness and luxuries it could purchase. Rather than enjoying the fruits of his labor, the righteous Protestant businessman was encouraged to live simply and to invest his excess capital in his business: "With the consciousness of standing in the fulness of God's grace and being visibly blessed by Him, the bourgeois business man . . . could follow his pecuniary interests as he would and feel that he was fulfilling a duty in doing so."[58] Anna Trapnel articulates the Protestant notion of calling when she exhorts the merchants not to permit their "mouthes" to "overflow" with earthly delights such as "Canded Ginger" and "Preserved Nutmegs" but to eat God's food. Nowhere does she suggest that they desist from trafficking in exotic foods altogether, rather she merely insists that they do not revel in the goods themselves.

What is so striking about Trapnel's materialism, and particularly her use of food imagery, is the extent to which it demystifies her body as a sign of divine power. By contrast, Sarah Wight appears much more committed to keeping the various groups of people who attend her bedside in awe of her body's special powers. Like Trapnel, Wight professes to be fed by supernatural means: "Bodily sustenance being offered to her, shee not having eaten any thing at all during twenty-four dayes last past, nor drunke any thing at all but fair water, and but very little of that. Shee thus answered: *Doe you think, I do not eat? How doe you think I live?* Being asked, what shee did eat? Shee said; *No eye of man sees it, but the eye of God. None could taste the sweetnesse of Manna, by looking on it, none but they that eat of it: or of the Honey out of the Rock*" (*ER*, 33). Indeed, she only uses food imagery, and she does so repeatedly, to describe the nourishment she receives from Christ: "but God hath given me Christ to feed upon; and his flesh is meat indeed, and his blood drink indeed" (*ER*, 57). However, she never calls upon God to nourish any of the despairing women who attend her bedside. Rather, she consoles them by telling them that they will receive assurance of grace from Christ. And while this may happen in terms of their bodies, it remains an abstract and mystical experience: "Christ will root you out of your sin, and root you out of your selfe:

and plant you in himselfe. He will doe it" (ER, 63). Wight's prefer-
ence for mystical imagery, as opposed to food imagery, focuses
her audience's attention not on the technical details of eating and
fasting but on the mystical union of human and divine. Her ability
to forego food for some seventy-six days is one extraordinary
manifestation of divine presence but not necessarily an exemplary one. Anna Trapnel, on the other hand, invites her audience
not merely to consider that her body conveys divine presence but
to consider how it articulates this. Her representation of her
body becomes legible precisely at the point when she calls upon
her audience to recognize not just that she is fed by Christ but
also that, in being fed by Christ, she does not eat secular food.
Sarah Wight, of course, implies as much. But, by making this
point explicit, Trapnel indicates that her physiological practices
are a sign of being chosen that can be borne by others as well
as by herself. Her body is exemplary because it illustrates the
abstemious food practices of the chosen. It does not merely convey her experience of divine presence but a collective experience
of grace. Trapnel's capacity to generalize her bodily experiences
takes them out of the miraculous realm and locates them in the
rational order. While her body is an extraordinary example of divine presence, it is nonetheless an example.

THE MOTHER OF THE STATE

Surprisingly, Trapnel's emphasis on her exemplarity and on
the representative status of her body suggests some affinities
with the ideas of the rationalist philosopher Thomas Hobbes. By
urging her auditors and readers to comprehend her body as an
index of being chosen, Trapnel implies that they should find as-
pects of her abstinent behavior in themselves. They too should
naturally prefer simple foods in modest quantities to the
"roasted meats" of the backslidden Cromwell. Hobbes's theory
of the state, of course, was not predicated upon the naturalness
of fasting but did depend upon another form of "natural" behavior. His "Representative" sovereign derived power from men
joining together to end the natural state of war that characterized social relationships before the advent of the commonwealth:
"The finall Cause, End, or Designe of men, (who naturally love
Liberty, and Dominion over others,) in the introduction of that
restraint upon themselves, (in which we see them live in Common-wealths,) is the foresight of their own preservation, and of a

more contented life thereby; that is to say of getting themselves out from that miserable condition of Warre, which is necessarily consequent . . . to the naturall Passions of men." Because men's "naturall Passions" make human society impossible, they must submit themselves to a "Power" in order to free themselves "from that miserable condition of Warre." They can establish a commonwealth when each man agrees to vest his authority in one man or assembly of men: "The only way to erect such a Common Power . . . is, to conferre all their power and strength upon one Man, or upon one Assembly of men, to beare their Person; and every one to owne, and acknowledge himselfe to be Author of whatsoever he that so beareth their Person, shall Act." [59] Just as Trapnel's fellow saints should see themselves in her, Hobbes's subjects can see themselves in their sovereign representative. For both Hobbes and Trapnel, political authority no longer derives from a divinely inspired great chain of being but from the capacity to define and represent the natures of individual men and women.

The correlation of political authority with representation, embraced by Hobbes and Trapnel alike, has strong philosophical ties to covenant theology. Sixteenth- and seventeenth-century covenant theologians understood history as comprised of two distinct covenants between God and humankind. The first was a covenant of works that joined God and Adam, the representative of all humankind. Because Adam failed to maintain his part of the agreement, all of humankind was damned. The second covenant was one of faith that joined God and Christ, the representative of some of humankind.[60] As Christopher Hill distinguishes the two covenants: "Man is born in debt to God: Christ has obtained easier terms for his clients." The "terms" that Christ has obtained for his "clients," his elect, require them simply to assent to the covenant of faith. In return, Christ promises that God will give them the grace necessary for faith. In essence, Christ's role in the new covenant resembles that of a lawyer representing his or her client in contract negotiations. And, as David Zaret notes, Puritan divines frequently used the language of secular contracts to explain covenant theology to their congregations. With "contractual transactions" becoming a "familiar feature of everyday economic life," these clergymen urged their followers to apply the "same patterns of methodical discipline and record-keeping" required by contractual arrangements to their spiritual lives.[61]

This use of contractual language was significant not only for serving to rationalize what was once the frighteningly arbitrary God of Calvinism but also for establishing Christ as a "public" or "representative" person. As Hill argues, this notion of representation permeated secular politics creating an intellectual climate in which groups such as Parliament, the New Model Army, and the Fifth Monarchists could deem themselves representatives of the people although they derived authority from neither noble blood lines nor popular elections. Because they had assented to the covenant of faith, they saw themselves as joined to Christ and therefore capable of serving as representative men and women. Trapnel's fellow sectarian, Mary Cary, elaborates how the close identification of Christ with his saints grants them an exclusive political prerogative: "God giving judgement to his saints, he brings to passe the great designs he hath in the world by them as his instruments: so that he does it, and they do it; and they must doe it, and are alwaies ready, and shall be so." Cary effectively justifies the ways of the saints to humankind: if they do it, it is God's will. For Cary, the contract between God and the saints means that all of the saints' deeds are righteous. And it is precisely this absolute sense of righteousness that, according to Alfred Cohen, sums up both Cary's career and Fifth Monarchist ideology: "Taken together Cary's works offer a view of the Fifth Monarchy mind as one that subordinated the spiritual elements in Christianity to an aggressive pursuit of this-worldly power by a group of militant saints who would rule in the name of Jesus for the good of all."[62]

Trapnel's self-representation encompasses the Fifth Monarchist idea that the saints "would rule in the name of Jesus for the good of all." In her capacity as "Representative" (to borrow a term from Hobbes) Fifth Monarchist, she considers herself chosen to broker the relationship between God and the saints. For instance, she portrays herself as pleading on their behalf from the "Mount": "Why is thy Handmaid so long with thee upon the Mount, seeing thy sparkling glory, and those reviving springs, but that thy Handmaid may plead with thee concerning thy Saints, thine Inheritance, and that her heart may take in the things concerning thy Saints" (35). As the divinely appointed representative of the saints, Trapnel hardly plays the role of a passive "Handmaid" but actively cajoles God to "reckon" with or punish those who "act nothing but darknesse, discover nothing but vileness and evill" (62). Moreover, she admonishes God that she will continue to badger him: "oh thy servant will not let thee alone till thou resist" (62). Clearly viewing herself as the spokesperson of the elect, she exhorts God to punish the godless who surround them. Moreover, in her song to Cromwell, she literally identifies herself as the embodiment of the contract between God and his people. She suggests that she sets aside her own interest (and that, presumably, of her fellow sectarians) to advocate for Cromwell, the man who, at that very moment, is responsible for holding Vavasor Powell as a prisoner:

> Thy servant said, Lord, that she would
>   lay aside her interest,
> And plead for him [Cromwell] on his sick-bed,
>   that he might see the breast,
> Where he should be restor'd to life,
>   and walk again on earth,
> And manage the affairs for thine.

(55)

Clearly, Cromwell's speedy recovery from his spiritual illness could benefit Trapnel's sect: "And manage the affairs for thine." Although she claims to "lay aside her interest," she calls upon God to recognize that restoring the Protector's spiritual well-being could redound to the benefit of the saints and therefore to himself. (By asserting that she acts against her own interests, she may mean that she pleads the case of one who has broken his "vows and promises" to the "most blessed Son" and the "flock of Jesus Christ" [55].) In effect, Trapnel is authorized to tell God how to act neither by God nor by the saints but by the common political agenda they share.[63] Her capacity to represent the union of human with divine authorizes her to explain the covenant's will to both the saints and God. In her vision of the Fifth Monarchist theocracy, she represents the contract between God and his people and serves as the independent judiciary, designed to preserve the state's constitution.

With regard to Hobbes, of course, the idea that the representative sovereign derives authority from contractual obligations is well known. What needs to be elucidated here is the extent to which Hobbes's notion of representative authority was influenced by the same covenant theology that informed Trapnel's self-presentation. Indeed, as Hill argues, "the doctrine of the public person [informed by covenant theology] may have had at least a negative influence on Hobbes, making him think out more carefully his own theory of representation." Hill bases his contention on the fact that Hobbes's political writings of the 1640s, *The Elements of Law* (1650, but written in 1640) and *De Cive* (1642), do not portray "the sovereign as a representative person such as is fundamental to *Leviathan*" but rather describe "the sovereign in passing as 'a person civil.'" Hill suggests that Hobbes's emphasis on the sovereign as "the only true representative of the people may owe something to the popularity of the covenant theology, and in particular of the claims made in the 1640s that Parliament and the Army were public persons." Hobbes, of course, disdained claims that groups such as these were particularly called to usurp sovereign authority: "And whereas some men have pretended for their disobedience to their Soveraign, a new Covenant, made, not with men, but with God; this also is unjust: for there is no Covenant with God, but by mediation of some body that representeth God's Person; which none doth but God's Lieutentant, who hath the Soveraignty under God."[64]

In contending that only the sovereign, *the* representative person in the commonwealth, could establish a politically authoritative covenant with God, Hobbes employs the methods of covenant theology to undermine the claims to political legitimacy of its radical practitioners. While his sovereign may establish a covenant with God, he may do so not, as the Fifth Monarchists might have, because he is divinely sanctioned but because he embodies the brutish passions common to all humanity:

> Hitherto I have set forth the nature of Man, (whose Pride and other Passions have compelled him to submit himselfe to Government;) together with the great power of his Governour, whom I compared to *Leviathan*, taking that comparison out of the last two verses of the one and fortieth of *Job*; where God having set forth the great power of *Leviathan*, called him King of the Proud. *There is nothing*, saith he, *on earth, to be compared with him. He is made so as not to be afraid. Hee seeth every high thing below him; and is King of all the children of pride.*

Because men are naturally proud, they authorize a fearsome beast, in their own image, to govern them.[65] Hence, Hobbes's representative sovereign, according to his version of the public person, can quite conceivably be an oppressive ruler. In essence, Hobbes "twists" the sectarians' arguments for their own elect status to urge the absolute authority of his representative sovereign. In Hobbes's theory of representative authority we have both the beginnings of "modern political thinking" and a direct link to the theology that shaped Trapnel's theocratic vision.[66] This connection is important because it suggests that in repre-

senting her body as a model for Fifth Monarchist political identity, Trapnel adopts a form of political representation akin to that
which founds the modern secular state.

Unlike Hobbes, however, Trapnel makes her version of representation into the basis for a vision of political order that gestures toward, in Catherine MacKinnon's terms, a "feminist
theory of the state"—a model of political authority that accounts
for the specific conditions of women's existence. This is suprising
on two counts. First, because, as Richard Helgerson has observed, the idea of the state, as opposed to that of the nation, appears quite literally to espouse a masculine sensibility:

> Compare, for example, Hobbes's frontispiece with Drayton's [to his
> *Poly-Olbion* (1612)]. The all-powerful state, as represented by
> Hobbes, is a man, erect, in armor, wearing an imperial crown, bear-
> ing a sword and crozier in his outstretched hands. He rises above the
> land and dominates it. The fruitful nation as depicted by Drayton, is
> a woman, seated, dressed in a loosely draped gown, one breast ex-
> posed, holding a cornucopia and a scepter. She is enclosed in a tri-
> umphal arch occupied by the men who have fought for possession of
> her. Rather than dominating the land, she wears it.

Further, Helgerson distinguishes discourses of the nation, with
their emphasis on union, community, and particularity, as friend-
lier to women than discourses of the early modern state that
privilege uniformity, central and, therefore, elite power, and ab-
straction. The second reason *Cry*'s politics are surprising is that
the idea of a feminist theory of the state is a new one. As Catherine MacKinnon wrote in 1989: "A feminist theory of the state has
barely been imagined, systematically it has never been tried."[67]
Trapnel does not, of course, explicitly articulate a feminist theory
of the state or even a theory of the state, but she does attest to
the political significance of representation and women's history—two components of a feminist theory of the state. Indeed,
she may have been able to imagine such a strikingly modern vision of women's political possibilities precisely because she was
not burdened with the legacy of Hobbes's political theory. His
highly influential rendering of the politics of representation gave
us the frontispiece of *Leviathan* portraying the state as "a man
erect, in armor . . . [who] rises above the land and dominates it."
For feminist scholars such as Carole Pateman and MacKinnon,
the decidedly masculine image of Leviathan has been reproduced in laws and political theories that claim to be neutral and

unbiased but which ultimately serve to perpetuate the male domination of women.[68]

Trapnel offers an alternative version of political representation in which her own female figure dominates the political arena. But while Leviathan's power is the sum total of all of his subjects' power, Trapnel's power is the composite of divine election and the historical legacy of female fasting. Although Trapnel never explicitly represents herself as part of any female tradition, she does invoke her mother's deathbed speech in *Cry* and in so doing reveals her latent historical consciousness of women's embodied speech. It is through her mother (as I demonstrate below) that Trapnel effectively invokes the legacies of fasting women such as Sarah Wight, Eve of Fleigen, and Catherine of Siena, and thereby situates herself in women's history. History, of course, is precisely the category that *Leviathan* claims to supercede. Hobbes's text professes to formulate a science of politics predicated upon a timeless, "mechanical system of matter in motion."[69] Nevertheless, history does have a place in *Leviathan*, but it is in the private not the public realm.[70] By examining history's place in *Leviathan* and its implications for gendered political authority, we can understand how Trapnel's use of history enables her to translate her version of political representation into a vision of female authority that anticipates MacKinnon's feminist theory of the state.

Hobbes turns to history when he reluctantly appeals to the tradition of paternal authority to explain why men should rule in the domestic realm. Indeed, in the chapter "*Of Dominion* Paternall, *and* Despoticall," Hobbes argues that parental authority over children does not derive from the fact of generation but from the child's "Consent." According to such a contract, the child would subject him or herself to the parent in exchange for protection. One difficulty of the parent-child contract, however, is the issue of which parent—mother or father—should have dominion over the child: both parents cannot possess this authority because "no man can obey two Masters." Surprisingly, Hobbes counters the "natural" assumptions of those who claim that dominion belongs to the man "as being of the more excellent Sex" by arguing that "there is not always that difference of strength or prudence between the man and the woman, as that the right can be determined without War." A woman could be stronger and more prudent than her male counterpart and so, exercising some of the attributes of the "more excellent Sex," she could earn the right to exercise dominion over the child. Hobbes's reasons for

positing a merit-based model for maternal authority begin to
emerge in his next positive affirmation of the mother's natural
right: where "there can be no Contract, the Dominion is in the
Mother" because "where there are no Matrimoniall lawes, it cannot be known who is the Father, unlesse it be deduced by the
Mother." In the state of nature, parental dominion *de facto* falls
to the mother because only her authorship of the child is certain.
Hobbes's competing claims about the origin of maternal authority—that it can be determined by strength/prudence or by physical authorship—underscore *Leviathan*'s attempts to undermine
paternal authority. As Pateman puts it: "The story of the original
contract is perhaps the greatest tale of men's creation of new political life . . . Now the father comes under attack. The original
contract shows how his monopoly of politically creative power is
seized and shared equally among men. In civil society, all men,
not just fathers, can generate political life and political right. Political creativity belongs not to paternity but to masculinity." By
pointing to the literal certainty of maternity, Hobbes implicitly
critiques a system of authority that depends on the transmission
of power from father to son; because paternity depends upon the
mother's word, paternal authority is always vulnerable to illegiti-
macy. The "labour" of contract theorists such as Hobbes, Pateman contends, was to establish "the civil body politic" as "an act
of reason" and not as "an analogue to a bodily act of procre-
ation."[71]

Immediately after asserting that women could be stronger and
more prudent than men in the state of nature, Hobbes proceeds
to illustrate how parental authority is determined in the commonwealth: "In Common-wealths, this controversie is decided by
the Civill Law: and for the most part, (but not alwayes) the sentence is in favour of the Father; because for the most part Common-wealths have been erected by the Fathers, not by the
Mothers of families." Fathers "for the most part" can rule over
families because they have been active in establishing common-
wealths. For Hobbes, paternal authority is not the origin of sovereign power but it does provide a pattern for the male domination
of women in the private realm. While men are no longer subject
to paternal authority, women are. According to Pateman, "the
sphere of natural subjection [or, of paternal dominion] is separated out as the non-political sphere."[72] Against the obedience
women must show to fathers, sons, Hobbes opines, should honour them because they formerly held political power: "originally

the Father of every man was also his Soveraign Lord, with power over him of life and death; and that the Fathers of families, when by instituting a Common-wealth, they resigned that absolute Power, yet it was never intended, they should lose the honour due unto them for their [children's] education."[73] Because they have "resigned that absolute Power," fathers warrant the honour of their sons. Hobbes does not banish fathers from his common-wealth because they embody a form, although not the current one, of masculine authority.

After illustrating that civil law would give the father, rather than the mother, dominion over the child, Hobbes speculates further that, in the state of nature, a man and woman might "between themselves dispose of the dominion over the Child by Contract." As an instance of this, he describes how the Amazons contracted with their male neighbors for the generation of children: "We find in history that the *Amazons* Contracted with the Men of the neighbouring Countries to whom they had recourse for issue, that the issue Male should be sent back, but the Female remains with themselves: so that the dominion of the Females was in the Mother." Why does Hobbes appeal to the Amazons to illustrate that men and women, in the state of nature, can contract with one another to determine parental authority? First, the Amazons were women who were stronger than many men, yet they chose to determine parental authority through contract. Thus, the Amazons are in accord with one of the express objectives of *Leviathan*, preferring rational accomodation to the law of the strongest. Second, Hobbes's Amazons may represent the threat of female power neutralized. In their anthropological study of the idea of the "wild woman," Sharon Tiffany and Kathleen Adams argue that "the Wild Woman has latent powers to discomfort or harm men, but, theoretically, she can be harnessed." Third, and perhaps related to their pursuit of civil contract rather than brute force, the Amazons choose only to keep the female children. And, Hobbes represents their choice as almost axiomatic: "so that the dominion of the Females was in the Mother." This is a most uncanny moment in Hobbes. On the one hand, he seems to be likening human reproduction to mechanical reproduction or copying. Birth, as it did under the rule of the fathers, no longer produces hierarchical distinctions between father and son, aristocrat and commoner, but instead gives rise to a race of equals fully capable, in theory at least, of entering into a contract with their mothers or fathers. So it is that like begets like: a proud race begets Leviathan, mothers beget daughters, fathers beget sons. On the other hand, Hobbes also tacitly implies that while the differences between fathers and sons, mothers and daughters, are negligible, those separating men and women are greater. According to Hobbes, they inhabit two distinct societies. And in practice, according to Pateman, these two realms prove to be separate but not equal: "Once the original contract is entered into, the relevant dichotomy is between the private sphere and the civil public sphere—a dichotomy that reflects the order of sexual difference in the natural condition, which is also a political difference. . . . The antinomy private/public is another expression of natural/civil and women/men."[74] Although within the context of *Leviathan*, the Amazons must be seen as, in part, referring to the hardening of gender distinctions that Pateman describes, they also, on a much quieter note, underscore the possibility of a female community with a distinct political identity.

Hobbes's tenuous suggestion of a female community aside, his near-axiom ("so that the dominion of the Females was in the Mother") is quickly succeeded by a pejorative image of maternal, pre-commonwealth dominion over the child. No longer the "representative" male child who populates the early part of his discussion of parental dominion, the child the mother dominates is an infant "it": "Again seeing the Infant is first in the power of the Mother, so as she may either nourish, or expose *it*, if she nourish *it*, *it* oweth *its* life to the Mother; and is therefore obliged to obey her, rather than any other; and by consequence the Dominion over *it* is hers" (emphasis mine). Expanding his fable of parental dominion, Hobbes implies that maternity itself does not give the mother power over the infant but protecting and caring for "it" does: "But if she expose it, and another find, and nourish it, the Dominion is in *him* that nourisheth it. For it ought to obey *him* by whom it is preserved; because preservation of life being the end, for which one man becomes subject to another, every man is supposed to promise obedience, to *him*, in whose power it is to save, or destroy *him*" (emphasis mine).[75] Abandoned by its mother, the nameless, formless infant is picked up by a man and grows to be a proper male subject. Like begets like: the natural, not contractually bound mother gives birth to an amorphous, infant "it," the sheltering man, and (significantly) not necessarily a father, raises the child to be a man. To mothers outside of the commonwealth, regardless of their ability to contend physically with men, Hobbes bequeathes nameless, ungendered infants. And to those who contract with their husbands for protection, he promises subjection. As for fathers, Hobbes restricts their authority to the domestic realm in which their children will honor them. Shadows of their former selves, they command the subjection of their wives and children because they once held absolute power: "For the Father, and Master being before the Institution of the Common-wealth, absolute Soveraigns in their own Families, they lose afterward no more of their Authority, than the Law of the Common-wealth taketh from them."[76] By keeping the memory of patriarchal domination alive, Hobbes can insist on the subordination of women and children.

Although Hobbes's theory breaks from the tradition of paternal authority, it does preserve the memory of the power that belonged exclusively to fathers. Trapnel's text also correlates authority and memory. But in her case, the female authority she instantiates is public and the historical figure it explicitly commemorates is her mother. Although Trapnel mentions her mother only once in *Cry*, it is clear that she served as a pattern for her daughter's avowedly political, prophetic career. Trapnel's mother appears in the opening paragraph of the autobiographical section of her text, in a context that clearly identifies her as an authoritative figure:

> I Am *Anna Trapnel*, the daughter of *William Trapnel*, Shipwright, who lived in *Poplar*, in *Stepney* Parish; my father and mother living and dying in the profession of the Lord Jesus; my mother died nine years ago, the last words she uttered upon her death bed, were these to the Lord for her daughter. Lord! Double thy spirit upon my child; These words she uttered with much eagerness three times, and spoke no more; I was trained up to my book and writing, I have walked in fellowship with the Church meeting as [sic] *All-hallows*, (whereof Mr. *John Simpson* is a Member) for the space of about four years; I am well known to him and that whole Society, also to Mr. *Greenhil* Preacher at *Stepney*, and that whole society, to Mr. *Henry Jesse*, and most of his society, to Mr. *Venning* Preacher at *Olaves* in *Southwark*, and most of his society, to Mr. *Knollis*, and most of his society, who have knowledge of me, and of my conversation; If any desire to be satisfied of it; they can give testimony of me, and of my walking in times past. (3)

For Trapnel, male authority figures provide her political identity: her father's name, occupation, and address literally define her while the various preachers whose names identify their (largely female) societies can provide "testimony" of her "walking in times past."[77] They appear as a list of names because, within the context of this paragraph, their only role is to name and authenticate her.

By contrast, her mother makes a dramatic entry onto the stage of her daughter's autobiography. Within the space of a few lines, Trapnel paints a portrait of a strong-willed woman calling upon God, moments before her death, to "Double" his "spirit" upon her daughter. Her mother does not passively ask but rather more assertively urges, nearly commands ("Lord!"), or, at the very least, exhorts God to perform her will. One influence of her mother on Trapnel's career is clear: she marks off the bed as a space of powerful female speech. While, as Phyllis Mack notes, Trapnel's contemporaries would have understood the "maiden who preached prone, holding forth from a sickbed" as the "ultimate manifestation of the prophet as a passive and entirely purified receptacle of divine energy," both Trapnel and her mother make the bed a site of female wilfulness.[78] By recuperating beds as sites of female authority, Trapnel and her mother effectively undermine a reading of history that views "the maiden who preached prone, holding forth from a sickbed" as a passive vessel. Instead, they promote women's speech from the sickbed as powerful. In so doing, they echo previous political uses of the form such as the medieval fasting women's challenge to male clerics' authority and Sarah Wight's efforts to teach "radical theology" to seventeenth-century men and women.[79]

Trapnel emulates her mother's dying speech not only by making the bed the site of her prophetic career but also by linking her own speech with fasting.[80] For Trapnel, fasting becomes a vehicle for remembering her mother's death bed prayer because it signifies a kind of living death to the self and to the body's desires. In her *Legacy*, she describes a period in June of 1646 when she desired "to be out of the body" because she feared the temptation to fleshly sin: "I was desirous to be out of the body, I longed to be dissolved, and while I continued pleading with God to be out of the body, entreating to go hence, that so I might be swallowed up in glory, lest continuing in the body, I should act in the flesh, and so dishonour my loving father."[81] For Trapnel, bodiliness leads to sin and eternal death, and being "out of the body" is the way to "glory." Fasting, she suggests in *Cry*, approximates the gloriousness of death and life everlasting: "Lord it is a Fasting day, indeed when thou art a Rest, when thou commest out with a sparkling Rest; if thou hadst given a rest in thy Ordinary way, that had been very sweet, oh but a rest in the Mount with thy selfe, a transfiguring Rest among Angels with the brightest sun"

(47). Fast days, like the Sabbath day that provides the initial referent for her meditation on "Rest," may serve (as they do in this case) as an earthly means for going to God on the Mount. A bridge between life and death, fasting enables Trapnel to establish a kind of intimacy with Christ, one that permits her (as death did her mother) to call upon him to respond to her entreaties.

Fasting is not the only means that Trapnel employs to reenact her mother's death-bed scene, but language, particularly in its written form, also serves as a vehicle for remembering her mother. Indeed, when she introduces the role of reading and writing in her life ("I was trained up to my book and writing"), it is that very text that *literally* comes between her recollection of her mother's death-bed wish and the various male preachers who can vouch for her past actions. On one level, reading and writing function in the masculine world of authorities she describes to communicate the knowledge of names, places, and associations. In such a world, to borrow from Hobbes, "words are wise mens counters, they do but reckon by them."[82] Moreover, the knowledge conveyed by such "wise mens counters" does not readily lend itself to dramatization. Trapnel's mother disrupts the busy enumeration which is the work of much of the paragraph by spectacularly announcing her dying wish. Trapnel's text permits her mother's intrusion into its orderly world of facts and figures, but it does not allow her to get carried away with herself. While her mother expends her dying breath to say "Lord! Double thy spirit upon my child; Lord! Double thy spirit upon my child; Lord! Double thy spirit upon my child;" the text merely records that "These words she uttered with much eagerness three times." As Hamlet would have it, there is no excessive "sawing of the air" here: Trapnel follows Wight's amanuensis who chooses not to copy out "Love him" nine times, preferring to report the information instead. Still, Trapnel does not dismiss her mother altogether but incorporates her mother's passionate voice into her catalogue of male authorities.

For Trapnel, writing provides both a way back to the mother and to her embodied voice, and a way into the rational world of men and their multiple and manifest authorities.[83] While Sarah Wight spoke her body, Trapnel speaks her body as a sign of the body politic. Trapnel prefers representation to repetition. And although the rational language of politics drives her away from union with her mother—she does not, after all, reproduce her mother's last words in their entirety—it is through this very language that, her text insists, this rupture can be healed; that her mother's wild voice can be linked to those authenticating voices of the various preachers; that stagecraft can be reconciled to statecraft. For instance, she warns the soldiers that the hand writing on the wall which predicts the downfall of the Babylonian King, Belshazzar, in Daniel, will also cause them to shake: "Though they [soldiers] may shake off faith and prayer, yet they shall not shake off thee: oh when the hand-writing is come up in their veins, will not their knees smite together" (62). Belshazzar's "knees smote one against another" because of the strange hand that wrote on the wall. The soldiers' knees, on the other hand, will be *literally* driven to "smite together;" like blood, God's message of doom will flow through their veins.[84] Once again, Trapnel insists that texts are experienced through the body, and that the body can be read like a text. For Trapnel, the interchangeability of word and body produces a striking literalness: God's word *really* will kill the soldiers just as it has transformed her own body.

In her literalness, Trapnel echoes her mother and the medieval and early modern religious women whose bodies spectacularly articulated the intensity of their relationships with Christ. By identifying with, as Bynum puts it, the "suffering humanity of Christ," such women might consume the fluids from the bodies of the afflicted in order, literally, to embrace Christ's pain. Margery Kempe, the medieval English mystic, gained both fame and notoriety because she was given to astonishingly loud weeping at the very thought of Christ's passion. Appropriately, her crying begins when, during a pilgrimage to Jerusalem, she is shown the *actual* places where Christ suffered his passion: "And when they came up onto the Mount of Calvary, she fell down because she could not stand or kneel, but writhed and wrestled with her body, spreading her arms out wide, and cried with a loud voice as though her heart would have burst apart, for in the city of her soul she saw *truly* and *freshly* how our lord was crucified" (emphasis mine). After her initial crying at Jerusalem, Kempe's cryings occur with increasing frequency and cause her to become "very weak in her bodily strength." For Kempe, Christ's passion continues to be very real: she sees Christ being crucified "truly and freshly" and responds with "such crying and roaring" that her health suffers.[85] Like Kempe, Wight also claims to have intimately experienced Christ's passion: "I was *really* crucified with Christ; though I was not in the appearance of any bodily eye, but as I was in the loyns of Adam when he sinned. I was the nailes in his hands and in his feet; and the speare in his side" (*ER*, 26;

emphasis mine). Although to the "bodily eye" she does not appear to be present at the crucifixion, she was *really* there in the "nailes" and the "speare" that killed Christ. Likewise, now that Christ has redeemed her through his death and resurrection, he *really* feeds her and hence she does not need to eat *real* food.

Like Wight and the medieval and early modern fasting women, Trapnel also claims that Christ feeds her when she appears, to the "bodily eye," not to be eating anything at all. She does not, however, identify as intensely as her forebears did with Christ's suffering humanity but with his humanity alone. For Trapnel, Christ's incarnation as well as his crucifixion are events that literally create opportunities for the saints. In her 1658 *A Voice for the King of Saints*, she calls upon her fellow sectarians to recognize that their willingness to bear witness to Christ's crucifixion grants them a "right" to participate in his power:

> Another note take to know vision,
> That you may not be decei'vd,
> And cousened of your right, and that to which
> A crucified Christ doth lead.[86]

While Christ's crucifixion prompts Kempe to tears and Wight to self-recrimination, it inspires Trapnel to claim her rights in the contract binding God and the saints. In *Cry*, Trapnel again identifies Christ's humanity as an attribute that literally nurtures his followers: she prays that Cromwell "might see the breast,/ Where he should be restor'd to life" (55). Christ nourishes her, and if Cromwell should "see the breast," Christ would sustain him also. Christ's humanity does not inspire Trapnel to lament his suffering but to celebrate the possibilities for divine conversation, for a "heavenly contract," that it creates. Like the handwriting that threatens the soldiers, Christ's word/food is real and could serve to identify Cromwell's body with those of the saints. Christ's word is as real and physically knowable as mother's milk.

Trapnel's spiritual autobiography, the *Legacy*, further strengthens the connection between Christ and maternity. Shortly after her mother's death in 1642, some of Trapnel's fellow saints attempt to console her by urging that Christ would be a substitute for her mother: "the Saints told me when I mourned the loss of my tender mother, that Christ would be more tender, and would be all to mee in the loss of earthly comforts; and he was more to me than they told me, he was a double comfort, and a Comforter that hath tarried and abided with me, and will abide with me for ever." Strongly echoing her mother's death bed wish: "Lord! Double thy spirit upon my child," Trapnel's text suggests that her mother's will is realized in the "double comfort" she receives from Christ who more than consoles her "loss of earthly comforts." Moreover, the passage also appears, through its allusion to John, to indicate that her mother literally engenders Christ. In John, Christ promises Philip that he will not leave his followers "comfortless" when he dies: "And I will pray the Father, and he shall give you another Comforter, that he may abide with you for ever." The Son's prayer produces the Spirit and, in Trapnel's writings, the mother's prayer produces the Son. In the interstices of Trapnel's theology, what becomes evident is that the mother embraces both the Word and the body. Christ was not merely "made flesh" through woman, but was made "Word " by her as well.[87] William Trapnel names his daughter, a token of a paternal authority that Hobbes himself admits is always speculative, but her unnamed mother confers the Word upon her in a spectacular instant.[88] And so, for Trapnel, the Word is always bound up with the flesh, coursing through her veins like her mother's blood and filling her mouth like her mother's milk.

Cry's brief but important description of her mother's influence on her prophetic career underscores the extent to which Trapnel's feminist consciousness pervades her understanding of her role as representative Fifth Monarchist. Using both words and her body to represent her sect's body politic, Trapnel emulates the way her mother bequeathes the Word to her daughter. In so doing, she makes her private relationship with her mother into a model for political relationships. Trapnel's translation of a private into a public bond puts her at odds with Hobbes whose theory of the state distinguishes the private realm from the public, political world and clearly identifies the public realm as politically superior to the private. Pateman understands the political isolation of the private realm to be characteristic of contract theorists who "primarily" create "social relationships constituted by subordination." In her eyes, distinguishing between the public and the private becomes another way of separating women from political life. Catherine MacKinnon argues further that the modern state similarly legislates male authority through laws that "appear" to be gender neutral: "So long as power enforced by law reflects and corresponds—in form and in substance—to power enforced by men over women in society, law is objective, appears principled, becomes just the way things are. So long as men dominate women effectively enough in society, without the support of positive law, nothing constitutional can be done about it." Mac-Kinnon asserts that the first step to righting laws which use the language of "objectivity" and "universality" to represent themselves as neutral and hence free from gender bias is "to claim women's concrete reality."[89] In other words, women need to assert the reality of their sexual subordination against laws that falsely legislate the reality of inequality out of existence. Thus, women must impose their point of view on what is essentially a male domain. Trapnel does just this when she incorporates her mother's voice into her catalogue of male authorities. In the political order she describes, her mother's memory and the particular bodily legacy it enjoins share pride of place with conventional modes of authority. When Trapnel moves, in the autobiographical introduction to the *Cry*, from the scene of her mother's death, through reading and writing, to the world of male authorities, she never *really* leaves her mother at all, rather she *realizes* her presence again and again as she utters her prophecies.

Trapnel gestures toward a feminist theory of the state when she appeals to her historical identity as a woman, as her mother's daughter, to make her female body the model chosen body. In making herself into the representative Fifth Monarchist, Trapnel effectively politicizes a distinctly female historical reality. It is precisely Trapnel's emphasis on her personal connection to the past that distinguishes her from Hobbes. What makes his model of the state aggressively masculine, and therefore misogynous, is its relationship to history. For Hobbes and, according to MacKinnon, for the framers of the Anglo-American legal tradition (so profoundly influenced by Hobbes), history appears to be a negligible and insignificant category, except as it impinges on the private realm. There, an emphatically masculine history is rigidly enforced. For Hobbes, this means that fathers, who have so graciously conceded their exclusive authority to the brotherhood of all men, remain in control over their wives and children so long as they are dependent upon them. (Wives, of course, will owe them obedience until they are parted by death.) In the modern state, MacKinnon contends, the legal system simply denies the categorical existence of a history of women's oppression in favor of a coolly objective and neutral law. Under the guise of sex equality, the law only allows "features women share with the privileged group" to substantiate "equality claims" rather than recognizing the "substantive" conditions of women's lives, such as their exposure to sexual abuse, as legitimating equality claims. In other words, the law negates the existence of the historical conditions that have subordinated women to men. The only history that matters is that of male dominance: "The legal process reflects itself in its own image, makes be there what it puts there, while presenting itself as passive and neutral in the process."[90]

History, and particularly histories of domestic relationships, prove to be an essential precondition for advancing a feminist theory of the state. Hobbes himself appears to testify to this when, in discussing family relationships, he appeals to the historical example of the Amazons. Judicious contracting by both the male and female parents involved, his text seems to suggest, enables the development of commonwealths organized according to gender distinctions. Even within the body politic imagined by *Leviathan*, gender difference remains an important structuring device. Only this time, women do not form independent commonwealths, but instead they are relegated to the private realm where they must submit to male authority as represented by the figure of the father, that holdover from a bygone age. Likewise, in *Cry*, the father possesses a limited authority over his daughter, but this is not due to the implementing of a new political dispensation but rather to the more expansive power of his wife. William Trapnel, it appears, only transfers his name and thus a political identity to his daughter, but his unnamed wife transmits the Word to her child, thereby providing the material for her daughter's prophetic career. It is precisely this awareness that personal relationships, and particularly those between women, can have political meaning which, some thirteen years later, will set the stage for Margaret Fell's defense of women's right to preach, *Womens Speaking Justified* (second edition, 1667). For too many years, Fell complains, church officials have made "a Trade of Womens words," including those of Elizabeth's joyful commendation of her cousin Mary's blessed pregnancy, "to get money by" and to insert in their "Common Prayer" and "Sermons," all the while demanding, "Women must not speak, Women must be silent." While Trapnel's text attests to the political significance of her dying mother's words, Fell's gender polemic asserts the material value of women's words. Fell extends Trapnel's vision of women's history by explicitly identifying a literary legacy of women's powerful speech. Where Trapnel implies a broad female tradition, Fell directly reveals a history of valued and valuable women's words. In doing so, Fell, like Trapnel, attests to the political import of "private" exchanges between women. After all, it is a conversation between two pregnant women that forms a core prayer in the Book of Common Prayer. The child leaps in Elizabeth's womb as she prophesies to Mary: "Blessed *art* thou among women, and blessed *is* the fruit of thy womb."[91]

4

Margaret Fell's *Womens Speaking Justified* and Quaker Ideas of Female Subjectivity

> Now *Moses* and *Aaron*, and the seventy Elders, did not say to those Assemblies of Women, we can do our Work our selves, and you are fitter to be at home to wash the Dishes, or such like Expressions; but they did encourage them in the work and Service of God, in those things which God had commanded them in the time of the Law.
>
> —George Fox, *This is an Encouragement to all the Womens-Meetings in the World* (1676)

ॐ

ON THE FACE OF IT, MARGARET FELL APPEARS TO HAVE HAD VERY LITtle in common with Anna Trapnel. While Trapnel was the daughter of a shipwright, Fell was the child of John Askew, "of an Ancient Family, of those esteem'd and call'd Gentlemen, who left a considerable Estate, which had been in his Name and Family for several Generations."[1] Moreover, Fell maintained the elevated social status she received at birth through her marriage in 1632 to Thomas Fell, a man who would become a prominent judge in Lancashire. And although Fell, like Trapnel, faced periods of imprisonment, she was never accused of vagrancy nor interrogated for being a single woman.[2] Rather, as the mother of nine children and as the lady of her then deceased husband's estate, Swarthmoor Hall, it was she who questioned the legal officials who persecuted her, in 1664, for holding religious meetings in her home: "What Law have I broken, for Worshipping God in my own House?" Eager as they were to suppress the members of her sect, the Quakers, the civil authorities were right to intrude upon activities at her home. According to one of Fell's biographers, Bonnelyn Young Kunze, Swarthmoor Hall played a major role in the sect's expansion, serving as "a haven for [its leader] George Fox, a clearing house for Quaker correspondence, and an important center for the organizational activities of the men and women in the rise of Quakerism."[3]

While Fell's birth and first marriage to Judge Fell granted her the material resources and political connections to contribute to the growth of the Quaker movement, her second marriage in 1669 to George Fox secured her legacy as the "mother of Quakerism." Phyllis Mack has commented extensively on the Quaker female ideal of the "mother in Israel" that celebrated women, such as Fell, who actively participated in church life through both the conventional female roles of wife and mother and through the public roles of preacher and missionary.[4] As the wife of the sect's leader, Fell came to symbolize for many of her cosectarians the archetypal mother figure, thereby complementing her fifty years of service to the movement. Between her conversion in 1652 and her death in 1702, Fell advanced the Quaker movement by tending to the material and spiritual needs of traveling and imprisoned Quakers, by exhorting first Oliver Cromwell and then Charles II to desist from persecuting her sect, by urging the conversion of the Jews, and by contributing to the creation of women's meetings. Of course, Trapnel had also been a central figure within her sect, the Fifth Monarchists, but, consistent with a movement that quickly declined when its millenarian expectations were not realized, her role was limited to prophecy. As the most influential female leader of seventeenth-century Quakerism, Fell's material resources and devotion to the cause enabled her to contribute both to her sect's early millennial enthusiasm and to its later turn toward increased institutionalization.

Although Trapnel and Fell came from different class backgrounds and played different roles in their respective sects, both shared the belief that women's prophetic, and hence political, authority derives from their female sexuality. Trapnel articulated this view, in part, by appealing directly to her body and her female-identified mode of prophetic delivery—fasting—to assert her legitimacy. Like most women prophets of the period, Trapnel deemed the issue of her authority as a woman to be a hurdle she had to leap in order to address other topics, and she never produced a self-conscious apology for women's prophetic legitimacy. This was not the case for Fell who devoted one of her twenty-four tracts, *Womens Speaking Justified,* to asserting women's right to preach in the church. First published in 1666 and then reissued with an important Postscript in 1667, *Womens Speaking Justified* predicates female visionary authority on the physical bond that women, both as mothers and lovers, share with Christ. Fell's claim that Christ makes the female body a site of revelation marks a radical departure from previous Quaker writings on women's speaking. As distinct from her fellow sectarians, Fell re-

sists arguments about female authority that efface the significance of the female body. For Fell, the body is what women have
and to take it away from them, whether literally or metaphorically, is to deprive them of their only material claim to speak publicly.

Today, *Womens Speaking Justified* is by far the best known of
the early modern prophetic tracts authored by women.[5] Although
clearly attractive to feminist scholars because it explicitly addresses gender issues, Fell's text has disappointed some critics
by not conforming to their vision of women's political radicalism.
Hilda Smith regards *Womens Speaking Justified* as a limited
feminist text because it "was strictly a scripturally based argument" that "did not touch upon women's social status" and did
not raise "the issue of women's role in the family or in society
more generally." Smith defines women's political radicalism as a
commitment to effecting social change on behalf of women, and
her *Reason's Disciples* privileges the secular writings of women
such as Mary Astell as examples of proto-feminism. Margaret
Olofson Thickstun argues that critics such as Smith prefer Astell
to Fell because she "values what they value, education and the
exercise of reason, while . . . Fell's impassioned claims of inspiration disconcert readers trained to equate religious enthusiasm
with either irrationality or fundamentalism." Unlike Smith,
Elaine Hobby is not troubled by religious fervor and, in fact, considers Fell's tract as less radical than other Quaker women's
writings because it is not enthusiastic enough. Hobby deems the
Quaker women's treatises of the 1650s radical because they reveal women claiming "a freedom to publish" and exploding "into
print with rage and joy." Priscilla Cotton and Mary Cole, who
briefly address the question of women's speaking in *To the
Priests and People* (1655), measure up to Hobby's standard of
radical writing because their text presents "a witty demolition of
the argument that women should be silent in church." Moreover,
Cotton and Cole express "glee" as "they whirl through their argument" and deftly "slip in and out of their bibles."[6] By contrast,
Hobby describes *Womens Speaking Justified* as "careful and
conservative," as a "judicious, rational presentation of Bible
verses which counter Paul's injunction to silence," and as devoid
of the "ecstatic fervour of Cotton and Cole."[7] So while Fell is not
rational enough for Smith, Hobby finds her too rational and too
dull to be a true radical.

As the work of Smith and Hobby attests, to approach Fell's text
in search of either a fully articulated political agenda for women
or enthusiastic fervor is ultimately disappointing. Rather, the

radicalism of *Womens Speaking Justified* is more readily apparent in the context of the Quaker discourse on gender as it emerges first in tracts advocating women's right to preach in the church and second in treatises describing the structure and purpose of women's meetings. Viewed from this perspective, Fell's text appears to be the work of a masterful polemicist who skillfully alternates between rationality and enthusiasm to suit her purposes. Ultimately, *Womens Speaking Justified* transcends the bounds of much Quaker gender polemic because it not only affirms the theological point that women may speak in the church but also attempts to change general perceptions of women's abilities. Although Fell does not write the explicitly secular text that Smith privileges, she does speak to the situation of women both within and without her sect. Moreover, her insistence that female sexual difference underwrites female prophetic authority marks a radical departure from the mainstream of Quaker gender polemic and reveals an enthusiasm for women that verges on heresy.

WOMEN'S WORDS

While *Womens Speaking Justified* represents the first treatise produced by a Quaker woman to be devoted to the topic of female authority, it is by no means the first female-authored, Quaker tract to consider the issue. As Elaine Hobby has observed, "from the 1650s onwards, brief defenses of female prophesying often appear in the midst of Quaker women's writings where the primary focus is on something else altogether."[8] The briefest of these mentions might consist of quoting one of two scriptural passages, from Galatians or Acts, that Quakers repeatedly cited to justify women's speaking. Their favorite proof-text was Paul's claim in Galatians that "there is neither male nor female . . . in Christ Jesus." Second to Galatians, they frequently invoked Joel's apocalyptic prophecy quoted in Acts: "And it shall come to pass in the last days, saith God, I will pour out my Spirit upon all flesh: and your sons and your daughters shall prophesy, and your young men shall see visions, and your old men shall dream dreams. And on my servants and on my handmaidens I will pour out in those days of my Spirit; and they shall prophesy."[9] These two passages, respectively, summarize the twinned emphases on spiritual equality and eschatological fulfillment that characterized Quaker attitudes toward gendered subjectivity. According to

Phyllis Mack, the "earliest Quakers were radical and democratic" because, in part, "they perceived the attributes of men and women to be fluid and interchangeable." The belief in the interchangeability of male and female attributes did not, however, result in "the glorification of weak and pious femininity" but rather predicated female authority upon the claim that "a woman preaching in public had actually transcended her womanhood."[10] Thus, women's spiritual equality with men derived not from a belief in gender equality but rather from the contention that through God women could exceed traditional ideals of womanhood.

Although the Quaker notion of spiritual equality may not have expressed a positive assessment of femininity, it did, in concert with the sect's millenarian theology, result in a positive attitude toward women. Catherine M. Wilcox has observed that women's speaking was not merely permitted by Quakers but was seen as fulfilling the Joel prophecy that confirmed the sect's identity as God's chosen people operating in the last days. Quakers saw "the widespread practice of women prophesying" as proof that the "last days" described in Joel and Acts had arrived. "Women's prophecy was therefore not simply tolerated amongst the Quakers. Instead it contributed to the Quakers' image of themselves as the true church in the last days, in whose midst the ancient prophecies were being fulfilled." For Hester Biddle, the Joel prophecy of the last days underwrites her vision of an England, blessed with God's bounty in the form of prophesying sons and daughters, on the cusp of millennial glory: "O *England*, that art the most fruitful and famous Land, in which the Lord hath been pleased to make manifest his . . . Glory, more than in any Nation under the Heavens; in so much, that he hath raised his sons and daughters from death to life, and hath made them bold and valiant Souldiers for his Testimony . . . and by the Glorious and Powerful Word of Life, which hath proceeded out of their mouthes . . . hath the Lord visited in this day of great Salvation, and everlasting love."[11] Clearly, Biddle understood the importance of women prophets such as herself in terms not of the realization of sexual equality but of millennial expectations.

As she emphasizes the appearance of women prophets to assert the imminence of the second coming, Biddle also tacitly suggests that the Joel prophecy authorizes her own visionary powers. She is implicitly one of the prophesying daughters whose presence marks the last days. Frequently, the tracts of early Quaker women who fleetingly allude to biblical passages that support their prophetic role do so without directly calling the reader's attention to their situation as female authors. This is certainly true of the imprisoned Anne Audland's *A True Declaration of The suffering of the Innocent.* Jailed on charges of blasphemy because she had publicly denounced the town of Banbury's priest and his congregation as being "out of the Doctrine of Christ," Audland appears to breeze through the reference to Galatians concerned with spiritual equality in order to make the point that true believers will always privilege divine over human law: "but they who were the servants of Christ, & *Ministers* of *Christ*, when they were commanded by the rulers that which was contrary to the command of Christ; they said whether is it better to obey God or man: judge ye, and I say the same, and they which command any thing contrary to the command of Christ, which rules and reigns in his people, and is one in the male and in the female; such are not just men fearing God and judging faithfully with a perfect heart."[12] Although her allusion to Galatians does not directly address her prophetic role, it suggests that because women participate equally with men in "the command of Christ, which rules and reigns in his people," they are equally obliged "to obey God" over man. Hence, her rancorous speech to the priest and his followers and her resulting prison term are not beyond her scope as a woman but represent the defiance of carnal law that all of God's chosen are called to practice. She is one of Christ's "servants," one of his "Ministers," and she can make this claim because Christ "is one in the male and in the female."

While Audland invokes scriptural passages that subtly underwrite her authority to challenge the beliefs of the Banbury congregation, Priscilla Cotton and Mary Cole address the question of women's public preaching directly. Writing from *"Exeter goal"* in 1655, they situate their defense of women's public preaching in the closing pages of a text, *To the Priests and People of England,* largely dedicated to persuading their fellow countrymen and women to desist from persecuting Quakers. Cotton and Cole compare their contemporaries to the members of Cain's generation who embrace a legacy of religious persecution: "Now People, this was the same generation of *Cain* in them after Christ's death, that persecuted the Apostles and put them to death . . . for *Cain*'s generation is now still envying, hating and persecuting the righteous *Abel.*" While their text complements this rather severe diagnosis of their peers' condition with exhortations to pursue the remedy of hearkening "to the light of Jesus Christ" within, their defense of women's prophetic powers emerges as a direct response to the machinations of "envious" priests. They claim that the people blindly obey their religious leaders and so when the priests falsely, they insist, teach that women may not preach in the church, the people will support them:

> if thou bid them fight and war, they obey it; if thou bid them persecute and imprison, they do it; so that they venture their Bodies and Souls to fulfil thy lusts of envy and pride, and in thy pride thou contemnest all others, thou tellest the people, Women must not speak in Church, whereas it is not spoke onely of a Female, for we are all one both male and female in Christ Jesus, but it's weakness that is the woman by the Scriptures forbidden.[13]

For Cotton and Cole, the priests' "lusts of envy and pride" cause them not only to condemn "all others" (namely, those who dissent from their views) but also to misread Scripture on the topic of speaking in the church. Cotton and Cole play Paul's writings off each other, using the Galatians passage to counter the Corinthians passage in which he forbids women's preaching: "Let your women keep silence in the churches: for it is not permitted unto them to speak; but they are commanded to be under obedience, as also saith the law. And if they desire to learn anything, let them ask their own husbands at home; for it is improper for a woman to speak in the church." Because Christ neutralizes gender difference, they imply, Paul does not forbid women from preaching in Corinthians but rather he prohibits anyone who speaks out of his or her carnal nature from preaching in the church: "Now the woman or weakness, that is man, which in his best estate or greatest wisdom is altogether vanity, that must be covered with the covering of the Spirit, a garment of righteousness, that its nakedness may not appear, and dishonour thereby come." Because the priests speak and act out of their carnal natures, Cotton and Cole contend that they are the "women" whom Paul forbids to speak in the church: "Indeed, you your selves are the women, that are forbidden to speak in the Church, that are become women; for two of your Priests came to speak with us; and when they could not bear sound reproof and wholesome Doctrine, that did concern them, they railed on us with filthy speeches, as no other they can give to us, that deal plainly and singly with them, and so they ran from us."[14] Confident that they speak "wholesome Doctrine" free from the taint of fleshly pride, Cotton and Cole comprehend the priests' unwillingness to "bear sound reproof" as a sign of vanity and sinfulness.

Like Cotton and Cole, Sarah Blackborow, in *The Just and*

Equall Ballance Discovered (1660), denounces the priests for leading the people astray. Blackborow introduces her discussion of women's prophetic authority while presenting guidelines for discerning true from false ministers. She suggests that one way to distinguish true from false ministers is to observe the behavior of a decidedly "true" group of ministers, the Apostles. They "were never found boasting above their own measure," and they forbid those, either men or women, from prophesying who were "out of the power": "and wherever they found either the Male or the Female out of the power, not learned of their Husband [Christ] their Head, they were forbid to Pray or Prophesie."[15] She proceeds to delineate the Apostles' attitude toward women prophets by turning to Paul's injunction in 1 Corinthians that women with covered heads and men with uncovered heads might prophesy. On one level, Paul's directive about the personal appearance of prospective male and female prophets serves to underscore men's closer resemblance to God: "For a man indeed ought not to cover *his* head, forasmuch as he is the image and glory of God: but the woman is the glory of the man."[16] Blackborow, however, does not consider Paul's rationale for his directives about the appearance of prophets but rather suggests that covered/uncovered functions as a distinction like female/male and thus is a difference that Christ's ministers and apostles, after Galatians, do not recognize as spiritually significant:

> And therefore the man whose head was covered, might not Pray nor Prophesie, for in so doing, he dishonoured his Head, but the woman having her head Covered, might Pray or Prophesie, as so she honours her Head, and that which [un]covereth the Head of the man, covers the head of the woman, and this is no mistery to those that are Ministers in the spirit, whose eye is in their Head; these saw both Male and Female, in the Gospell were true labourers with them; And therefore writ that those women should be helped that laboured with them in the Gospell, and these knew that Christ was one in the Male and in the Female.[17]

In bypassing Paul's own explanation for his insistence on women prophets' covered heads, Blackborow subtly creates another ending, using Paul's words, to the story of women's headwear. As she would have it, those who are "Ministers in the spirit" find nothing mysterious about Paul's directives because their "eye is in their Head [Christ]." Indeed, their advanced powers of perception enable them to see that "both Male and Female, in the Gospell were true labourers" and to know "that Christ was one in the Male and in the Female."

While Blackborow, like Cotton and Cole before her, focuses much of her argument for women's prophetic authority on women's spiritual equality, her final statement on the topic curiously gestures toward the idea that women possess a particular claim to prophesy. Again, she returns to Paul, juxtaposing his guidelines for female subordination in Timothy: "Let the woman learn in silence with all subjection. But I suffer not a woman to teach, nor to usurp authority over the man, but to be in silence" to his obscure statement linking a kind of female power to angels: "Neither was the man created for the woman; but the woman for the man. For this cause ought the woman to have power on *her* head because of the angels." According to Blackborow, these two passages, taken together, suggest that women, through prophetic speech, may *appear* to usurp authority over the man. She concludes, however, that they do not because the angels confer power on their heads: "If this power moves to declare its own mind and will, whether in the Church or out of the Church, this is a true Ministry in the will of God, in his Spirit and Power; Christ Jesus the everlasting Gospell, and here the Woman Usurps not Authority over the man, but hath power on her head because of the Angells; And who shall appoint in what place or in what Vessell this power shall Minister forth it self in, or what Spirit is that which would limit it."[18]

On the one hand, she appears to argue (as did many Quakers) that mortals should not constrain women's prophetic speech because in so doing they attempt to limit the Spirit's power. Her allusion to Paul's "Angells," taken from his meditation on women's need to cover their heads while prophesying, serves, however, to complicate the passage's meaning. Indeed, the significance of Paul's statement that "the woman" has "power on her head because of the angels" is itself cryptic. Regarding this passage, the Geneva Bible's commentator simply notes: "What this meaneth, I doe not yet understand." More recently, William F. Orr and James Arthur Walther have suggested that the angels are the guardians of the notion of order the passage affirms: "A woman who participates in Corinthian worship leadership *ought* to exercise her freedom responsibly. Guardian angels watch over the churches . . . and they are concerned about spiritual and natural order. So the wife ought to lead in public worship in such a way (with such traditional decorum) that she will not bring disgrace or dishonor to her husband." Blackborow appears not to read the passage in such a, from a feminist perspective, conciliatory way. Rather, she seems to use the angels to say that God grants woman power, through them, that makes her the equal of man and so she cannot usurp authority over him when she prophesies. Blackborow's reading radically departs from the general tone of the Pauline text. Paul appears to be tempering his previous statements about women's inferiority by urging his male readers to recognize that women do play a role in spiritual community: "Nevertheless neither is the man without the woman, neither the woman without the man, in the Lord."[19] For her part, Blackborow reads the passage as conferring a special power on women that makes them the equals of men. On the whole, Blackborow focuses on asserting women's spiritual equality with men, and her peroration on the "Angells" proves yet another way for her to make this point. Still, her suggestion that God effaces women's inferiority by giving them power on their heads through the angels tenuously indicates that female authority bespeaks the particular circumstances of being a woman. More than any other of the early Quaker women's writings on women's speaking, Blackborow's *Just and Equall Ballance* approaches Fell's contention that female prophetic authority is linked to exclusively female attributes.

Like the earliest Quaker women's writings on gender, the first Quaker tract devoted to female prophetic authority, Richard Farnworth's *A Woman Forbidden to Speak in the Church* (1655), addresses women's visionary authority in conjunction with general theological truths. Indeed, for Farnworth, as for Cotton and Cole, the preconditions for women's speaking do not differ from those for men: both may only speak in the church when the Spirit inspires them to do so. Farnworth insists that because the Spirit transforms the whole body of the Saints or the Church into a "fit Habitation" for God, speech which does not derive from the Spirit must be forbidden in the church: "the Woman or wisdom of the Flesh is forbidden to speak in the Church." Instead, only the Spirit "may speak in the Temple, either in male or female, nothing must speak in the Church but the Spirit of God." This conflict between spiritual and carnal speech is the central concern of his text. He devotes very little attention to accounts of historical women's speech, and when he does, he is careful to document its spiritual origins: "and the Spirit of the Lord was made manifest through the Female kind, as Women in former Ages, and it was profitable; for *Deborah* she had the manifestation of the Spirit of God ruling in her, by which she, or the Lord in her, did administer Justice to the *Israelites*." Farnworth leaves little question but that Deborah's greatness was firmly linked to the Spirit acting in her. The only other historical women to appear in his text are Phoebe and Priscilla who are commended in Paul's letters and in Acts and whom Farnworth uses to counter Paul's letters that "appear" to forbid women's speaking. As Farnworth puts it: "*Paul* would not have commanded *Phebe* to have been a Minister, or Servant to the Church . . . if he had forbidden the Spirit of Truth for [from?] being declared through Women in the Church."[20]

George Fox's first contribution to the Quaker discourse on female prophetic authority, *Concerning Sons and Daughters*, brought the subject into much stronger historical focus than did Farnworth or any of the early Quaker women writers. Fox did not employ the language of flesh and spirit to distinguish between those who could and could not prophesy rather he separates the authorized from the deluded on the basis of whether they are "under the Law" or in the Spirit. For Fox, "Law" and "Spirit" signify both a period of time and a spiritual state. Following Paul's famous disquisitions on the topic, Fox claims that the appearance of Christ brings the period of the Law (typically represented by the figure of Moses) to a close and ushers in the period of the Spirit. Just because one technically lives in the period of the Spirit, however, does not necessarily mean that one has the Spirit and hence the right to prophesy. Fox grudgingly observes that some who technically lived under the Law had a stronger sense of the Spirit than some of his own contemporaries: "And whereas *Moses* said I would all the Lords people were Prophets, and there were women that were the Lords people as well as men and women Prophetesses in his days and in the time of the Law. Therefore you who are called Christians have a minde unlike *Moses*; and shew that you have not the Spirit of the Lord poured upon you (according to *Joel* 2.) to prophecy [sic] withall who appear to be such as vex & grieve it."[21]

While Fox's contemporaries may not recognize that they live in the age of the Spirit, Paul certainly did and, according to Fox, he articulates this knowledge in his writings on women's public speaking. When Paul forbids women from speaking in the church, he actually forbids women who are under the Law from prophesying. According to Fox, Paul's concern that a woman might usurp authority over her husband is directed toward women under the Law: "there she is to learn in silence and not to usurpe Authority over the man, but to ask her Husband at home: that which usurp authority the Law takes hold on, but if

you be lead of the Spirit then you are not under the Law." Moreover for Fox, to be "lead of the Spirit" is to be engaged not merely
in obeying the Word but in producing the Word and therefore to
be removed from the possiblity of usurping authority: "for the
speaking as moved of the Lord in the obedience to the power &
spirit which does not bring to usurpe over the man . . . which he
[Christ] in the male and in the female may speak, which is one,
which ends the Law, and throwes down that which usurped Authority." To speak according to the spirit is to become one with
the "Authority" or Christ and therefore to negate the possibility
of usurping Authority. Indeed, as Fox cannily suggests, true believers might deem themselves authorized to counter some of
Paul's dictates on women with some of their own divinely inspired meditations on the topic: "And it is a shame for a woman
to speak in the Church 1 Cor. 14. 34. that which the Law forbids,
and commands silence it is a shame to suffer them to speak in
the Church. What? Came the word of God out from you or came
it unto you only?"[22] The Word of God, as Quakers repeatedly attested, is not limited to the pages of the Bible but continues to
speak to individual believers. So, when Paul "commands silence"
in women, his may not be the last word on the topic. To live in
the age of the Spirit is ultimately to inhabit a radical era that,
despite its temporal definition, defies time and all other worldly
constraints including gender and even, if only tentatively, biblical
authority.

The radically liberating possibilities of the Spirit notwithstanding, Fox remains essentially committed to a biblically based, historical vision. After all, he takes the title of his text from Joel's
famous correlation between women's speaking and apocalypse,
and he rebukes the ignorance of those who fail to recognize contemporary women's prophesying as fulfilling Joel's prophecy:
"you that are ignorant of the Lord's work, and the voice of his
Prophets who are wondring at the Prophecying [sic] of the
Daughters who make your selves ignorant of the Scriptures, and
are wondring at the Lords Prophetesses, or his Daughters contrary to *Joel* the Lords Prophet."[23]

In addition to using history to identify his as an age of prophecy, he also appeals to historical figures who were exemplary
men to attempt to challenge his male readers to change their attitudes toward female prophetic authority. Throughout his text,
he repeatedly pairs portraits of women under the Law who
prophesied with those of the men who endorsed them. Fox opens
with the accounts of four Old Testament women—Miriam, Hul-

dah, the mother of Ma-her-shal-al-hash-baz, and Deborah—who prophesied and who were regarded as authoritative.[24] The case of Miriam, with which Fox begins the tract, illustrates how he appeals to historical examples to criticize his male contemporaries: "*Miriam* was a Prophetess the sister of *Aron*, and *Moses* a Magistrate, and *Aron* the Priest did not judge this Prophetess nor other Women for they came forth praysing God together . . . now are not Christian Priests, Rulers and Magistrates worse then *Moses* and *Aron* which would stop a prophetess from prophesying? Yea worse than those that were under the Law." For Fox, Moses, "a Magistrate," demonstrates how his seventeenth-century male contemporaries who occupy positions of authority should respond to women prophets. Moses appears throughout Fox's text as possessing the openness to prophecy that Fox thinks his peers should have: "how backward *Moses* was from limmitting the Spirit that he would have the Lords spirit put upon them all, and said would that the Lords people were all Prophets, some of which [the Lord's people] were women. Now hear you Magistrates, Priests and people, which do put into Prison Sons and Daughters for prophecying [sic]; and the Lords people: you shew a contrary spirit, you shew a spirit that hath erred from *Moses* spirit."[25]

Despite his support for female visionaries, Fox's approach to the issue remains focused on male authority figures. While Fox provides numerous examples of historical women who prophesied, he generally describes them in terms of the way significant men responded to them. In essence, Fox attempts to justify the Quaker practice of permitting women to preach by enumerating the great men throughout history who have endorsed women prophets. Fox does not delve into biblical history to find exemplary women but exemplary men. Although Fox's approach is not woman-centered—he rarely celebrates the women prophets themselves—it does attempt to make the recognition of biblical messages of spiritual equality a prerequisite for male political and spiritual greatness.

While Fox paints a clear portrait of enlightened masculinity, his vision of female identity remains fuzzy. What is Fox's attitude toward women? He certainly views women as his spiritual equals, but does he view them as his political and social equals? Because of the theological nature of his writings, we may never be able to glean precise answers to these questions. Still, what is evident is that throughout Fox's career, he appears reluctant to urge female subordination in any realm of life. Ironically, in *Con-*

cerning Sons and Daughters, he rather surreptitiously articulates his antipathy toward endorsing female subordination in a passage in which he quotes at length from Paul's writings on the inferior position of women in marriage:

> Husbands love your wives and be not bitter against them: Wives submit your selves first to your Husbands as unto the Lord; the Husband is the head of the Wife even as Christ is the head of the Church, *Ephe.* 5. & is the saviour of the body, therefore as the Church is subject to Christ so let the Wives be subject to their own Husbands in every thing, *Ephe.* 5. Husbands love your Wives even as Christ loved the Church and gave himself for it, that he might sanctifie and clense it by the washing of water by the word: that he might present it a glorious Church without spot or wrinckle, or any such thing that it should be holy and without blemish, so ought men to love their wives as their own bodys, he that loveth his wife loveth himself; for no man ever hateth his own flesh, but nourished it, and cherished it, even as the Lord the Church.

As Catherine Wilcox has observed, it is not clear here whether Fox quotes from Scripture "in order to expound it, or in order to show that he is in simple agreement with its surface meaning."[26] Immediately following his catalogue of Paul's statements on matrimony, however, he attaches, what might from a feminist perspective be seen as a disclaimer. In it, he appears to imply that all of Paul's writings on properly ordered relationships between husbands and wives exist to illustrate the relationship between Christ and his Church: "This is a great mistery, I speak concerning Christ and the Church; he that hath an ear, let him hear this great mistery; now the unlearned men wrest it, and the unstablished who know not this great mistery; you that are ignorant of the Lords work, and the voice of his Prophets who are wondring at the Prophecying [sic] of the Daughters who make your selves ignorant of the Scriptures, and are wondring at the Lords Prophetesses, or his Daughters contrary to *Joel* the Lords Prophet."[27]

Wilcox proposes two possible interpretations of the passage: "that the application of this passage on husbands and wives to the issues of women's speaking is a 'wresting of Scripture'; or, on the other hand, that those who interpret the 'great mistery' which refers solely to Christ and his church as referring to human husbands and wives are guilty of wresting his [Paul's] meaning." Fox's text supports both readings as well as a generally ambivalent attitude toward Paul's misogynous writings themselves. Fox had opened the paragraph by indicating that Paul's writings on the "shamefulness" of women's speaking in the church might not represent *the* complete version of revealed truth: "What? Came the word of God out from you or came it unto you only?" Moreover, as Wilcox notes, Fox quotes Peter on the difficulty some of Paul's epistles pose: "*Paul* according to the measure given to him in all his Epistles . . . speaking in them of things which some are hard to be understood, which they that are unlearned and unstable wrest, as they do also the other Scriptures, to their own destruction."[28] Fox quotes Peter again at the close of his catalogue of Pauline passages on matrimony and/or the relationship between Christ and his church: "This is a great mistery, I speak concerning Christ and the Church; he that hath an ear, let him hear this great mistery; now the unlearned men wrest it, and the unstablished who know not this great mistery." Paul, Fox suggests, writes on the relationship between Christ and his church in terms of matrimony and this is a mystery that some "wrest" for private purposes. These "wresters" of Scripture are the same individuals who "are ignorant of the Lords work, and the voice of the Prophets who are wondring at the Prophecying [sic] of the Daughters." In other words, the "wresters" of Scripture are those eager to suppress women. Although Fox never says so directly, he appears to read Scripture as a text that does not endorse the subjugation of women. Moreover, he seems to believe that Paul's apparently misogynous writings need to be seen properly so that they are not "wrested" to support such private ends as the oppression of women.

Fox further reveals his disdain for misogynous attitudes, and again in an understated and indirect manner, in his treatment of the prophet, Anna (whom he refers to as "Hannah"). He mentions her four times in the course of his treatise. He observes that Simon and Zachary "did not finde fault with *Hannah* for preaching Christ, to all them that looked for Redemption in *Jerusalem*" and that Anna can serve as a model for female prophets in his own generation. More importantly, however, for understanding Fox's views on the political status of women is the fact that he twice remarks on the respect the Jews pay Anna despite her advanced age: "And you do not read that the Jews were offended at old *Hannah* the Prophetess, who prophecyed [sic] in the Temple, which if an old woman should come and prophecy [sic] in your Synagogs or Temples, you would cry to the Stocks with her; or to Prison with her, and haile and persecute her, though you be called Christians and so do shew your selves worse then the Jews." And again, the account of Anna prompts Fox to dwell on the mistreatment of older women in his own society: "Here was a large Testimony born of Jesus by *Hannah* the Prophetess . . . here you may see a daughter which did give Testimony of Jesus, which would be as a wonder in this our age to see a woman of four score years of age to speak of Jesus, to all them that looked for redemption in *Jerusalem*, as she did: put her into Prison would wicked ones say; into Prison with her would the Priests say."[29]

In emphasizing Anna's age, Fox may indirectly comment on the particular disrespect meted out to his elderly female contemporaries. Within his own immediate social context, Fox's interest in Anna's age might speak to his sorrow and rage at the way elderly Quaker women prophets, such as Elizabeth Williams and Elizabeth Hooton, were treated by the ruling authorities. In 1653, the fifty year old Williams and a younger woman, Mary Fisher, were arrested for preaching in Cambridge. As punishment, they were both stripped naked to the waist and whipped "far more cruelly than is usually done to the worst of Malefactors, so that their Flesh was miserably cut and torn." An early convert to Quakerism and the first Friend to be imprisoned for the cause, Hooton endured years of harsh treatment from the authorities. Frequently described as "old Elizabeth Hooton," she was a woman of nearly fifty years when she joined the movement in 1647, and she was probably close to sixty years old when, in the late 1650s, "she embarked on a missionary voyage to America in the company of another old woman, Joan Brooksop. There she offended magistrates in Massachusetts and Rhode Island by returning to preach again and again, after being stripped, whipped from town to town while tied to the back of a cart, and abandoned in the forests."[30] Doubtless, Fox himself was aware of further instances of egregious physical abuses suffered by elderly Quaker female prophets.

More broadly, as the historian Keith Thomas has illustrated, elderly, poor women frequently bore the brunt of witchcraft accusations. According to Thomas, the increased number of witch trials and hence legal attacks on old women in early modern England represent a complex crisis in which traditional forms of charity and social obligation to the poor were beginning to collapse just as developments such as enclosure were worsening the position of the destitute. Those convicted of witchcraft were often old women to whom traditional forms of neighborliness and poor relief had been denied and who were then seen as having

just cause to curse or pronounce evil upon their would-be bene-
factors. The sixty-year-old widow, Margaret Harkett, was executed as a witch in 1585 after a number of her neighbors had, with
ill consequences, refused her basic forms of charity: "She had
picked a basketful of peas in a neighbour's field without permis-
sion. Asked to return them, she flung them down in anger; since
when, no peas would grow in the field . . . A neighbour refused
her a horse; all his horses died. Another paid her less for a pair
of shoes than she asked; later he died. A gentleman told his servants to refuse her buttermilk; after which they were unable to
make butter or cheese." Like the downtrodden Harkett, Hooton
herself was in her sixties when, in 1662, she too was accused of
witchcraft.[31] Fox's comments about Anna and her age reveal him
to be fully aware of and in disharmony with a specific kind of misogyny present in his own day. Again, he never directly urges his
fellow Englishmen to desist from sexist and ageist practices, but
he implicitly advances an egalitarian ideal with respect to the
treatment of older women.

Fox's *Concerning Sons and Daughters* strongly influenced
Fell's *Womens Speaking Justified*, but unlike Fox, Fell advances
a model of women's prophetic authority predicated not on egalitarian principles but on female sexuality. She celebrates not the
men who endorsed women's speaking but the women preachers
themselves. Her text shares Fox's historical vision of a time before and after the law, but rather than making these distinct ep-
ochs a premise of her argument, she narrates the movement
from one period to the next. While Fell, like Fox, provides examples of women such as Hagar and the New Jerusalem who are
decidedly affiliated with the Law and the Spirit respectively, she
emphasizes the role women play in the transition between the
period of the law and the period of the spirit. The linchpin in this
historical transition is Christ, and Fell is particularly interested
in tracing women's roles in the Christ-centered narrative of redemption.

In the first and lengthiest section of *Womens Speaking Justified*, she begins to illustrate how women contribute to salvation
history with, ironically enough, Genesis and the story of Eve's
fall. Fell naturally considers Eve's transgression an unfortunate
event but directs her reader's attention to God's promise that ultimately a child of Eve would crush Satan: "Let this Word of the
Lord, which was from the beginning, stop the mouths of all that
oppose Womens Speaking in the Power of the Lord; for he hath
put enmity between the Woman and the Serpent; and if the Seed

of the Woman speak not, the Seed of the Serpent speaks; for God hath put enmity between the two Seeds, and it is manifest that those that speak against the Woman and her Seeds Speaking, speak out of the enmity of the old Serpents Seed"(4). To counter those who would hold Eve and all of her sex eternally guilty of humanity's first act of disobedience, Fell offers an interpretation of God's curse on the serpent that strongly identifies the vehicle of redemption—the woman—with the redeemer (the Woman's Seed) himself. For Fell, the woman is no mere vessel through which historical change, in the person of Christ, enters the world but rather woman is intimately linked with the production of history. Without the woman, there would be no Christ and should she be forbidden from speaking, "the enmity of the old Serpents Seed" would rule. According to Fell, the woman must speak in order to give birth to Christ because otherwise Christ simply could not exist: woman's inspired speech and maternal power are one and the same.

She makes this point clearer in subsequent paragraphs in which she elaborates her statements about the strong tie between the woman and her seed by appealing to numerous scriptural passages that liken the Church to a woman: "Moreover, the Lord is pleased when he mentions his Church, to call her by the name of *Woman*"(4). Rather than regarding passages such as Revelation's description of the "woman clothed with the Sun" as metaphorical representations of the relationship between Christ and his Bride, the Church, she sees them as literally identifying the Church as a woman: "Thus much may prove that the Church of Christ is a woman" (5). Because the Church is a woman, speaking against a woman's speaking is tantamount to speaking against the Church and Christ himself: "those that speak against the womans speaking, speak against the Church of Christ, and the Seed of the Woman, which Seed is Christ" (5). Her entire discussion of woman as the mother of Christ and as the Church points toward a particular and historical role unique to woman. Coming toward the beginning of her tract as they do, her suggestive discussions of the woman's seed and the female church underscore her thoroughgoing commitment to marking out a particular historical and political territory for women's speaking.

In addition to insisting that because women have intimate relationships with Christ, as his mother and his wife, they have a right to prophesy, Fell appeals to unique moments of Christ's self-representation to assert female visionary authority. For instance, she observes that when he revealed himself as the messiah to the Samaritan woman at the well, he revealed more of himself than he had previously: "This is more than ever he said in plain words to Man or Woman (that we read of) before he suffered" (5). Fell presents the interaction between Christ and the Samaritan woman as a dialogue in which the Woman's statements about the messiah lead Christ to reveal himself: "and when the Woman said unto him, *I know that when the Messiah cometh . . . when he cometh, he will tell us all things*; Jesus saith unto her, *I that speak unto thee am he*" (5). Fell's portrait of the meeting of Christ and the Samaritan woman tacitly suggests that Christ's decision to reveal himself to her is not wholly arbitrary. She is no mere vehicle for Christ's self-revelation but an individual who merits this honor because of her faith.

Fell's sense that women not only play significant roles in salvation history but also cultivate and merit such prominent positions is most fully elaborated in her discussion of the women who announce Christ's resurrection. Fell views the message of Christ's resurrection delivered by Mary Magdalene, Joanna, and Mary the mother of James as central to the redemption of humankind and exaggerates its significance: "Mark this, you that despise and oppose the Message of the Lord God that he sends by women, what had become of the Redemption of the whole Body of Mankind, if they had not believed the Message that the Lord Jesus sent by these women, of and concerning his Resurrection?" (7).[32] Of course, two of the gospel writers—Mark and Luke—explicitly remark that the women's announcement was not believed.[33] Indeed Fell herself quotes Luke on the topic: "*And their words seemed unto them as idle tales, and they believed them not*" (7). As for Matthew and John, they indicate that the women either planned to or did announce the news of Christ's resurrection, but neither records the disciples' response to the women's message.[34] Thus while no evidence exists that the women's words were believed, and some exists to the contrary, "the Redemption of the whole Body of Mankind" appears not to have been seriously imperiled by anyone's failure to believe the women. (Indeed, according to all four gospel writers, Christ appears before all of his apostles shortly after his resurrection.)[35] As overstated and extravagant as Fell's claims for women's role in salvation history may be, they are important in and of themselves because they reveal her ambition not merely to justify women's speaking but to assert its historical centrality.

Perhaps even more striking than Fell's inflated assessment of women's role in spreading the news of the resurrection is her suggestion that women earned the privilege of disseminating this information:

> And if these women had not thus, out of their tenderness and bowels of love, who had received Mercy, and Grace, and forgiveness of sins, and Virtue, and Healing from him, which many men also had received the like, if their hearts had not been so united and knit unto him in love that they could not depart as the men did, but sat watching, and waiting, and weeping about the Sepulchre untill the time of his: Resurrection, and so were ready to carry his Message, as is manifested, else how should his Disciples have known, who were not there? (7)

Once again Fell exaggerates the significance of the women's message: although the disciples "were not there," they ultimately learned the news of the resurrection from Christ himself. What makes this passage significant, however, is Fell's observation that the women were prepared to carry Christ's message: "they could not depart . . . but sat watching, and waiting, and weeping about the Sepulchre . . . and so were ready to carry his Message." Unable to depart "as the men did," the women committed themselves to the tedious labor of "watching, and waiting, and weeping" in order to be "ready" to convey Christ's word. These women are not arbitrary vessels of the word but individuals who through their committed devotion to Christ have revealed themselves to be his loyal servants. Moreover, they were possessed of some of the same gifts that men had also received from Christ—"Mercy, and Grace, and forgiveness of sins, and Virtue, and Healing"—and yet the women's hearts were "so united and knit to him in love, that they could not depart as the men did." In other words, the women actively identify with Christ in such a strong way that they cannot separate themselves from him. Their devotion seems to be comprised of an absolute love for Christ that finds them fixated on his sepulcher and unable to leave. Fell's rendering of the nearly literal inseparability of the women from Christ makes their self-sacrifice and devotion appear to be almost as momentous as that of Christ. Indeed, her account of their not only weeping but also watching and waiting at his tomb suggests that they share Christ's knowledge of his imminent return and in their anticipation of the "the time," they once again show their hearts to be "so united and knit to him in love."

Fell continues to trace the ways in which Christ has manifested himself to women by following the order of the Bible through Acts, Paul's controversial epistles on women's speaking, and Revelation. From beginning to end, her text maintains, the Bible documents divine sanction for women's prophetic authority. While she musters numerous examples from Scripture to prove her case, she emphasizes the biblical events and figures that constitute her narrative of women's central role in salvation history. Her "closing arguments" summarize this narrative as they encapsulate a feminized vision of biblical history that centers on women's connection to Christ's corporal nature:

> and since that the Lord God in the Creation, when he made man in his own Image, he made them *male* and *female*; and since that Christ Jesus, as the Apostle saith, was made of a Woman, and the power of the Highest overshadowed her, and the holy Ghost came upon her, and the holy thing that was born of her, was called *the Son of God*, and when he was upon the Earth, he manifested his *love*, and his *will*, and his *mind*, both to the Woman of *Samaria*, and *Martha*, and *Mary* her Sister, and several others, as hath been shewed; and after his Resurrection also manifested himself unto them first of all, even before he ascended unto his Father. (12)

While God may not distinguish between the male and the female, Christ clearly does and this may be due to his own inseparability from the woman: "and the holy thing that was born of her, was called the Son of God, and when he was upon the Earth, he manifested his love, and his will, and his mind, both to the Woman of Samaria, and Martha, and Mary her Sister, and several others, as hath been shewed." Remarkably, Christ first appears as "the holy thing" born of woman before he is identified as Christ. His period of being a "thing" prior to being named suggests that he had been a rough composite of holiness and earthiness. Thus, his temporary identity as a "holy thing" may serve to illustrate his connection to his mother. And because Fell does not identify Mary as *the* mother of Christ but rather refers to Christ's mother as "a Woman," she implicitly extends the corporal bond between Mary and Christ to all women. Moreover, although Fell ultimately identifies the "holy thing," his fleshly connection to the woman tacitly accounts for his special relationship with women: Christ begins life as a "holy thing" born of woman and never quite forgets that originary relationship as he manifests "his love, and his will, and his mind" to women. In closing the first part of *Womens Speaking Justified* by asserting the physical bond linking women to Christ, Fell materializes the unique sense of union that women have with Christ. Unlike his male disciples, the women simply could not, were physically unable to, leave him as he suffered on the cross and was buried in the tomb.

Fell's emphasis on the connection between Christ and women suggests the broader philosophical shift in the understanding of both divinity and humanity that Christ inaugurates. In many ways, her portrait of the unique bond between Christ and women represents a feminized version of Elaine Scarry's account of the change in the relationship between God and humankind that Christ's incarnation establishes: "The body in the Old Testament belongs only to man, and the voice, in its extreme and unqualified form belongs only to God. Across the cross, each of these retains its original place but simultaneously enters the realm from which it had earlier been excluded . . . God's acquisition of a body . . . is accompanied by its counterpart . . . man's acquisition of a voice."[36] While Fell would certainly agree that all of humankind gains the possibility of a "voice" or inspired speech by virtue of Christ's death and resurrection, she insists that women experience the union of body and voice on a far more intimate level. Indeed as Fell would have it, the mutuality of the relationship between women and Christ is most fully revealed in women's speaking: Christ has derived part of his substance from woman and confers part of his unique nature on her in the form of inspired speech.

Although the first part of *Womens Speaking Justified* consists of ambitious, bordering on extravagant, claims for female authority, it speaks less to the political situation of women than both of the text's additions do. In *"A further Addition in Answer to the Objection concerning Women keeping silent in the Church"* and the 1667 Postscript, Fell is much more committed to creating a new, more politically engaged image of women and their capacities than she had been previously. This is not to say, however, that the main body of her text lacks material relevant to women's political status. She had opened the first part of *Womens Speaking Justified* by observing that opposers of women's speaking had levied accusations of female meddlesomeness: "Whereas it hath been an Objection in the minds of many . . . against Womens speaking in the Church; and so consequently may be taken, that they are condemned for medling in the things of God" (3). The main body of her text attempts to dispel charges of female meddlesomeness not only by emphasizing the unique connection between Christ and women but also by identifying moments in Scripture when women's faithfulness surpasses that of men. She, for instance, commemorates the woman with the "Alabaster Box of very Precious Oyntment" who pours it on the head of Christ much to the chagrin of his disciples who argue that the money spent on the ointment would have been better spent on the poor.

For his part, Christ chastises the disciples and praises the woman for her foreknowledge of his imminent death: "Why trouble ye the woman? for she hath wrought a good work upon me. For ye have the poor always with you; but me ye have not always. For in that she hath poured this ointment on my body, she did *it* for my burial."[37] Fell reads the episode as manifesting "that [the] Woman knew more of the secret Power and Wisdom of God, then his Disciples did, that were filled with indignation against her" (5). Although the act of this apparently frivolous woman fills the disciples with "indignation," her use of the ointment reveals her to be particularly wise. Christ himself recasts an act of apparent female meddlesomeness as a testimony to penetrating wisdom.

Fell's interest in women's achievements, already apparent in the main body of *Womens Speaking Justified*, becomes the focal point of her first addition, *"A further Addition in Answer to the Objection concerning Women keeping silent in the Church."* She claims to direct her "Addition" to refuting interpretations of the Pauline epistles on women's speaking that identify these texts as enjoining women to learn in silence and not to speak in the church. She briefly addresses the epistles, rehearsing some of the same arguments Fox had used in *Concerning Sons and Daughters*: Paul's injunction that women learn from their husbands does not take into account women without husbands; Paul's prohibition against women's speaking applies only to those under the Law; and Paul's writings in Galatians assert the oneness of Christ in the male and in the female (13).[38] Fell also appears to follow Fox's lead as she identifies three women—Huldah, Miriam, and Hannah—who were under the Law but who were not forbidden to speak. In contradistinction to Fox, however, Fell is interested not only in the fact that they spoke or that they were taken seriously as prophets but also in how well and how effectively they spoke. Indeed, her "Addition" almost reads like an anthology of women's words in which Fell provides brief commentaries on scriptural passages—representing the words of women such as Huldah, Elizabeth, and Mary—that she reproduces in her text.[39] After quoting at length Huldah's prophecy concerning the destruction of Jerusalem,[40] Fell remarks: "Now let us see if any of you blind Priests can speak after this manner, and see if it be not a better Sermon than any of you can make, who are against Womens speaking?" (14). What makes Huldah's sermon "better" than anything the "blind Priests" might have to offer is not entirely clear. At times, Fell appears to celebrate women's words for aesthetic reasons: "And see what glorious expressions Queen *Hester* [Esther] used to comfort the People of God" (15). Esther's words function to comfort the people yet they are "glorious expressions." More frequently than she emphasizes beauty, however, Fell addresses the effectiveness of women's words. When the two newly pregnant women, Elizabeth and Mary, greet each other, Fell insists that they preach well because they prophesy accurately: "Now here you may see how these two women prophesied of Christ, and Preached better than all the blind Priests did in that Age, and better then this Age also" (14). One of Fell's reasons for insisting on the effectiveness of women's words becomes clear in her appraisal of the woman whose speech resulted in the rescue of the City of Abel: "And this deliverance was by the means of a Womans speaking; but tatlers, and busie bodies, are forbidden to preach by the True Woman, whom Christ is the Husband, to the Woman as well as the Man, all being comprehended to be the Church" (16–17). The reference to "tatlers" and "busie bodies" comes from Paul's first letter to Timothy, and these are the women, Fell reports, whom Paul enjoins to silence.[41]

By incorporating biblical women's words into her "Addition" and then by admiring both the quality and effectiveness of these words, Fell appears to be attempting to revise conventional notions of women as "meddlesome," as "tatlers," and as "busie bodies." Certainly, she makes this point clear in terms of religious matters: Huldah, Elizabeth, and Mary make important prophecies which prove consequential long after they are uttered. Moreover, Fell appears interested in asserting that women's words matter in secular contexts as well. Many of Fell's own writings and those of her fellow sectarians denounce priests who receive money for preaching God's word. Quakers frequently deemed these individuals "hireling Priests" who secularized their faith by "making a Money-Trade of Religion." According to Fell's contemporary, Jeane Bettris, God condemns the "priests" because they "teach for hire" although they "lean upon the Lord and say, is not the Lord amongst us."[42] In *Womens Speaking Justified*, Fell suggests that the very priests who denounce women's speaking, turn around and use women's words as part of their trade: "yet you will make a Trade of Womens words to get money by, and take Texts, and Preach Sermons upon Womens words" (16). Clearly, the priests recognize that some women's words are far from frivolous but have a bankable market value. Fell's attention, in her "Addition," to ideas of secular value serves to underscore her point that women have preached some of the "better"

sermons ever uttered and that their words are effective and surpass the expectations of those who deem women to be trouble-
some meddlers.

As Fell continues her attack on the priests who forbid women's
speaking, she continues to move further into the field of practical
politics. While the first part of her tract had been concerned with
locating women within salvation history and the second section
with asserting female achievements in the field of preaching and
prophesying, the final section seeks to affirm that women may
indeed be called upon if not to usurp, to exercise authority over
their husbands or over military leaders. Her short Postscript
represents the most cogently political and savvy moment in her
entire text perhaps in part because it appears as an afterthought.
She, of course, added the Postscript to the second edition of
Womens Speaking Justified, suggesting that the only thing ca-
sual about it is its presentation. Further she structures the Postscript with very little commentary to make it appear as though
the Bible speaks for itself and in so doing speaks in support of
female authority. Without any thematizing note, the Postscript,
although clearly referring to Paul's letter to Timothy, simply exhorts the "dark Priests" to observe three biblical accounts in
which the authority of a woman takes precedence over that of a
male superior (18). Fell remarks that, in the case of Abraham and
Sarah, *"the Husband must learn of the Woman . . . and so* Abraham *did obey the voice of* Sarah" (18). Barack, the commander
of the Israelite militia, wisely *"did not bid* [Deborah] *be silent,
for she Sung and Praised God, and declared to the Church of*
Israel" (18). And Manoah learns from his wife not to fear the vision of the *"Angel of the Lord"* which appears to her (18). (Perhaps because the account in Judges does not name the wife, Fell
does not name Manoah but identifies him as the "Husband" of
the "Woman" to whom "the Angel appeared" (18). In fact, Fell
never refers to her as a wife at any point in her rendering of the
narrative.) With its three examples of women teaching men and
its spare commentary, the Postscript enables Fell to strengthen
the overall political tone of the tract. She began by proposing to
justify women's prophetic authority—"But first let me lay down
how God himself hath manifested his Will and Mind concerning
women, and unto women"—and closes by emphasizing the political significance of such inspiration.

In *Womens Speaking Justified*, Fell not only argues for wom-
en's right to participate in the political realm but also presents a
positive vision of female difference. "Difference" itself is a key

term in Fell's text signifying, on the one hand, the hierarchical distinctions men make between male and female and, on the other hand, the attributes of femininity God uses to convey his will. For Fell, women are indeed different from men but different, in God's eyes at least, in ways that make them unique rather than inferior. These two senses of difference come to the fore in Fell's text in her discussion of "weakness." Her initial foray into the topic focuses on the conventional hierarchical distinctions between weak and strong and implies, but does not directly state, that weakness is a female attribute. After quoting the Priestly version of the Genesis creation narrative, in which *"God created Man in his owne Image: in the Image of God created he them, Male and Female,"* she observes that God does not make distinctions between the sexes: "Here God joyns them together in his own Image, and makes no such distinctions and differences as men do; for though they be weak, he is strong" (3).[43] Oddly, Fell moves from asserting spiritual equality into a discussion of weakness that may pertain to men and women but more likely concerns only women. The remainder of the passage quotes Paul on God's capacity to make the weak powerful: *"His Grace is sufficient,* and his *strength is made manifest in weakness,* 2 Cor. 12.9. And such hath the Lord chosen, even *the weak things of the world, to confound the things which are mighty* . . . And God hath put no such difference between the Male and Female as men would make" (3). From the point of view of effectively using the egalitarian principles established in the first Genesis creation narrative, Fell's rhetorical strategy seems inexplicable: she opens with a strong scriptural proof text for spiritual equality, introduces a "distinction" and "difference" that men make, and concludes by suggesting that God attends to the weak and so puts no "difference" between men and women. Already in the second paragraph of her text, Fell appears to be more interested in justifying women's speaking on the grounds of sexual difference rather than on the basis of spiritual equality. The features that make women weak or inferior in men's eyes make them strong in divine terms.

She develops this sense of divinely sanctioned weakness further when she observes that indeed Eve was a weak woman who was "more inclinable to hearken to" the serpent (3). Still, God does not utterly reject her because of her weakness but promises that her seed will ultimately overpower that of the serpent. Fell does not, as did Cotton and Cole and Farnworth, attempt to separate women from their identification with weakness by making weakness a feature of wretched carnality, rather she asserts women are indeed weak but that feminine weakness is not necessarily a negative attribute: "And as God the Father made no such difference in the first Creation, nor never since between the Male and the Female, but alwayes out of his Mercy and loving kindness, had regard unto the weak" (5).[44] Men may indeed be stronger than women but that is of little consequence to God because "the weakness of God is stronger than men, and the foolishness of God is wiser then men" (8). Moreover those men who denounce "the weakness of Women" prove themselves to be fools. For Fell, the case of the Apostles who dismiss the women's message of the resurrection as "idle tales" proves the point. The Apostles fail to believe the women because they see them only as women and the bearers of "idle tales" instead of recognizing Christ's capacity to use their femininity: "Mark this, ye despisers of the weakness of Women, and look upon your selves to be so wise: but Christ Jesus doth not so, for he makes use of the weak" (7). Fell does not criticize the Apostles for identifying women with excessive, meandering speech but rather for failing to realize that female prolixity could be made to serve divine ends.

According to Fell, weakness is not the only feminine attribute that Christ honors. For instance, in elaborating her claims "that the Church of Christ is a woman," Fell reads David and Solomon as proclaiming Christ's interest in female beauty:

> And *David*, when he was speaking of Christ and his Church, he saith, *The Kings Daughter is all glorious within, her cloathing is of wrought Gold; she shall be brought unto the King: with gladness and rejoycing shall they be brought; they shall enter into the Kings Pallace.* Ps. 45. And also King *Solomon* in his Song, where he speaks of Christ and his Church, where she is complaining and calling for Christ, he saith, *If thou knowest not, O thou fairest among women, go thy way by the footsteps of the Flock*, Cant. 1. 8. c. 5. 9. (4)

Another female image of the church, the Lamb's wife, also appears to be a beauteous presence: "and the joy of the morning is come, and the Bride, the Lambs *Wife*, is making her self ready, as a Bride that is adorning for her Housband, and to her granted that she shall be arrayed in fine linnen, clean and white, and the fine linnen is the Righteousness of the Saints" (11).[45] In all three of these accounts of the Church/ Woman's erotic attractiveness, female beauty becomes a way of expressing the joy that attends the union of Christ with his Church. Fell seems to be saying that women contribute beauty to the union of Christ with his Church and that female beauty is an integral part of this union. She articulates this point much more clearly when she discusses the union of the Spirit and the Bride in Revelation's closing chapter.[46] For Fell, the "bride" illustrates the fact that the church is not solely composed of men and that as members of the church women are called upon to contribute to it:

> And here Christ is the Head of the Male and Female, who may speak; and the Church is called *a Royal Priesthood*; so the Woman must offer as well as the Man, *Rev.* 22. 17. *The Spirit saith, Come, and the Bride saith, Come*: and so is not the Bride the Church? and doth the Church only consist of Men? you that deny Womens speaking, answer: Doth it not consist of Women as well as men? Is not the Bride compared to the whole Church? And doth not the Bride say, *Come*? Doth not the Woman speak then? the Husband Christ Jesus, the *Amen* . . . for the Bridegroom is with the Bride, and he opens her Mouth. (17)

As members of the "Royal Priesthood," women "must offer" and, according to Fell, what the woman offers may well be illustrative of her gendered identity. Her divinely inspired speech, for instance, may well appear to be nothing more than "idle tales." She may speak as an expectant bride and say the word "come" to which her groom, Christ, would reply "Amen." For Fell, woman's inspired speech is not distinct from her gendered identity but rather emerges from her femininity to offer itself and female difference to the broad community of believers.

In justifying women's speech, Fell does not rely on, as did her predecessors, the gender-neutralizing power of the spirit. Rather, she constructs a narrative in which woman falls because of her "inclinable" nature but is redeemed by Christ, in whose essence she intimately participates. As the "holy thing" to whom she gives birth grows into manhood, he and she repeatedly express the special tie that binds them. She finds herself unable to "depart" from him as he suffers and dies on the cross, and he, for his part, rewards her devotion by making her the bearer of the news of his resurrection. Once he has ascended into heaven, he continues to cherish her by making her his bride, his church. As his bride, her beauty comes to represent the union of Christ and his people. Just as Christ was brought into the world through a woman so he is brought into union with his people through the bride. Fell does not disdain female carnality as Cotton and Cole had but rather she embraces it as productive of both the uniquely female bond to Christ and the uniquely female voice the bride-groom Christ expects to hear when he calls for his bride. Although Fell constructs a feminine model of women's speaking, she does not, by any means, assert female subservience to men. Rather she asserts that, women may be called upon, as Sarah was, to exercise authority over their husbands. In essence, Fell's text seeks to celebrate the "distinctions and differences" that link women to Christ while dismantling the hierarchical "distinctions and differences" between the sexes that men make.

WOMEN'S WORK

Although Fell herself and her *Womens Speaking Justified* would play an important role in the development of women's monthly and quarterly meetings, it was George Fox, with the publication of his 1671 circular letter on the topic, who inaugurated the sect-wide system of women's meetings[47] designed to enable women to, in his words, "come into the practice of pure religion, which is to visit the widows and fatherless and to see that all be kept from the spots of the world."[48] The system of men's and women's separate meetings that evolved created a classically gendered, two-tiered system in which men devoted themselves to magisterial and theological concerns while women tended to the material and emotional needs of the poor, infirm, and imprisoned; the discipline of wayward Quakers; the apprenticeships of young Friends; and the supervision of marriages. All of these tasks, as Fox himself would write, drew on women's greater expertise in domestic matters. So while women were given a specific political role or "office" within the sect, they were given one that was consistent with traditional notions of gendered identity.

Indeed, one reason women's meetings were created in the first place was to limit women who previously felt free to follow the leadings of the Spirit and who, in so doing, engaged in disruptive behavior. In the 1660s, after enduring years of cruel persecutions, the Quakers increasingly avoided challenging their contemporaries either with apocalyptic warnings or with prophesying women and sought to pursue an accommodation with English society at large. As numerous Quaker petitions written from prison in the years between 1660 and 1689 (the year of the Toleration Act) attest, the Friends simply wanted to be set free so they could go about their daily business. In "*A few Words to the* Magistrates," a group of imprisoned Friends at Northampton represented their desire to return to their jobs as a commitment to the national good: "we only seek that we might but enjoy the Happiness of living among you in Peace and Quietness, under the King, in the Land of our Nativity, to be an Help according to our Ability for the Prosperity of all that dwell therein." The following year, in 1685, a second group of Northampton prisoners noted how before being persecuted their labors were so productive that they could contribute to the relief of the poor, although now it was they who were in need of financial support: "most of us having been here above two Years, and some three or four Years; which Sufferings greatly tend to the ruining and undoing of many industrious Families that have helped to bear the Charge of the Nation, and they who have been in a capacity to relieve others, may by such Means be reduced to stand in Need of Assistance themselves."[49]

In their eagerness to reconcile with their fellow citizens, the Quakers were willing neither to pay tithes nor to take oaths of allegiance but they were willing to issue a peace testimony affirming their loyalty to the king and to suppress some of the unconventional activities of their women. Phyllis Mack considers the sect's increasing concern with order a necessary phase of development in any religious movement: "the history of late seventeenth-century Quakerism presents the observer with a virtual ideal type of radical religious movement: a loose, egalitarian group under charismatic leadership evolving into a tightly knit, bureaucratized, hierarchical church." In short, the Quakers had to form a more organized body if they were to survive. And for women, this transformation proved to be a mixed blessing that "changed the setting of women's spiritual creativity from the home and the street to the women's meeting, and, in so doing, it introduced a political dimension into the discussion of the proper vocation of female Friends."[50]

Although she did not write any formal treatises on the topic, Margaret Fell is frequently described as one of the prime organizers of the women's meetings. She inaugurated the women's meeting at Swarthmoor in 1671 and "then began a tour through the north of England, most probably to do the same in other communities."[51] While none of her treatises published after 1671 addressed the women's meetings, her *Womens Speaking Justified* exerted a powerful influence over the creation of the system of men's and women's separate meetings. As the first Quaker apologist for women's speaking to argue that female prophetic authority was linked to female sexuality, she implicitly condoned the emphasis on "differences and distinctions" that the meeting system formally established. Still, while she had attested to female sexual difference, she did not recognize this "difference" as necessarily delimiting women's role. Her understanding of the political implications of sexual difference was much more open-ended than it would become for the proponents of women's meetings including their leading apologist George Fox himself.

Fox's attitude toward the male-female hierarchy that the women's meetings established can only be called equivocal. His writings produced a two-tiered system of meetings that called upon women to assume an active role in intra-sect politics but one more consistent with conventional gender norms, yet he remained loathe to promote the subordination of any human being's conscience to the will of any other human being.[52] Ultimately, Fox negotiates the impasse between practical necessity and his philosophical commitment to egalitarianism by emphasizing the value of women's work for the sect at large. As he had in *Concerning Sons and Daughters*, he, in his writings on women's meetings, concentrates on the overarching needs of the sect rather than on gender difference.[53] In other words, Fox understands that the sect needs to accomplish a certain amount of work and the only way the sect's work can be completed is through the combined efforts of men and women. What matters for Fox is not who does which work but that the work gets done. Ironically then, while Fox creates a system of meetings in which women gain a political role, he subordinates the distinctions between men's and women's political authority that his system formalizes to a vision of the sect's greater good. In Fox's writings, the value of both men's and women's political roles can only be measured in terms of the sectarian community's goals and not in the conventional language of power, in terms such as "overlord" and "subordinate." As Fox himself would put it: "And some men and women there are that fear, if women should meet in the Order of the Gospel, the Power of God, they would be too high, but such men and women are too high already, and would be a ruling Spirit over men and women's Possessions, and waste their own; for if they were in the Power and Spirit of God, they need not fear any ones getting over them."[54] In Fox's vision of "the Order of the Gospel," the only power that matters is "the Power of God."

The focal point of Fox's writings on women's meetings is that women like men are called to manifest their calling through labor. For Fox, laboring for Christ's church is an essential component of an individual's calling and so every man and woman must represent his or her calling through labor. He justifies the creation of separate men's and women's meetings as a way of demonstrating that Quaker men and women have been "restored" by Christ and so are able to work together, as prelapsarian Adam and Eve had, to be each other's "helps-meet": "For man and woman were helps-meet in the image of God, and in righteousness and holiness, in the dominion, before they fell; but after the fall in the transgression, the man was to rule over his wife; but in the restoration by Christ, into the image of God, and his righteousness and holiness again, in that they are helps-meet, man and woman, as they were before the fall."[55] Fox's vision is remarkably egalitarian in its claim that "the restoration by Christ" ends the period when "the man was to rule over his wife" and opens the period when men strive not to dominate women but to work with women to maintain the gospel teachings. In his view, the fact that Quaker men and women work together as they did before the fall clearly marks them out as God's chosen people.

On an individual basis, the idea of cooperative labor between the sexes means that Friends now saw work as an integral part of their identity and recognized their labor for the sect as both a responsibility and an entitlement. Fox exhorts women to recognize their meetings as their possession: "Keep your women's meetings in the power of God, which the devil is out of; and take your possession of that which you are heirs of, and keep the gospel order."[56] Women, like men, are heirs of Christ and so must "keep the gospel order" and pursue practices that are consistent with scriptural teaching. Eve, for instance, was out of the gospel order when she usurped authority over Adam by drawing him away from God:

> Now for a Woman to preach or teach such a Teaching as *Eve* taught *Adam*, such a Sermon as she had from the Serpent, that drew her self, and *Adam* her Husband from God's Teaching, here, in this Teaching she usurpt Authority over the man, and therefore God set the man to rule over the woman, but they were meet Helps before while they were under God's Teaching.
>
> Now to usurp Authority over the man by such Teaching, is out of the Unity, which Teaching is forbidden both by Law and Gospel. (*Encouragement*, 75)

Eve was not at fault, however, for teaching Adam but for what she taught Adam. Indeed, teaching may be precisely the work a woman may be required to do as part of her "inheritance": "And there were elder women in the truth, as well as elder men in the truth; and these women are to be teachers of good things; so they have an office as well as the men, for they have a stewardship, and must give an account of their stewardship to the Lord, as well as the men."[57] Women's meetings, Fox implies, allow women to "have an office" so that they can "give an account of their stewardship to the Lord."

For Fox, one of the chief values of women's work in the sect is that it enables them to serve Christ and thereby to prove themselves worthy of redemption. Indeed, the work women do is important enough to require the material support of men. At one point, Fox urges men to share their wealth with their spouses so that women can both tend to the poor and share in the disbursement of the earth's goods: "And there is no Believing Husband will hinder his Believing Wife, being heirs of Life, to administer some of their temporal things to them that are in Necessity; he will not have all the Earth to himself, but let her have the disposing of some of it, as well as himself, whilest they do enjoy it" (*Encouragement*, 79). Perhaps, more than any other, this passage suggests that Fox understands the system of men's and women's meetings to be about the sharing of power. Men have traditionally controlled the disposition of "temporal things," but now that women's work has taken a political form, resources need to be devoted to its objectives. By insisting that women and men should both "enjoy" earthly riches and participate in the "disposing of some of it," Fox locates women's meetings on the continuum of political power occupied by male authority and men's meetings. Fox, of course, would not have wanted power to become the object of the meeting system. He did, however, recognize that power could become an effect of his system and so sought to translate it, like labor, into something shared between ideal helpmates.

While Fox's central objective in his tracts on women's meetings is to justify the system of separate meetings as a means of replicating pre-lapsarian working conditions, he also attempts to explain why women meeting together function as men's helpmates. As a result, Fox creates a fuller image of woman than he had in *Concerning Sons and Daughters* and one derived, in part, from Fell's *Womens Speaking Justified*. Indeed, much of the structure and content of the lengthiest of his writings on women's meetings, *This is an Encouragement to all the Womens-Meetings in the World* (1676), bears the marks of Fell's influence.

In the manner of *Womens Speaking Justified*, Fox's *Encouragement* provides a chronological survey of biblical examples of women, working singly or in groups, who served God and his people in important ways. Like Fell, he constructs a history of female accomplishment to assert the legitimacy of women meeting together to perform the sect's work. Nevertheless, his history of female accomplishment remains tied to affirming the central historical concern of *Concerning Sons and Daughters* that the movement from the time of the law to the time of the spirit strengthens the connection between each individual and Christ and so gives each a greater share in carrying out Christ's work. Applied to women's meetings, this produces Fox's insistence that since women's meetings took place under the law they absolutely must occur now: "And so the Assemblies of the Women, whom God hath poured out his Spirit upon, are to be in the time of the Gospel, as well as in the time of the Law, that they may be Helps meet to the men in the time of the Gospel, in the Restoration, as they were in the Biginning [sic], and time of the Law" (*Encouragement*, 26). While the distinction between the old and the new dispensations is a component of Fell's historical vision, she is more inclined to celebrate the accomplishments of her female exemplars both for their own sakes and for the purpose of promoting the relationship between women's visionary authority and female sexuality.

Although not predominant in Fox's tract, purely celebratory moments of female achievement do appear. He, for instance, almost directly quotes his wife when he expounds upon Christ's response to the Pharisee, Simon, who silently and to himself questions Christ for allowing a woman known to be sinful to touch him, let alone wash his feet with her tears:

> And in *Luke* 7. Christ turned him to the woman, and said unto *Simon, Seest thou this woman? I entred into thy House, but thou gavest me no Water for my Feet; but she hath washed my Feet with Tears, and wiped them with the Hair of her Head* . . .
> So here you may see how Christ justified the woman's Actions above *Simon*, whose Faith hath saved her, which is chronicled to her Renown, and the Honour of God. (*Encouragement*, 63–64)

Indeed Fox's treatment of this particular incident is perhaps more celebratory than Fell's who sees the episode as yet further evidence for her claim that "Jesus owned the Love and Grace that appeared in Women, and did not despise it" (6). Yet, in general, while Fox's *Encouragement* celebrates the actions of women much more so than *Concerning Sons and Daughters* did, it remains focused on justifying women's meetings in terms of the broader goals of the sect.

Biblical examples in Fox's tract serve to legitimate his contention that women should have an office in the church, but they do not adequately address the character and content of that office. To explain why women, for instance, should tend to the poor, Fox has to discuss ideas of gender identity. This appears to be a far less engaging topic for Fox than it had been for Fell who readily justified women's right to prophesy in terms of the special relationship that they as women had with Christ. Where Fell had defined female difference in terms of female sexual difference, Fox addresses difference in terms of gendered difference. In the language of feminist analysis, both Fell and Fox understand female difference in terms commensurate with what Gayle Rubin has identified as the "sex/gender system," "the set of arrangements by which a society transforms biological sexuality into products of human activity."[58] What distinguishes Fox from Fell is that he emphasizes "the products of human activity," while she underscores "biological sexuality" itself. Because Fox tends to define women in terms of their social role, he insists, for example, that the work of women's meetings center around domestic concerns because women tend to be in the domestic arena: "So the Women in the time of the Light, Grace and Gospel, are to look into their own selves and Families, & to look to the training up of their Children; for they are oft-times more amongst them then the Men, and may prevent many things that may fall out" (*Encouragement*, 20). Likewise, "women many times know that Condition more of poor Families, and widows, and such as are in distress more then the men, because they are most conversant in their Families and about such things" (*Encouragement*, 80). Fox's view of gendered identity is both essentialist and sociological. On the one hand, he assumes, as did most of his contemporaries, that men and women see their gendered roles as natural, as simply a reflection of the way things are. On the other hand, he suggests that women's skills in the domestic arena come from practice rather than nature: women might know more about children because they are "more amongst them then the Men" and they might better serve the poor because "they are most conversant in their Families and about such things." In other words, women have historically been positioned in the domestic sphere so they tend to be more adept at addressing matters related to the home and the family. Rather than viewing traditional female behaviors or work as the basis for female inferiority, Fox makes it the basis for female authority. Women should have the "office" of giving money to the poor because they are better skilled at such tasks.

In another tract, "To the Men and Women's Monthly and Quarterly Meetings," Fox similarly appeals to the female trait of modesty to explain why women should be placed in charge of supervising other women: "All things must be done in [God's] power and name: and there is many things that is proper for women to look into both in their families, and concerning of women which is not so proper for the men, which modesty in women cannot so well speak of before men as they can do among their sex."[59] The passage suggests that for a woman to expose her indiscretions before a male tribunal would directly contradict her gender's behavioral trait of "modesty." Fox does not specify modesty as a natural or socially motivated behavior, although he presents it as a generally assumed (and hence to some degree, natural) attribute of women with clear social consequences: women's innate desire to keep themselves properly concealed from men makes all-female supervisory councils absolutely essential. For Fox, women's natural tendency to modesty is both an attribute that should separate them from the monitory eyes of men and a shared experience that rightly makes them subject to the authority of other women. Like his arguments for women's greater experience in the home, Fox's discussion of female modesty serves to justify the specific political roles women gain in the meeting system of Quaker government.

Again and again, Fox insists on the political significance of women's work. In one of his most charming asides, he contends that women are capable of far more than menial domestic chores: "Now *Moses* and *Aaron*, and the seventy Elders, did not say to those Assemblies of Women, we can do our Work our selves, and you are fitter to be at home to wash the Dishes, or such like Expressions; but they did encourage them in the work and Service of God, in those things which God had commanded them in the time of the Law" (*Encouragement*, 12). The women Fox refers to here are those who contributed to the construction of the tabernacle through gifts of jewelry and through spinning.[60] Fox sees in the attitude of Moses and Aaron toward the women a model for Quaker church order: women should not be separated from the work of the church but should be encouraged to participate as they are called. Through the institution of women's meetings, Fox like Moses and Aaron seeks to legislate a means through which women can contribute their special domestic skills—spinning in the case of the Israelites and awareness of the poor in the case of the Quakers—to the building of the tabernacle. In a later epistle, Fox envisions women's meetings as conferring a broader political significance to women's domestic roles. He invokes Paul who commands older women to " 'teach the young women to be sober and discreet, chaste, and good, to love their husbands, and their children, that the word of God be not blasphemed.' So these were to be as mothers to the younger women, and were public women in their public services, and charge that was committed to them." The women were to be "as mothers to the younger women" and through "their public services" transformed a domestic role into a public one. As compared to *Concerning Sons and Daughters*, Fox in his tracts on women's meetings expresses a clearer vision of gender difference and one that approximates the way Fell links specific attributes to women. Yet Fox's sense of gendered identity does not, as did Fell's, focus on female sexuality. While Fox compares Quaker women to "mothers in spiritual Israel" who have the "breasts of consolation, which are full of the milk of the word, to suckle all the young ones," he does not literally mean that Quaker women's breasts are full of the "milk of the word."[61] For her part, when Fell describes the mother-son link that binds Christ to the archetypal woman, she literally means that all women share with Mary a unique physical bond with Christ. For Fell, Christ serves to legitimate women's prophetic authority by legitimating women's sexual identity. Fox's sense of women's gendered identity focuses on women's social role and never directly links female behavior with female sexuality.

Indeed, Fox's emphasis on women's gendered rather than sexual identity diverges, at times, quite sharply from some of Fell's more radically literal claims about the link between Christ and women. On the topic of women being redeemed of the aspersion cast upon them by Eve's transgression, he, like Fell, points to the promise that "The seed of the woman should bruise the serpents head." His treatment of women's redemption, however, parts company with Fell's when he attributes the birth of Christ to Mary's individual and singular act of faith: "Now, here comes the reproach to be taken off from women, which were first in transgression, who are not suffered to speak in the church; but here Mary did speak, and believe that which was spoken to her." Fox celebrates Mary, and Mary alone, not for her capacity to give birth but for believing "that which was spoken to her." Moreover, Fox asserts that Mary not only redeemed women but also men: "and also the reproach and transgression taken off men, that believe in the seed Christ Jesus, who bruises the head of the serpent, that has brought man and woman into his image, and his works."[62] In Fox's broad historical vision, Eve's transgression turns out not to be just about women but about all humankind and hence all benefit from Mary's redeeming act of faith. Likewise, the tenderness that Mary displays toward her sacred infant is a pattern of the tenderness all should display upon receiving Christ in their lives:

> And you may see in *Luke* 2.7. how *Mary* wrapped Christ in Swadling-Clothes, and how tender she was of the Heavenly Birth conceived by the Holy Ghost.
> And so must all true and tender Christians that receive him in the Spirit; and how she kept all the Sayings that were spoken of Christ, and pondered them in her Heart. (*Encouragement*, 51)

While Fox deems the birth of Christ the faith act of one historical figure, Mary, whose tenderness all can emulate, he makes the women's announcement of Christ's resurrection the product of a women's meeting. Unlike Fell, Fox emphasizes neither the neglect of Christ's male disciples during his suffering nor the mystical bond that links Christ and the women but rather emphasizes the collective achievement of the women. For instance, Fox does not note that Christ's male disciples abandoned him during his crucifixion but only that the women attended him: "And you may see when Christ was crucified, how many women were there, as *Mary Magdalen*, and *Mary* the Mother of *James*, and many others, which came up to *Jerusalem*, that were about Jesus at the time of his being crucified" (*Encouragement*, 55). Fox, like Fell, does observe that the disciples did not believe the women's message of Christ's resurrection, but he also recognizes that their disbelief does not prevent them from ever learning of the resurrection: "And here was a joyful woman's-meeting indeed, of Messengers and Preachers of Christ's Resurrection, which is recorded to Posterity to their Renown, that all should believe; though their Message & Speech were as idle Tales to the Disciples; but they were owned by Christ the Head of the Church, as aforesaid, though their preaching was slighted by the Apostles, and counted as idles [*sic*] Tales; but they came to believe afterwards" (*Encouragement*, 60–61). The importance of the women's role in spreading the news of the resurrection for Fox is that a group of women collaborated to serve the church. That the leaders of that church did not credit them was certainly unfortunate although not nearly as critical as Fell might have us believe, for "they came to believe afterwards." Still the fact that "they were owned by Christ the Head of the Church" and did convey an important message attests to the significant role women, joining together, can play in the church.

Strikingly, when Fox addresses the "women's meeting" that delivered the message of Christ's resurrection, he in no way attempts to link the women's service to their gendered identity. Indeed, where Fell had chastised the apostles for failing to recognize the good use God makes of women, Fox scolds them for failing to remember, as the women did, Christ's own prophecy about himself. Just after reporting that the apostles deemed the women's words to be "idle tales," Fox indirectly admonishes not the apostles but anyone who might discredit women because they are women: "Now mark their [the women's] Message, and to whom it was, and who they were that were the Messengers, the weaker Vessels, and to whom, to the Apostles; and what they preached was what they remembred Christ had spoken to them before, to wit, that Christ should suffer, and rise again" (*Encouragement*, 58). Fox, although he does not berate the apostles in a heavy handed way, appears to be astonished that they could discount the women's words since their "tales" represent Christ's own prophecy about himself. Moreover, the structure of the passage indicates that Fox intends his reader to understand the identification of women as "weaker Vessels" ironically: He exhorts his reader to note the message, the addressees, and the messengers and then reveals the identities of all three in reverse order. The women, the so-called weaker vessels, tell the apostles that Christ's prophecy has been fulfilled. The women do not passively report news but rather they, unlike the apostles, actually "remember" Christ's words. Fox's recounting of the narrative suggests that the apostles regard the women in conventionally gendered terms as "weaker vessels" and as purveyors of "idle tales" to conceal their own inattention to Christ's word. In contradistinction to Fell's positive emphasis on conventional female attributes, Fox suggests that when women are divinely inspired they may transcend traditional norms of female behavior.

As was true of *Concerning Sons and Daughters, Encouragement* is very much about men, the only difference being that *Encouragement* is explicitly directed to "all the Women that are gathered by and in the Power of God" (*Encouragement*, 3). Indeed, the title page of *This is an Encouragement to all the Womens-Meetings, in the World* indicates that the text will show women "how the Holy Men Encouraged the Holy Women both in the Time of the Law, and in the Time of the Gospel." As the author of a tract that encourages women, Fox clearly locates himself in the long tradition of men, which includes figures such as Moses and Christ, who have encouraged women. And while, following Fell, Fox's text provides a history of female achievement, it also chronicles male characters from the Bible who have encouraged women. Indeed, many of the women who have notably served Christ were implicitly strengthened by male encouragement: "Now here you may see all these renowned, faithful Women, were encouraged by Christ and his Followers" (*Encouragement*, 68). Throughout *Encouragement*, Fox's emphasis on encouragement suggests that he views women as reticent and reluctant to act unless they receive approval from men. He, for instance, sees John's second epistle, directed to and commending the "Elect Lady" as "an Encouragement to all faithful Women, to see that their Children do walk in the Truth, and abide in the Doctrine of Christ" (*Encouragement*, 80, 81). In Fox's eyes, John's encouragement serves to prompt both the Elect Lady and women in general to recognize that they are called to attend to the spiritual life of their children.

On the one hand, Fox's emphasis on encouragement belittles women by suggesting that women thrive in conjunction with male approval. What appears to be his text's account of female achievement proves to be a record of male-sanctioned female achievement. On the other hand, Fox may well have been addressing a real need some Quakers, both male and female, may have had to believe that the sanction for women's meetings and the public role they conferred upon women could be traced to major biblical figures such as Moses and Christ. First, as historians have documented, the women's meetings were a great source of division and controversy within the Quaker movement. The Separatist movement, led by the Wilkinson/Story party, opposed Fox's attempts to impose greater institutionalization on Quakerism generally.[63] They viewed themselves as "defenders of the Quakers' original spiritual mission," defying the "juggernaut of bureaucratization" in favor of advancing "the valiant forces of spiritual charisma and social equality."[64] As the tract of one of the dissenters suggests, however, their opposition to women's meetings did not derive exclusively from their ideas about freedom and equality but also from their contempt of female political authority:

> Can there be greater imposers in the world, than those that judge all people, *not to be of God*, for not submitting to a *female government* in marriage? A thing never heard of ... except the government of the *Amazons* ... And whether such *women-judges* ever did any good, who come into the seat of counsel, rustling in gaudy flowered stuffs, or silks, from top to toe, mincing with their feet ... [We are not] against a woman's declaring in a religious meeting, what God has done for her soul, by silently waiting at the feet of Jesus, as *Mary* did ... Nor are we against women meeting by themselves, upon a particular occasion, but not monthly for government.[65]

Second, documentary evidence exists to suggest that some women may have reluctantly participated in the meetings because of both the controversy surrounding them and concerns about their seemliness. Theophila Townsend addresses both concerns in her testimonial to Anne Whitehead when she exhorts women "to withstand all the false pretenders to love and unity" who "are in a dividing Spirit, and secretly endeavoring, to disturb the Churches peace" and to "stand up in the strength of the Lord" to resist those who "would destroy your comly Order."[66] The multiple female authors of *A Living Testimony* affirm that women "have a Heavenly propriety in the *Light, Power* and *Spirit* of *Grace*, and the *Gospel*, being *Heirs* of the same; so by Grace we are called into the Work and Service of God and Jesus Christ, that they require of us in our Age and Generation." Beyond asserting the "propriety" of women's meetings, these authors also appear to have detected a kind of reticence among some Quaker women: "we are not to put our Candles under a Bushel, not to hide our Talents in a Napkin, as the sloathful do; but we are to have Oyl in our Lamps, like Wise Virgins to the Lord; and our Lamps are to burn, and our Lights are to shine, that we may all see clearly our Work and Service."[67] As the female authors of *A Living Testimony* aver, Fox was not the only Quaker who felt compelled to "encourage" women to participate in women's meetings.

While Fox may certainly "encourage" women as a way of undoing a tendency to hide "Candles under a Bushel," encouragement also functions, after the early modern legal expression "femme couverte," to cover women. In both *Concerning Sons and Daughters* and *Encouragement*, whenever women do or say anything significant a man, whether Christ or Moses, is usually standing nearby to sanction or encourage them. It is this relationship between men and women that, according to Fox's contemporary, William Loddington, the system of separate men's and women's meetings is designed to maintain. Loddington contends that separate meetings preserve male "Headship" because "Women Friends meeting by themselves, may without the least suspition of usurping Authority over the Men, confer and reason together, how to serve Truth in their places, in such things as are most proper and suitable for them, still submitting to the Wisdom of God in the Mens Meetings."[68] As Loddington suggests and as appears to have been the case, male encouragement of women's meetings meant that men allowed women to act but within bounds determined by men.

Still, despite the fact that men frequently sanction or encourage women in Fox's tracts, his writings do not imagine an oppressive atmosphere of surveillance but rather memorably testify to women's potential. Particularly noteworthy is his treatment of the two Hebrew midwives, Shiphrah and Puah, in Exodus who defy the Egyptian pharoah's command to kill the Hebrews' male children at birth. Fox formalizes their defiance and suggests that their deeds are not the acts of two women but of a women's meeting: "And do you think that these honourable women did not meet often together, and took Counsel together, to stand together and adventure their own Lives and Estates to preserve the Lives of those Male-Children?" (*Encouragement*, 33). The Bible, of course, does not indicate that they actually met together in any formal way; this is merely Fox's speculation. Still Fox's rendering of the narrative transforms these two women, who perform a decidedly traditional kind of women's work, into calculating architects of subversion. They do not merely resist the pharoah but carefully deceive him using the terms of their trade. Asked why they had saved the male children despite the king's command, the women respond that the Hebrew women "are lively, and are delivered ere the midwives come in unto them."[69] Fox notes their deception and observes that if women did this in his own day, they would be deemed "bold women to answer the king after such a manner" (*Encouragement*, 33). Women's deeds, even those that appear confined to the domestic sphere, can have a political impact, and Fox through the women's meetings attempts to create an institution that enables women to perform their work in ways that best benefit the sect. What makes Fox's attempt to ennoble women's work believable and politically significant is that while he does maintain conven-

tional gender distinctions, he does not assert the superiority of
men's work over that of women.

MARRIAGE AND PROPERTY RIGHTS

In 1669, a fifty-five-year-old Fell and a forty-five-year-old Fox
married. According to Isabel Ross, theirs was "no ordinary marriage," both partners believing "that their union was primarily,
and indeed preeminently spiritual." (And, as Mack observes, debate exists as to whether their marriage had a physical component at all.)[70] Fox, in a letter that Friends so "resented, and so
much disliked that it was called in again, and a rare thing it was
to get a sight thereof," depicted his marriage to Fell as emblem-
atic of the union of the Church and the Lamb. As Braithwaite describes the letter: "Fox wrote that the marriage was commanded
him as a figure or testimony of the Church coming out of the wilderness and of the marriage of the Lamb before the world was.
He witnessed this marriage of the Lamb in the restoration which
had come to him out of the Fall and in the Seed of Life. Its nature
had been seen by him for many years past, but the command
from God to fulfil the thing had only come of late."[71]
   The turns of Fox's mystical mind here are not altogether clear,
but the passage suggests that Friends' resentment of the letter
may well have stemmed from Fox's identification of himself with
the Lamb and of Fell with the Church. As possessors of grand
historical visions of themselves, Fox and Fell were well-matched.
After all, she had asserted in *Womens Speaking Justified*, that
the "Church is a woman" and Fox had enlivened her claims, although not in literal terms, by suggesting Fell herself as a figure
of the Church. Fox viewed his marriage to Fell not only in novel,
if inflated, spiritual terms but also in anachronistic material
terms. Prior to the marriage, he produced a written document in
which he promised not to interfere with Fell's considerable estate and which affirmed that Fell's daughters would continue as
her primary heirs. Needless to say, Fox's decision "that his marriage to a well-to-do woman should not make him a wealthy man"
was an unusual determination for a seventeenth-century En-
glishman to make.[72] Moreover, his attention to this worldly detail
of their union further underscores the well-developed political
sensibility of this Quaker leader who carved out a political role
for women from an essentially mystical and charismatic theology.

Although the union of Fell and Fox produced no biological off-spring, Fell's daughter Sarah wrote a letter sometime between 1675 and 1680, "From our Country Women's meeting in Lancashire to be Dispersed abroad, among the Women's meetings everywhere," that could be said to be the intellectual offspring of the two Quaker luminaries' marriage.[73] The fourth of Fell's seven daughters, Sarah assumed a leading role in the early women's meetings. She served as the clerk of the Swarthmoor and Lancashire Women's Meetings from 1671 to 1680. Following her marriage to William Meade in 1681, she moved to London where she also served as the clerk of the Box Meeting and the Plaistow and Barking Women's Meeting. As clerk of these various meetings, she took very detailed minutes and her accounts serve as important historical records of early women's meetings.

Written while she was still the clerk of the northern women's meetings, "Country Women's meeting," "is both a summation of advanced Quaker thought about women and instruction to the far-flung women's meetings as to responsibilities and functions."[74] Her text is very much influenced by Fox and Fell, embracing both her stepfather's socially oriented and her mother's biologically focused understanding of gender difference. Like Fox, she recognizes that now is the time that Quakers must organize; they can no longer afford simply to be Quakers and revel in their new life in the Spirit. Rather, they need to work to keep their sect afloat. Women play an important role in perpetuating the sect's existence, and Sarah Fell calls upon her sisters to continue to guide their families because, in so doing, they contribute to the Quakers' overall well-being: "And dear sisters it is duely Incumbent upon us to look into our families, and to prevent our Children of running into the world for husbands, or for wives, and so to the priests: for you know before the womens meetings were set up, Many have done so, which brought dishonour, both to God, and upon his truth and people." In their roles as mothers, women influence whether their children will continue in the sect and, according to Sarah, women working together in meetings have already significantly reduced the rate of attrition. Like Fox, Sarah regards women's experience in the family as making them particularly suited to attend to family related matters: "For you know, that we are much in our families amongst our children, maids, and servants, and may see more into their inclinations; and so see that none indulge any to looseness and evill, but restrain it."[75] Women's business focuses on family matters because their skills are best employed in that arena.

While Sarah Fell's understanding of the politics of women's work bears the marks of Fox's influence, her understanding of women's right to preach and to work for the church derives from her mother. In her epistle, Sarah evokes the particular relationship between Christ and women that her mother had created, but the tie the younger Fell imagines is much more subdued. Sarah addresses many of the same biblical passages that her mother does—the promise that the woman's seed will bruise the serpent's head, the church as the bride of Christ, the woman of Samaria, the female messengers of the resurrection, and Christ's regard for the weak—but she does not stridently feminize them. Of the seed destined to bruise the serpent's head, the younger Fell contends that "all live and dwell in the sensible feeling thereof" and "all nations of the earth" are blessed by this seed. Still, when Sarah more directly links the seed to woman and to the figure of the church as woman, the sound of her mother's voice can be heard: "the Seed of the Woman should bruise the Serpents head, and this is fullfilled and fullfilling, in the day of the lords power, and of the restoration, and redemption of his seed and body, which is his church, which is comming out of the wilderness, leaning on her beloved, who is coming in his power and great glory." In *Womens Speaking Justified*, Fell had appealed to the Song of Songs and Revelation to prove that the Church is a woman, and she had used the discussion of the church as a woman to clarify her representation of the relationship between woman and the seed. The younger Fell does not predicate female authority upon a literal connection between the seed and woman, and the church and woman as her mother had but rather more subtly deploys this very female imagery to affirm her claims that women are "in Christ Jesus," are "Abrahams seed," and are "heires according to promise . . . of the free Jerusalem from above, which is the mother of us all."[76] She does not make women the center of her narrative of salvation history but makes them central to that narrative.

Likewise, Sarah's account of the women who delivered the message of Christ's resurrection celebrates the fact that women are the first to learn the good news, but she does not emphasize the honor the event brings to women at the expense of men: "Soe here the lord Jesus Christ, sends his first message of his resurrection by women unto his own disciples: And they were faithfull unto him, and did his message, and yet they could hardly be believed." True, the disciples dismissed the women's message but the more important point for Sarah is that Christ "first" asks women to proclaim the news of his resurrection. Unlike her mother's account, however, the women in Sarah's narrative do not earn the honor of bearing this message through an intimate connection to Christ that leaves them unable to "depart" from him as he suffers and dies. Rather, their role in disseminating the news is yet another example of the special regard that Christ has for women. Like her mother, the younger Fell frequently concludes vignettes about female biblical figures by observing "here the Lord makes use, and had a service for the women" or "See what love and plainess he [Christ] manifested unto this woman." She appeals to Scripture to prove that Christ "had a dear and a tender care and regard unto women," but she does not intensify the nature of this bond by suggesting that Christ's "regard" for women stems from his being of a woman born. In the younger Fell's text, Christ's "regard" for women serves rather to dispel assumptions that Christ, like mortal men, would be contemptuous of women because of their supposed inferiority. As Sarah notes, when Christ addressed the woman at the well, he was "not despising her, nor undervalluing her, in the least."[77]

Sarah most closely approximates her mother's insistence that Christ and women are linked by a physical bond when she addresses women's weakness. She discusses weakness twice, at the beginning and at the closing of her text. She initially claims that Christ equally regards the strong and the weak: Christ "is no respecter of persons, but hath a care, and a regard unto all, the weak as well as the strong, that he may have the glory of his own work, who treadeth the wine-press alone." Unlike her mother, she never claims that Christ has a particular regard for the weak. Nevertheless, she closes her text with an extended description of Christ's capacity to construct a spiritual warrior woman out of "weaker vessels": "And though we be looked upon as the weaker vessels, yet strong and powerfull is God, whose strength is made perfect in weakness, he can make us good and bold, and valliant Souldiers of Jesus Christ, if he arm us with his Armour of Light, and give unto us the sword of his Eternal Spirit which is the word of the Eternal God, and cover our hearts with the breast-plate of righteousness, and crown us with the helmet of Salvation, and give unto us the Shield of Faith, with which we can quench all the fiery darts of Sathan."[78]

Her portrait of the warrior woman for Christ follows directly after her exhortation to women to recognize that women's meetings have their origins in Scripture and are "no new thing, as some raw unseasoned spirits would seem to make" them. Her warrior woman serves to counter any tentativeness with respect to women's meetings that female Quakers may experience and to redefine the new woman her sect celebrates. As powerful as she appears, Sarah's warrior woman decidedly does not, on her own, possess the attributes of masculine strength. Rather, as she contends, women's natural weakness means that their strength can only come from Christ; men, on the other hand, might be more likely to rely on their own physical strength: "our sufficiency is of him, and our Armour, and strength is in him: and all the great strength that is in men, if they want this Armour, they can do nothing for God, nor he will have none of their Service, who will have no flesh, to glory in his presence."[79]

For Sarah, female weakness can prepare women to become dependent on Christ, while masculine strength can prove a hindrance to union with the divine. Indeed, her assessment of strength and weakness reverses conventional gendered binary oppositions by making excess fleshliness a feature of male strength rather than an attribute of the carnality more typically identified with women. She deems female weakness to be a positive physical attribute because it makes women less embodied, and so, like her mother, the younger Fell predicates, if only rather tenuously, female authority upon female sexual difference. While the elder Fell had emphasized female weakness along with maternity and erotic attractiveness as feminine traits that sutured women's special tie to Christ, Sarah focuses on weakness, on women's diminished physicality, alone. Because her warrior woman derives power from a notion of female sexual difference predicated directly upon the body but that, at the same time, derogates bodily presence, Sarah proves herself to be heir to the intellectual legacies of both Fell and Fox. Fox and the system of women's meetings would recast sexual difference in terms of work: women attend to domestic matters while men focus on theology. Clearly, conventional notions of sexuality informed the two-tiered system Fox's writings established, but Fox never spoke of women's physical difference directly, preferring to assert that the specific nature of women's work is the result of their gendered identity. On the other hand, Fell's vision of an embodied female sexuality would create, for instance, the figure of the looming maternal presence who shapes Christ's existence. With her warrior woman, her daughter would create another such looming female presence but one whose power would derive from the absence rather than the presence of physicality. Sarah is capable, like Fox, of relinquishing property rights—and in her case these are in her body—to pursue spiritual objectives; but she is determined, like her mother, to celebrate the properties of the female body.

Sarah Fell's warrior woman serves as a metaphor for the union of the two visions of female authority constructed by Fox and Fell. In idealizing a diminished but specifically female physicality, she produces a paragon of female power who appears decidedly masculine. On the one hand, this sort of cross-dressing, in which women assume male garb, is one of the tacit objectives of the system of women's meetings through which political meaning, typically reserved for men's work, is applied to women's work. Fox, of course, would argue that the system of men's and women's meetings is nothing new, having originated in Eden with Adam and Eve's shared labors, and so does not confer power upon women but merely restores the political role they played before the fall. But, practically speaking, the system of women's meetings served to confer political status on women. On the other hand, Sarah and Margaret Fell (although to varying degrees) understood female authority as an essential attribute of female sexuality. Women can become warriors for the Lord not despite but because of their physical weakness that teaches them not to overvalue their physical power but to depend on Christ for strength. Confident that her female sexuality contributes to her power, Sarah's warrior woman can self-consciously dedicate herself to engagement in the male political world. While Margaret Fell had celebrated the role of female sexuality in underwriting female authority, her daughter goes one step beyond her to consider what it means for women to be actively engaged in the business of politics. Women, she maintains, will need strength and they can count on God to arm them for the fray. Although her female warrior assumes a masculine appearance, she possesses a specifically gendered need for divine succor that serves to perpetuate her female identity in the hurly burly of male politics. Politics, both Fells aver, may indeed be a man's game, but women possess innate qualities that enable them to engage the field.

Epilogue: Mary Astell's "History of Women"

SARAH FELL'S WOMAN WARRIOR REPRESENTS THE CLOSING MOMENTS of a unique epoch in women's literary history. Never again would such an extensive canon of women's writing create models of female political authority through prophetic discourse. And never again would women appeal to the female body as a conduit for special access to the divine will and hence as a material claim to political right. In many ways, the political dynamism of the women prophets stems from their failure to measure up to Hilda Smith's definition of feminism as the self-conscious commitment to advancing the rights of women as a group. Although the women prophets did not attend to women's issues with the same self-consciousness of later feminists, they attempted to create central political roles for women. Claiming to derive authority from the same source—God—that empowered monarchs, the women prophets sought to intervene in the political sphere not on behalf of women but as women. While Margaret and Sarah Fell, whose work most nearly approximates later feminists' concerns with explicit "women's issues," do not preoccupy themselves with, in Smith's terms, exhibiting "a general understanding of women as a whole," they do affirm women's divine mandate to participate in the political sphere.[1]

Smith's observations notwithstanding, even feminists who celebrate the political activism and achievements of the women prophets struggle to explain their relevance to the history of feminism and particularly to their immediate successors, the better known late seventeenth- and early eighteenth-century feminists. The legacy of the female visionaries is difficult to identify for two reasons. First, the group of Restoration feminists who immediately follow the women prophets appear to share little in common with them. They were much more intellectual and, from an activist perspective, much more subdued. They present a stark contrast to the women prophets who sought, with a fiery zeal, to be in the thick of political events. Second, the religious origins of the prophets' politics strike many feminist scholars as out of place in a secular feminist agenda. This view, while relevant to contemporary feminism, fails to account for, in earlier periods, the central political role of divine authority. For the women prophets, claims to divine authority brought political capital. Indeed, religion provides a crucial link between the women prophets and the Restoration feminists for whom religion was a less potent but still significant force. For the Restoration feminists, the women prophets serve to illustrate how women might invoke divine authority to advance their own political ambitions. Another subtler legacy of the women prophets is the way in which their politics of female sexuality anticipate later feminists' politics of sexual difference. While the women prophets emphasize the positive characteristics of female sexuality to advocate their right to participate in the political realm, later feminists underscore the differences between male and female to illustrate the unfair limitations imposed upon female advancement. Although Restoration feminists do not consciously embrace the women prophets for either their union of spiritual and secular politics or their politics of female sexuality, these attributes persist and illustrate consecutive developments in the history of feminist consciousness.

Surprisingly, one early feminist who embraces the legacy of the women prophets is Mary Astell.[2] This is unexpected because she was a Tory and High Church Anglican who wrote on a number of occasions about her deep disdain for radical sectarians, like Mary Cary, who supported the execution of Charles I.[3] Moreover, she identifies the religious dissenters of her own generation as descendants of the rebellious crew who "brought a Royal-Head to the Block" and therefore urges that nonconformists be banned from holding public office. Yet, in her 1706 Preface to her *Some Reflections upon Marriage* (first published in 1700), she addresses questions of female political authority in language that would have been familiar to the female prophets. In the Preface, she turns to the "Oracles of God" to disprove the customary belief in women's "natural inferiority." The Bible, she contends, contains a "History of Women famous in their Generations" that proves women to be as qualified as men to assume positions of power and influence. Although not as politically transgressive as the writings of Lady Eleanor and Anna Trapnel, Astell's Preface similarly encodes a plea for female authority in terms of divine sanction. Indeed, her 1706 Preface to her *Some Reflections upon Marriage* bears a striking resemblance to Margaret Fell's *Womens Speaking Justified*. As Margaret Olofson Thickstun has observed, both texts "deploy a 'hermeneutics of remembrance,' recovering women in Scripture as positive role models for contemporary women."[4] While Fell had turned to female exemplars to illustrate that women's preaching was consistent with the divine will, Astell insists that the Bible contains a "History of Women" to disprove the misogynous claim of women's "natural inferiority."[5] Moreover, the Preface's concern with politics and divine authority represents a significant departure from her earlier feminist tracts, the well-known *Serious Proposal to the Ladies* and *Some Reflections upon Marriage*. (While the Preface is appended to a later version of *Reflections*, the two should be read as separate texts.) Critics of these two texts have observed that Astell promoted women's rational equality with men only to insist steadfastly on women's political subordination. While Smith contends that Astell's adherence to "Christian dogma" limited her feminism, the Preface proves otherwise.[6] Precisely by appealing to divine authority—the very engine that drove the Civil War female prophets—does Astell come, in the Preface, to make her most aggressive demands for female political right. This is not to say that Astell's Preface can replace the politically engaged and enthusiastic women's writing of the revolutionary era. Rather, reading the Preface in terms of the rhetoric of the female visionaries illustrates the persistence of prophetic discourse as a means through which women have staked some of their strongest claims to political power.

Although I argue that Astell's Preface embraces an activist spirit akin to the writings of the women prophets, the hallmark of her career as a female apologist is commonly understood to be her emphasis on women's rational equality with men and her belief that training in rational principles confers upon women a sense of their value as beings created for God. In her famous treatise on women's education, *A Serious Proposal to the Ladies* (1694), Astell explains that grounding in rational principles promotes female piety: "Whereas she whose Reason is suffer'd to display it self, to inquire into the grounds and Motives of Religion ... and cleaves to Piety, because 'tis her Wisdom ... she who is not only eminently and unmoveably good, but able to give a Reason *why* she is so; is too firm and stable to be mov'd by the pitiful Allurements of sin, too wise and too well bottom'd to be undermined and supplanted by the strongest Efforts of Temptation."[7] She promises her male readers women who understand why they are "eminently and unmoveably good" and who therefore can ably resist the "strongest Efforts of Temptation." While men stand to gain from her proposed academy "wise" and "well-bottom'd" wives and daughters, women acquire the "understanding" of the importance of being "unmoveably good."

Reason has typically been seen, in the words of Ruth Perry, as the "cornerstone of her feminism," but political activism has not. For Astell, education in rational principles enables women to gain control over self but not over men: "The Men therefore may still enjoy their Prerogatives for us, we mean not to intrench on any of their Lawful Privileges . . . our only endeavor shall be to be absolute Monarchs in our own Bosoms." Her commitment to conservative social values persists in the second of her two feminist tracts, *Some Reflections upon Marriage*, in which she observes that although women might be cruelly mistreated by their husbands, they must adhere to the terms of the marital obligation and remain subordinate: "She then who Marrys ought to lay it down for an indisputable Maxim, that her Husband must govern absolutely and intirely, and that she has nothing else to do but to Please and Obey." While Astell maintains that women are men's equals as rational beings and therefore capable of occupying positions of power and influence, she equally believes that traditional social roles must be preserved. In a disquisition against marrying outside of one's class, Astell observes the beauty of the social hierarchy: "For since GOD has plac'd different Ranks in the World, put some in a higher and some in a lower Station, for Order and Beauty's sake, and for many good Reasons." Correspondingly, she frames the relationship between men and women in terms of this class-based hierarchy: "Superiors indeed are too apt to forget the common Privileges of Mankind; that their Inferiors share with them the greatest Benefits, and are as capable as themselves of enjoying the supreme Good; that tho' the Order of the World requires an *Outward* Respect and Obedience from some to others, yet the Mind is free, nothing but Reason can oblige it, 'tis out of the reach of the most absolute Tyrant."[8] Women, like members of the lower classes, are inferior to their "Superiors" or men. Yet, because "Inferiors" share with their "Superiors" in the "common Privileges of Mankind," they can possess a kind of interior independence from their overlords' wills. Astell's vision of rational liberty offers some, if small, consolation to the woman who finds herself subjected to a tyrannical husband.

Unlike *Serious Proposal* and *Reflections*, Astell's Preface does not skirt the political implications of her belief in women's rational equality. It, like Fell's Postscript, proves to be an addition that contains some of its author's most pointed claims for female authority. While her earlier feminist treatises address women's issues of education and domestic life, her Preface participates in the wide ranging political postulating of the women prophets and presents a complex meditation on political, divine, and even literary authority. The text opens with the original Preface's explanation of why in 1700 she does not reveal her identity when she publishes *Reflections*: "'Tis a very great Fault to regard rather who it is that Speaks, than what is Spoken; and either to submit to Authority, when we should only yield to Reason; or if Reason press too hard, to think to ward it off by Personal Objections and Reflections" (7). Despite her principled refusal to identify herself as the author of *Reflections* in 1700, by 1706 she reveals herself as the author of the tract. She asserts that her decision to do so was spurred by a male author who claims her text as his own (8).

By this point in her career, following the publication of her feminist treatises and her pamphlets on Occasional Conformity, Astell may also have felt more confident about her literary authority. According to Perry, the years between 1700 and 1706, and particularly 1702 through 1704, mark the period of "Astell's greatest public reputation. She became a figure in London society. Her pamphlets were read widely and discussed."[9] In any event, once she asserts her authorship of *Reflections*, she proceeds to develop a model of female political authority that appeals to the example of Deborah to insist upon the naturalness of the "Sovereignty of a Woman": "But Deborah's Government was confer'd on her by GOD Himself. Consequently the Sovereignty of a Woman is not contrary to the Law of Nature; for the Law of Nature is the Law of GOD, who cannot contradict Himself; and yet it was God who Inspir'd and Approv'd that great Woman, raising her up to Judge and to Deliver His People *Israel*" (24). Later in the Preface, Astell identifies Deborah as one of the "great Prophetesses" and thus links her divinely ordained political authority with her spiritual authority (26). In so doing, she evokes the writings of Lady Eleanor and Lady Eleanor's beloved James who similarly celebrated the figure of the prophet-king. On the one hand, she adheres to a traditional model of divine right. For instance, she insists that Anne derives her royal prerogative from God: "that GREAT QUEEN . . . is the chief Instrument in the Hand of the Almighty to pull down and to set up the Great Man of the Earth" (30). Yet her apotheosis of the prophet-judge Deborah

suggests a more radical model of political and spiritual authority—one that evokes Fifth Monarchists such as Anna Trapnel
and Mary Cary who deemed themselves called to govern their
people.

Much of the impetus for the Preface's focus on the politics of
spirituality may well derive from Astell's participation in the
major politico-religious controversy of her era, the debate over
Occasional Conformity. In two tracts of 1704, *Moderation Truly
Stated* and *A Fair Way with the Dissenters*, Astell defended the
Tory and High Church position that religious dissenters should
be banned from holding public office. Ruth Perry observes that
Astell's controversial writings significantly emboldened her feminist politics: "The pamphlet writing was a kind of political and
literary apprenticeship for her, forcing her to formulate her
views in relation to the other opinions arrayed before the public,
and giving her a sense of agency in political matters." Perry further identifies the Preface as the direct beneficiary of Astell's
newly politicized sensibility: it "bears the earmarks of her pam-
phleteering and demonstrates the politicization of her thinking in
the intervening six years. In this preface, which has about it the
ring of the debating hall, she protests that she is not seditious—as indeed she is not."[10] When Perry asserts that Astell "is
not seditious," she refers to Astell's brief disclaimer about the
political intentions of *Reflections*: "Far be it from her to stir up
Sedition of any sort, none can abhor it more . . . she did not in
any manner prompt them to Resist, or to Abdicate the Perjur'd
Spouse, tho, the law of GOD and the Land make special Provision
for it" (8–9). Certainly, her *Reflections* does support this limita-
tion of female freedoms, but the same cannot be said of the Preface to her *Reflections*. There, she develops a more politicized
feminist idiom, in part, because she turns to "debating hall" tactics and correspondingly abandons the preoccupation with class
difference that had marked her earlier feminist writings.

In *Reflections*, she had strenuously objected to marrying outside of one's class, and in *Serious Proposal* she promoted her
women's academy as a means through which the daughters of
wealthy families could be trained to protect their reputations:
"One would be apt to think indeed, that Parents shou'd take all
possible care of their Childrens Education, not only for *their*
sakes, but even for their *own*. And tho' the Son convey the Name
to Posterity, yet certainly a great Part of the Honour of their
Families depends on their Daughters." Her concern with class
in both *Serious Proposal* and *Reflections* serves to dilute her

feminism because it forces her to accommodate her progressive views to a hierarchical system that depends upon women's inferiority to men. Rather than framing her feminism in terms of class politics in the Preface, Astell takes a more direct and antagonistic approach, identifying male misogyny as the enemy. At one point, she even goes so far as to lament that women lack the collective will to rebel against men: "I do not propose this to prevent a Rebellion, for Women are not so well united as to form an Insurrection" (29). Her strident tone echoes that of her straightforward denunciation, in her 1704 *A Fair Way with the Dissenters*, of the religious dissenters and their quest to obtain the right to hold public office: "I shall frankly own with an Ingenuity they would do well to practise, that the *Total Destruction of Dissenters as a Party* . . . is indeed our Design."[11] Astell's feminism in the Preface shares with her tracts on Occasional Conformity the same single-minded devotion to her cause and the same unwillingness to appease those who oppose her.

While the vituperative terms of party politics may contribute to the more aggressive feminist tone of the Preface, Astell insists that she regrets the existence of party politics themselves.[12] In both the Preface and one of her tracts on Occasional Conformity, *Moderation truly Stated*, she attempts to assert female authority as transcending party politics. For Astell, party politics are inimical because they signal the existence of "factions" that frequently contribute to lawlessness: "Faction is therefore either the making of a Party in Opposition to the Laws and the Established Government; or else the pursuing of a Publick Good by Unlawful Means." Of course, according to Astell, because her party supports the established constitution, it is not a faction. Indeed, it is the party that represents not an opposing political view but the truth. Thus, the "Prince" himself may belong to her party because it espouses the founding values of the nation: "*The Prince may very safely and Honourably put himself at the Head of these ["hearty Friends to the Constitution"] without danger of a* Civil War. *Nor is this the* Heading of a Party, *'tis only setting himself at the Head of the Constitution, the only Place that becomes a Prince*."[13] Astell's professed distaste for party politics, however, does not preclude her from adopting its "debating hall tactics" to pursue her cause.

In *Moderation truly Stated*'s "Prefatory Discourse to Dr. D'Avenant," Astell incorporates a feminist excursus in which she masterfully invokes her stated ambivalence toward party politics in order to establish the naturalness of female authority as an

absolute truth. There, in the course of a debate on Occasional
Conformity, her two representative politicoes, John a Nokes the
Tory and William a Styles the Whig, suddenly take up the topic
of female authority. The discussion begins when Styles suggests
that the dissenters should be permitted to participate in the political system because otherwise they may, backed by their multitudes of supporters, simply usurp authority. More frightening
still, the significant numbers of women who support the dissenting cause may lead this threatened mob action: *"if the Ladies
should put themselves in the Head of* these Multitudes, *what a
formidable Insurrection would it make! What a shock would it
give the Throne! and how Fatal might the Consequences
prove!"* And once women have seized power, he admonishes,
men have historically struggled to wrest it back: *"You know how
hard it was for the Men to recover their Dominion from the famous* Ulasta, *or as some call her,* Valasca of Bohemia, *even
when she had none but Female Troops."* He further elaborates
his warning by recounting tales of other women—Agrippina,
Mary of Lalain, Donna Maria wife to Padilla, and Margaret,
Countess of Mountfort—who wielded considerable military and
political power. The urbane Nokes responds by claiming that
while women should not participate in politics, their gaining
power would not be totally disastrous, first, because women can
only act "above their Sex" for a brief time, and second, because
women's general good naturedness would prevent them from en-
acting atrocities: "Besides the Ladies are *inclin'd to pity,* they
are not of an *unforgiving Temper,* but will treat their Enemies
well when they have subdued them."[14]

Nokes and Styles are interrupted by *"a Lady in the Company"*
who chastises both and particularly Nokes for suggesting that
women's great achievements come from acting "above their
Sex": *"So again, if Women do any thing well, nay should a hundred thousand Women do the Greatest and most Glorious Actions, presently it must be* with a Mind *(forsooth)* above their
Sex!" Further, Astell's Lady undermines Nokes's "above her
sex" argument by claiming that Queen Anne belongs to a tradition of great female rulers: she possesses *"that undaunted Courage and Royal Magnanimity, that has never been wanting to
those Ladies that have adorn'd the English Throne."* On the one
hand, in asserting the femaleness of her great women, Astell
evokes her sectarian predecessors Trapnel and Fell. On the
other, her response to Styles's pro-woman arguments denounces
the sexual egalitarianism professed by the ideological heirs—the

dissenters—of the Civil War sectarians. Seeing a political opportunity in the Lady's speech, Styles proposes that England enact an "Anti-Salique Law" because *"such a Law as this may charm the Dissenters, who you know Love Novelties, have had great Influence over the Female Sex."* Exasperated by Styles's changeableness, Nokes urges him to *"leave these Fancies"* and conclude their debate. Styles indicates that he took the Lady's part in order to curry favor, behavior typical, Astell implies, of the dissenters: *"O Sir, there's nothing like* Compounding, *especially for Men who are Modest and not over confident of their Cause."*[15]

Part satire and part gender polemic, the dialogue between Styles and Nokes with the interjection from the Lady illustrates Astell's efforts to transcend the terms of party politics while advancing the cause of women. Entering the scene with the righteous femaleness of Anne's authority, the Lady (seemingly unaware of Styles's earlier discussion of dissenting women) genders party politics masculine and truth feminine. Indeed, the Lady goes so far as to claim that women have an abiding commitment to the Constitution, and thus she implicitly attributes political changeableness to men: "Women know very well, that England is not now to Chuse what shall Be *the Constitution,* but honestly and vigorously to Maintain that which is so. At least till these great Politicians have thought fit to inform us what is wanting to its Perfection."[16] And while Astell's "fellow" Tory Nokes ascribes a similar quality of moderation to women, he fails to assess female virtues accurately. Astell's Lady must chastise him for insisting that when women accomplish great deeds they act above their sex. Through the figures of Nokes and the Lady, Astell asserts that female authority, like the Constitution, transcends the realm of party politics. In particular, Astell appears to use the Lady's interjection to urge her readers to recognize female authority as distinct from the political controversies of the day. Indeed, the figure of the Lady reinforces Astell's commitment to the naturalness of and constitutional sanction for female authority.

In addition to revealing Astell's self-conscious efforts to distinguish female political right from party politics, the excursus on female authority in *Moderation truly Stated* represents the one instance when she invokes the legacy of the Civil War female prophets. Astell does not directly refer to the women prophets *per se* but she does, through the character of Styles, attest to the

prominent role of women among the dissenters. This is significant because she repeatedly insists throughout her writings on
Occasional Conformity that the dissenters of her own day are
heirs to the legacy of the Civil War regicides: "But when their
Forefathers had got the Purse and Power into their hands, which
is all that is wanted by their Successors, what followed? I tremble
to think! . . . the most detestable Murder of the best of Kings."[17]
Further, her critique of contemporary dissenting women evokes
satirical descriptions, such as Swift's in *A Discourse Concerning
the Mechanical Operation of the Spirit*, of the feminine and
lower class character of the enthusiasts who wreaked, by conservative lights, such havoc at mid-century.[18] Styles urges Nokes to
recognize that many women participate in the dissenting "faction," a group whose power derives from numbers and not social
position: "*I grant you, Sir, that to* contemplate them [dissenters]
in their proper Forms and Ranks, *they are not very considerable. For* they have in Communion with them none of the Nobility
. . . However, they seem very far from despicable as wanting
Numbers. *For you are to know, that they have* not a few of the
Female Sex, more Sea-faring Men, likewise very many Tradesmen, or Retailers, Artificers, Manufacturers and Day-Labour-
ers." Styles's portrait of the relationship between class and
gender strikingly allies women with the lower sort. Clearly, Astell
does not identify with these women in the way that she does with
the upper-class and gentry women who constitute *Serious Proposal*'s intended audience. In her mind, dissenting women are,
to borrow a phrase from a diatribe against women prophets, a
"brazen-faced" lot much like those "Tradesmen" and "Day-
Labourers" who similarly do not respect the conventions of traditional social order.[19] This gaggle of women and laborers, she implies, attempts to make up in numbers for what they lack in
social position.

    While Astell criticizes the seditious character of the dissenting
women, she also, as Perry observes, admires their bold assertions of political authority: "It is as if Astell could allow herself to
imagine rebelliousness only in the ranks of the Dissenter women,
but that once imagined, she was carried away by her enthusiasm
for women's power."[20] On one level, the Dissenter women spur
her to contemplate female authority and serve as the anti-type of
Astell's vision of female right. Against these women, she presents Anne and legions of unnamed women who uphold the Constitution. Yet, on another level, Perry is right to suggest that

Astell is entranced by Styles's vision of women putting themselves at "the Head of . . . Multitudes" and making "a formidable
Insurrection." The accounts of women such as Agrippina, whose
authority surpasses that of men, certainly do, as Perry would
have it, capture Astell's imagination: "Did not Agrippina the Wife
of Germanicus oppose her Courage to the Cowardice of the Men,
and in the time of a great Consternation among the Roman
Troops discharge all the Duties of a General? Review the Legions, march amidst the Roman Ensigns, make Donatives to the
Soldiers, having more Authority in the Army than all the Generals, for she appeas'd a Mutiny, when the Name of the Emperor
had been of no Consideration?"[21] While Astell derides the politics
of mob violence, her portrait of Agrippina suggests that the
dissenting women's bid for authority may not be an entirely out-
landish proposition. She does not celebrate Agrippina's extraor-
dinariness but rather her ability to guide the army as any
comparable man might: she reviews troops, marches amidst the
ensigns, and makes donations to soldiers. For Astell, powerful
women do not act above their sex but rather, they simply act, and
in so doing reveal the naturalness of female authority.

Perhaps informed by her rendering of Agrippina and other formidable women in *Moderation truly Stated*, the Preface appeals
to Scripture to assert that female authority need not always be
viewed as extraordinary. For Astell, as for Fell, the enlightened
attitudes toward women found in Scripture do not mirror her
contemporary milieu but they do suggest the enhanced authority
God permits women. While men have restrained women for
ages, Scripture, she insists, points to a better way. Although
Astell reveals the Bible to be full of instances of women who governed husbands and even nations, she initially undercuts Scripture as an authoritative source for arguments about women's
political status. At the outset, she pointedly contends that the
purpose of Scripture is to fashion "excellent Moralists and Perfect Christians, not great Philosophers" (13–14). Further, she insists "that Disputes of this kind, extending to Human Nature in
general, and not peculiar to those to whom the Word of God has
been reveal'd, ought to be decided by natural Reason only" (13).
The debate over the natural inferiority of women is not a question for Scripture although her adversaries might fly "to Authority, especially to Divine, which is infallible, and therefore ought
not to be disputed" (14). Immediately prior to launching her "History of Women," however, she will pronounce Scripture the perfect source for information about God's views of women: "And

because there is not any thing more certain than what is delivered in the Oracles of GOD, we come now to consider what they offer in favour of our Sex" (22). Although she initially repudiates Scripture as a source of knowledge in the debate over female inferiority, she now deems it the most "certain" vessel of such knowledge.

How might we account for Astell's opposed attitudes toward Scripture as an authority on general matters of human nature? Two strategies—one philosophical and the other rhetorical—seem to be at work. Her initial concern about the scope of Scripture's authority stems from her ambivalence toward Paul as an authority on women's place within the church and the domestic order. (This is not a position unique to Astell but one that echoes George Fox's approach to Paul.) She questions Scripture as an authority on "Human Nature" precisely at the points in her text in which she attempts to redress conventional misogynous readings of Paul's letters to the Corinthians and to Timothy.[22] She suggests, for instance, that Paul's insistence on "Woman's" subjection to men refers only to wives and not women in general and illustrates not female inferiority but the Church's inferiority vis-à-vis Christ (20, 21). Despite her efforts to present Paul's writings as favorable to women, she may wish to lessen their force in the debate over women's "natural inferiority," and so she diminishes their status as a valid source of commentary on the topic. Moreover, she observes that Paul's arguments against women's speaking in the church are not expressed as divine commands but as his own opinions: "Now by this Comparison we find, that tho' he forbids Women to teach in the Church, and this for several Prudential Reasons, like those he introduces with an *I give my Opinion, and now speak I not the Lord,* and not because of any Law of Nature, or Positive Divine Precept, for that the words *they are Commanded* (I Cor. 14.24.) are not in the Original, appears from the *Italic* Character" (20). Paul's writings on women's role in the church should be received then as a matter of prudence and custom and not as a "Positive Divine Precept."

The second reason Astell initially eschews Scripture as a means for pursuing her case for female authority may be purely rhetorical. Her strategy appears to be to demonstrate why Scripture contains instances of misogynous diatribe and then to show that despite this tendency she can still find numerous examples in Scripture which support female authority. For instance, early in the Preface, she insists that Scripture has typically served to advance her male adversaries' arguments against women because men control its text and interpretation: "But Scripture is not always on their side who make parade of it, and thro' their skill in Languages and the Tricks of the Schools, wrest it from its genuine sense to their own Inventions" (14). Because men possess the "tricks" to "wrest" Scripture "from its genuine sense," they may all the more easily use it to argue for the "natural inferiority" of women. When she finally does appeal to Scripture on behalf of women, she makes much of Scripture's supposed misogyny in order to make greater claims for the pro-woman examples she illuminates:

> Let it be premis'd . . . that One Text for us, is more to be regarded than many against us. Because that *One* being different from what Custom has establish'd, ought to be taken with Philosophical Strictness; whereas the *Many* being express'd according to the vulgar Mode of Speech, ought to have no greater stress laid on them, than that evident Condescension will bear. One place then were sufficient, but we have many Instances wherein Holy Scripture considers Women very differently from what they appear in the common Prejudices of Mankind. (22–23)

Because Scripture bears testimony not only to God's word but to the "common Prejudices of Mankind," one might expect few affirming examples of female authority, but surprisingly Astell discovers "many Instances." Astell emphasizes secular influences on Scripture to illustrate the authenticity of its pro-woman examples. Indeed, she suggests that Scripture is most clearly of God when it shows women assuming leadership roles and being presented "very differently from what they appear in the common Prejudices of Mankind."

Astell's vision of Scripture as both a record of God's will and of human nature makes her "History of Women" very different from Fell's account of God's will "concerning women." When she proclaims her intention to write a "History," Astell signals her interest in Scripture as both sacred and secular history: "Considering how much the Tyranny shall I say, or the superior Force of Men, keeps Women from Acting in the World, or doing any thing considerable, and remembering withal the conciseness of the Sacred Story, no small part of it is bestow'd in transmitting the History of Women famous in their Generations" (23). Although she had previously proposed to invoke Scripture as the "Oracles of God" to defend women from charges of natural inferiority, she now deems the Bible a "sacred" text that also contains historical accounts of women "Acting in the World" and becoming "famous in their Generations." Her celebration of fame surprisingly allies her with Milton's Dalila who, when she relinquishes her penitential posture before Samson, insists that her memory will be revered by the Philistines: "I shall be nam'd among the famousest/ Of Women, sung at solemn festivals."[23] Indeed Astell's set of examples of "famous" women includes not only admirable female figures such as Deborah, Elizabeth, and Anna but also women who were at odds with God's will. For instance, she does not denounce Miriam for her part in the unsuccessful uprising against Moses: "Is she to be blam'd for her Ambition?" (23). Rather, she commends Miriam's capacity to earn the respect of her peers: "nor cou'd she have mov'd Sedition if she had not been a considerable Person, which appears also by the Respect the People paid her, in deferring their Journey till she was ready" (23–24).[24] Miriam is not the only woman to wield power at cross purposes to the divine will whom Astell praises. She also observes that "the wicked *Athaliah* had power to carry on her Intrigues so far as to get possession of the Throne, and to keep it for some Years" (25). Clearly, the fact that Asa felt compelled to remove his mother from the throne illustrates her power. He would not have had to take such an action had her authority been "merely Titular" (25). And finally, Jezebel proved herself to have "Influence . . . in *Israel* . . . to her Husband's and her own Destruction" (25). As she insists throughout the Preface, the Bible articulates the mores and values of those who produced it, hence its accounts of influential and powerful women prove all the more surprising and authoritative.

While Fell's reading of Scripture locates female authority in a unique bond between women and Christ, Astell locates female authority in the fact that women have wielded power. Some of the women she documents gain power through sheer determination, and others receive their authority from God. She, as female readers of Scripture before her, places special emphasis on the account of Deborah: "But *Deborah's* Government was confer'd on her by GOD Himself. Consequently the Sovereignty of a Woman is not contrary to the Law of GOD, for the Law of Nature is the Law of GOD, who cannot contradict Himself" (24).[25] Fell also appealed to Deborah but only to notice that "God made no difference, but gave his good Spirit, as it pleased him both to Man and Woman, as *Deborah*" (11). For Astell, on the other hand, Deborah illustrates more than God's willingness to confer his "good Spirit" on both men and women. She becomes the vehicle through which God proclaims the naturalness of female sovereignty. The key difference between Fell and Astell is that the for mer implies the political significance of God's attentions to women while the latter emphasizes the secular consequences of divine intervention. Her secular concerns notwithstanding, Astell is every bit as preoccupied with providence as her Quaker counterpart. Hers is a providential vision, however, that prizes individual agency to a much greater extent. Deborah and Miriam belong in the same history because both acted in the world. Although Miriam exercised her authority in a manner that contradicted God's will, her possession of authority itself was not outside the bounds of divine sanction or of the Hebrews' social milieu. In Astell's vision, divine authority is not the absolute standard it was for her Quaker predecessor. Fell could celebrate female sexuality but only because Christ celebrated it too. Whereas, by Astell's reckoning, God may not have approved of the form that Miriam's quest for power took but would not necessarily have opposed her possession of power.

The second distinction between Fell's and Astell's interpretations of the role of women in Scripture centers on their approaches to the female body. Fell instantiates a politics of female sexuality while Astell develops the politics of sexual difference. Astell does not celebrate female sexuality as a wellspring of political possibility as Fell had but deems it an ontological fact that should not but does influence women's social position. Unlike Fell, she does not revel in the female body electric but wants to negate the significance of the female body as a determinant of political authority. In response to claims that greater physical strength gives men the right to rule over women, she sarcastically presents a vision of government dominated by the "Highway-Man so long as he has strength to force" (16). Still as much as she believes that political authority should be determined according to rational principles she recognizes that physical force, although not to the degree suggested by her ironic promotion of the highway man's authority, does influence the structure of political power in her own age: "and let the Reason of things be what it may, those who have least Force, or Cunning to supply it, will have the Disadvantage. So that since Women are acknowledg'd to have the least Bodily strength, their being commanded to obey is in pure kindness to them" (15). Women's lack of "Bodily strength" may make them subject to men but this does not necessarily make them their intellectual inferiors: "But does it follow that Domestic Governors have more sense than their Subjects, any more than that other Governors have?" (15–16).

Where Fell had embraced weakness as a feature of female sexuality that granted women a kind of authority, Astell views it as a wholly overvalued mark of sexual difference. Indeed, in a perfect world, she opines, not strength but reason would be the arbiter of political authority. Because of the fall, however, women like the Jews and Christians described in Scripture must continue to be subjected to those who may not be their "natural superiors": "But what says the Holy Scripture? It speaks of Women as in a State of Subjection, and so it does of the *Jews* and *Christians* when under the Dominion of the *Chaldeans* and *Romans*, requiring of the one as well as of the other a quiet submission to them under whose Power they liv'd. But will any one say that these had a *Natural Superiority* and Right to Dominion?" (14). Throughout her writings, Astell pointedly avoids emphasizing the significance of the body. Nevertheless, she espouses a highly reified vision of gender—women are a people apart like the Jews and Christians of old. While Fell commended the specific attributes of women, she did not focus to the same degree on women's difference from men. She merely illuminated the positive attributes of female sexuality. Astell, on the other hand, wants very much not to talk about the female body, yet, at the same time, she maintains that the female body makes women different from men and constitutes women as a distinct people. Where Fell had underscored the politics of the female body, Astell recasts the female body in political terms. As historian Thomas Laquer might put it, Astell inhabits a two sex world in which the differences between male and female prove incommensurable while Fell, although certainly moving in the same direction, does not articulate a definitive rupture between male and female.[26]

For Mary Astell, female sexual difference is much more bound up with female identity than it was for Margaret Fell. While Fell certainly celebrated female sexual difference, she did not imagine this difference as a source of otherness but rather as a means through which women could enjoy a unique intimacy with Christ, a means through which they could experience mystical union. This is not the case for Astell. Indeed, when she refers to Mary's relationship to Christ—an instance which assumes strong mystical overtones in Fell's rendering—she portrays the mother-son bond as a kind of exchange: "the Holy Virgin receiving the greatest Honour that Human Nature is capable of, when the Son of GOD vouchsafed to be her Son and to derive his Humanity from her only" (26–27). Like two parties in a contract negotiation, Christ offers honor while Mary provides humanity. Astell's vision of the female body is one devoid of mystical possibility. Rather, it is a source of political facts, the capacity to give birth being one of these. Although she presents a disembodied image of sexual difference, the female body remains present in her thoughts as she defines her political identity in terms of sexual difference.

While she insists that women's political and sexual difference has resulted in their subjection, Astell does not view the fact of difference as an essentially negative attribute. At the close of the Preface, she enthusiastically projects a vision of the future in which women's difference persists but no longer signifies subjection. In one of the most enthusiastic moments of her entire *oeuvre*, she looks forward "to the Halcyon, or if you will *Millennium* Days, in which the Wolf and the Lamb shall feed together, and a Tyrannous Domination which Nature never meant, shall no longer render useless if not hurtful, the Industry and Understandings of half Mankind!" (31). She hopes that God's intervention in secular affairs will bring about not a celebration of female sexuality but a world order in which the two very different sexes coexist as equals—"the Wolf and the Lamb shall feed together." Significantly, Astell draws her apocalyptic vision of sexual equality from an Isaiah who seeks to comfort a people recently returned from exile in Babylon: "For, behold, I create new heavens and a new earth: and the former shall not be remembered, nor come into mind." Like the prophet himself, she encourages her *people*—women—with the promise of sexual equality, of a new Jerusalem in which "the voice of weeping shall be no more heard."[27] Astell embraces apocalyptic as a vehicle through which she imagines an earthly paradise for women. Although not in such explicitly feminist terms, the Fifth Monarchist prophet Mary Cary similarly invokes apocalyptic, and in her case the prophecies of Joel, to imagine women assuming the traditional male role of preacher: "And if there be very few men that are thus furnished with this gift of the Spirit; how few are the women! Not but that there are many godly women, many who have indeed received the Spirit: but in how small a measure is it? how weak are they? and how unable to prophesie? for it is that I am speaking of, which this text says they shall do; which yet we see not fulfilled."[28] For both the radical sectarian and the conservative Tory, apocalyptic provides a unique religio-political language for articulating female ambition.

Astell's vision of the wolf and the lamb peacefully coexisting comes directly out of Isaiah but her enthusiastic rendering of the image appears spurred as much by secular as sacred influences. She leads up to her vision of sexual equality through a lengthy meditation on Queen Anne's role as standard bearer for the female sex. In a passage that evokes Lady Eleanor's praise of the first Stuart monarch, James, Astell enumerates the accomplishments of the last Stuart:

> To conclude, if that GREAT QUEEN who has subdu'd the Proud, and made the pretended Invincible more than once fly before her; who has Rescu'd an Empire, Reduc'd a Kingdom, Conquer'd Provinces in as little time almost as one can Travel them, and seems to have Chain'd Victory to her Standard; who . . . is the chief Instrument in the Hand of the Almighty to pull down and to set up the Great Men of the Earth; who Conquers everywhere for others . . . whilst she only reaps for her self the Lawrels of Disinteressed Glory, and the Royal Pleasure of doing Heroically. (30–31)

Of course, Anne's monarchical power was far less than that of James, but Astell focuses on her position as the leading political authority in the nation to fashion her into a second Elizabeth. In addition to detailing Anne's various accomplishments on the national and international scenes, Astell emphasizes her role as a galvanizing force for women: "To all the great things that Women might perform, Inspir'd by her Example, Encourag'd by her Smiles, and supported by her Power! To their Discovery of New Worlds for the Exercise of her Goodness, New Sciences to publish her Fame, and reducing Nature itself to a Subjection to her Empire!" (31). Astell celebrates Anne as the embodiment of "all the great things Women might perform." From her apotheosis of her Queen, she tellingly moves to her vision of a millennium in which sexual equality prevails. For Astell, Anne attests to the imminence of a "New Jerusalem" free from sexual oppression in the same way that the presence of preaching "daughters" signals, for the Quaker Hester Biddle, Joel's prophesied "day of great Salvation." The combination of Anne's achievements coupled with the language of divine providence found in Isaiah stirs Astell, in words that resounded powerfully for so many of the women addressed in this book, to "dream dreams" and "see visions."

With Astell's paean to the last Stuart, we have come full circle from Lady Eleanor's devotion to the first Stuart. Unlike Lady Eleanor, Astell did not profess to derive her authority from her monarch but rather held up the Queen as a model upon whom she and other women might found their identities as political actors. For Astell, Anne provides a link between the Bible's "History of Women" and her millennial vision of sexual equality. The structure of the Preface tacitly identifies women such as Deborah and Miriam as evidence that women have acted (and at times under God's direct command) in the world, while the example of Anne proves that the tradition of female achievement, despite being suppressed by men, is far from dead. Indeed, at the end of time, she hopes, this latent yet ever present tradition will finally come into the light and gain universal acceptance. From an apocalyptic perspective, her myth of origins of a female tradition resembles the early Protestant appeal to the account of the travails of the woman clothed with the sun in Revelation to explain why the true church had remained dormant for so many centuries. Their faith was not a wholly new thing but merely something that had been suppressed by the evil dragon.[29] At the same time that Astell constitutes a recognizably secular female tradition, she relies heavily upon providential history in order to articulate fully her vision of female equality. Her narrative links women's advancement and divine authority in a manner akin to the female prophets of the English Revolution and in so doing attests to the integral role of visionary poetics and politics in early feminism.

Appendix: Provisional Checklist of Women Prophets' Published Writings, 1625–1667[1]

1625   Lady Eleanor Davies, *A Warning to the Dragon and All his Angels*

1633   Lady Eleanor Davies, *Woe to the House*
———. *All the kings of the earth shall prayse thee*

1641   Katherine Chidley, *The Justification of the Independent Churches of Christ*
Lady Eleanor Davies, *The Lady Eleanor, Her Appeale to the High Court of Parliament*

1642   Lady Eleanor Davies, *Samsons Fall*

1643   Lady Eleanor Davies, *Amend, Amend; Gods Kingdome is at Hand*
———. *To the Most Honorable the High Court of Parliament*
———. *Samsons Legacie*
———. *The Star to the Wise*

1644   Lady Eleanor Davies, *Apocalypsis Jesu Christi*
———. *The Brides Preparation*
———. *From the Lady Eleanor, Her Blessing to her beloved Daughter*
———. *A Prayer or Petition for Peace*
———. *Prophetia de die*
———. *The Restitution of Reprobates*
———. *The Word of God, To the Citie of London*
Sarah Jones, *To Sions Lovers*

1645   Katherine Chidley, *Good Counsel, To the Petitioners for Presbyterian Government*
———. *A New-Yeares-Gift, Or a Brief Exhortation to Mr. Thomas Edwards*
Lady Eleanor Davies, *As Not Unknowne*
———. *Of errors joyned with Gods word*
———. *Great Brittains Visitation*

215

————. *I am the First, and the Last*
————. *A Prophesie of the Last Day*
————. *The Second Comming of Our Lord*
————. *For Whitson Tyds Last Feast*

1646   Dorothy Burch, *A catechisme of the several heads of Christian religion*
        Lady Eleanor Davies, *For the Blessed Feast of Easter*
        ————. *The Day of Judgments Modell*
        ————. *The Gatehouse Salutation*
        ————. *The Lady Eleanor Her Appeal*
        ————. *Je le tien: The general Restitution*
        ————. *The Revelation Interpreted*
        Elizabeth Warren, *The Old and Good Way Vindicated*

1647   Elizabeth Avery, *Scripture-prophecies opened*
        Mary Cary, *A Word in Season*
        Lady Eleanor Davies, *The Excommunication out of Paradice*
        ————. *Ezekiel, Cap. 2*
        ————. *Ezekiel the Prophet*
        ————. *The Mystery of General Redemption*
        Mary Pope, *A Treatise of Magistracy*
        Elizabeth Warren, *Spiritual Thrift*

1648   Mary Cary, *The Resurrection of the Witness*
        Lady Eleanor Davies, *Apocalyps, Chap. 11*
        ————. *Of the general Great Days Approach*
        ————. *Given to the Elector*
        ————. *The Lady Eleanor her remonstrance*
        ————. *Reader, the heavy hour at hand*
        ————. *Wherefore to prove the thing*
        ————. *And without proving what we say*
        ————. *The Writ of Restitution*
        Elizabeth Poole, *A Vision*
        ————. *An Alarum of War* (1648/9)
        Sarah Wight, *The Exceeding Riches of Grace* (Henry Jessey, ed.)

1649   Lady Eleanor Davies, *Her Appeal from the Court to Camp*
        ————. *The Bill of Excommunication*
        ————. *The Blasphemous Charge Against Her*
        ————. *The Crying Charge*
        ————. *A Discovery Unto what Nation the last Day aforehand*
        ————. *The Everlasting Gospel*
        ————. *For the most Honorable States*
        ————. *The New Jerusalem At Hand*
        ————. *For the Right Noble, Sir Balthazar Gerbier Knight*

————. *A Sign Given them being entred into the day of Judgment*

————. *Sions Lamentation*

————. *Strange and Wonderful Prophesies*

Anne Hall, *A Brief Representation and Discovery*

Thomasine Pendarves, "A Letter" in Elizabeth Poole's *An Alarum* (1649)

Elizabeth Poole, *An Alarum of War*

————. *A Prophecie Touching the Death of King Charles*

Mary Pope, *Behold, here is a word*

Elizabeth Warren, *A Warning-Peece from Heaven*

1650   Lady Eleanor Davies, *The Appearance or Presence of the Son of Man*

————. *The Arraignment*

————. *Before the Lords Second Coming*

————. *Elijah the Tishbite's Supplication*

————. *The Lady Eleanor Douglas, Dowger, Her Jubilees Plea or Appeal*

Sarah Jones, *This is the Light's Appearance*

1651   Mary Cary, *Little Horns Doom & Downfall*

————. *A new And More Exact Mappe Or, Description of New Jerusalems Glory*

Lady Eleanor Davies, *The Benediction. From the A:lmighty O:mnipotent*

————. *The benidiction. I have an errand*

————. *The Dragons Blasphemous Charge*

————. *Hells Destruction*

————. *The Restitution of Prophecy*

————. *The Serpents Excommunication*

————. *Of Times and Seasons Their Mystery*

1652   Lady Eleanor Davies, *Bethlehem Signifying the House of Bread: Or War*

————. *Tobits Book*

Mary Fisher, Jane Holmes, Elizabeth Hooton et al, *False Prophets and Their False Teachers Described*

Jane Holmes. *See* Mary Fisher

Elizabeth Hooton. *See* Mary Fisher

1653   Mary Cary, *Twelve New Proposals*

Elinor Channel, *A Message from God (by a Dumb Woman) To his Highness the Lord Protector* (Arise Evans, ed.)

Martha Hatfield, *The Wise Virgin* (James Fisher, ed.)

Jane Turner, *Choice Experiences*

1654   Anna Trapnel, *The Cry of a Stone*
        ———. *A Legacy for Saints*
        ———. *Strange and Wonderful News from White-Hall*
        ———. *Report and Plea*

1655   Anne Audland and Jane Waugh, *A True Declaration of the Suf-*
            ferings of the Innocent
        Anne Audland, "A Warning from the Spirit of the Lord," in *The*
            Saints Testimony Finishing through Sufferings
        ———. "A Testimony against False Prophets," in *The Saints*
            Testimony Finishing through Sufferings
        Hester Biddle, *Wo to thee City of Oxford*
        ———. *Wo to thee town of Cambridge*
        Margaret Braidley and Christopher Taylor, *Certain Papers which*
            is the Word of God
        Mary Cole. *See* Priscilla Cotton
        Priscilla Cotton and Mary Cole, *To the Priests and People of En-*
            gland
        Margaret Fell et al., *False Prophets, Anticrists*
        Martha Simmonds, *A Lamentation for the Lost Sheep*
        ———. *When the Lord Jesus Came*
        Jane Waugh, *See* Anne Audland

1656   Priscilla Cotton, *As I was in the Prison-house*
        Margaret Fell, *For Manasseth Ben Israel. The Call of the Jewes*
        ———. *A Loving Salutation to the Seed of Abraham*
        ———. *A Testimonie Of The Touch-Stone*
        Ann Gargill, *A Brief Discovery of that which is called the Popish*
            Religion
        ———. *A Warning to all the World*
        Margaret Killin and Barbara Pattison, *A Warning from the Lord*
            to the Teachers & People of Plimouth
        Barbara Pattison, see Margaret Killin
        Martha Simmonds et al., *O England; thy time is come* (1656–65)
        Hannah Stranger, "Consider I beseech you" in Martha Sim-
            monds et al. *O England*
        Dorothy Waugh, "A Relation" in *The Lambs Defence*
        Sarah Wight, *A Wonderful Pleasant and Profitable Letter*

1657   Susannah Bateman, *I matter not how I appear to man*
        Jeane Bettris, *A Lamentation for the Deceived People of the*
            World
        ———. *Spiritual Discoveries*
        Margaret Greenway, *A Lamentation against the Professing*
            Priest and the People of Oxford
        Mary Howgill, *A Remarkable Letter of Mary Howgill to Oliver*
            Cromwell

1658   Sarah Blackborow, *A Visit to the Spirit in Prison*
       Anna Trapnel, *A Voice for the King of Saints and Nations*
       ———. Untitled book of verse in Bodleian Library, Shelf-mark
       S.1.42.Th.

1659   Margaret Abbott, *A Testimony Against the False Teachers*
       Grace Barwick, *To all present Rulers*
       Hester Biddle, *Oh! wo, wo, from the Lord*
       ———. *To the inhabitants of the town of Dartmouth*
       ———. "Something in short" in Thomas Woodrow's *A brief*
       Sarah Blackborow, *Herein is held forth the Gift and Goodwill of
           God to the World*
       Priscilla Cotton, *A Briefe Description by way of supposition
           holding forth to the Parliament*
       Judith Eedes, *A Warning to All the Inhabitants of the Earth*
       Margaret Fell, "Concerning ministers" in her *A Paper*
       ———. *A Paper concerning such as are made ministers*
       ———. *To the Generall Councill of Officers of the English Army*
       ———. *To the General Councel*
       Mary Forster et al., *These several papers was sent to Parlia-
           ment*
       Ann Gould et al., *An Epistle to all Christian Magistrates*
       Margaret Lynam, *For the Parliament sitting at Westminster*
       Susannah Parr, *Susanna's Apologie against the Elders*
       Rebeckah Travers, *For Those that meet to worship at the Stee-
           plehouse*
       ———. *Of that Eternal Breath*
       ———. *This is for any of that generation* (1659/60)
       Mary Webb, *I being moved of the Lord*
       Dorothy White, *A Diligent Search against Rulers, Priests, Pro-
           fessors and people*
       ———. *This is to be delivered to the Counsellors*
       ———. *Upon the 22nd day of the 8th month, 1659*

1660   Hester Biddle, *A warning from the Lord God of life*
       Sarah Blackborow, *The Just and Equal Balance discovered*
       Anne Clayton, *A letter to the King*
       Margaret Fell, *The citie of London reprov'd*
       ———. *A Declaration And An Information*
       ———. *An evident Demonstration to Gods Elect*
       ———. *This is to the Clergy*
       ———. *This Was Given to Major Generall Harrison*
       ———. *A True Testimony*
       Elizabeth Fletcher, *A few Words in Season To all*
       Dorothy White, *A lamentation unto this nation*
       ———. *Unto All Gods Host in England*
       ———. *A Visitation Of Heavenly Love*

1661   Mary Booth, "Preface" to James Nayler's *Milk for Babes*
       Priscilla Cotton, *A visitation of love unto all people*
       Dorothea Scott Gotherson, *To all that are Unregenerated*
       Dorothy White, *An Alarm Sounded To Englands Inhabitants*
       ———. *An Epistle of Love, and of Consolation*

1662   Mary Anderdon, *A Word to the World*
       Hester Biddle, *The trumpet of the Lord God*
       ———. *The trumpet of the Lord sounded*
       Sarah Blackborow, *The oppressed prisoners complaint*
       Joan Brooksop, *An Invitation of Love*
       Sarah Cheevers. *See* Katharine Evans
       Katharine Evans and Sarah Cheevers, *This is a Short Relation*
       Anne Gilman, *An Epistle to Friends*
       ———. *To the Inhabitants of the Earth*
       Mary Howgill, *The Vision Of The Lord of Hosts*
       Dorothy White, *An Alarum Sounded forth*
       ———. *A Call from God out of Egypt*
       ———. *Friends. You that are of the Parliament*
       ———. *Greetings of pure Peace*
       ———. *A Trumpet of the Lord*
       ———. *The Voice of the Lord*

1663   Sarah Blackborow, "Dear Friend" in Richard Hubberthorne's *A Collection*
       Sarah Chevers, *To all the people upon the face of the earth, a sweet salutation*
       Katharine Evans, *A Brief Discovery of God's Eternal Truth*
       ———. *A True Account*
       Rebeckah Travers, *A testimony concerning the light*
       Dorothy White, *To all those that Worship*
       Judith Zins-penninck, *Some Worthy Proverbs*

1664   Margaret Fell, *To the magistrates and people of England*
       ———. *Two General Epistles To the Flock of God*
       Rebeckah Travers, *This is for all or any*

1665   Judith Boulbie, *A Testimony for Truth against all hireling priests*
       Margaret Fell, *A Call to the Universall Seed of God*
       Dewans Morey, *A true and faithful Warning*

1666   Margaret Fell, *A Letter Sent to the King*
       ———. *Womens Speaking Justified*

1667   Margaret Fell, *The Standard of the Lord Revealed*
      ———. *A Touch-Stone, Or, A Perfect Tryal*
      ———. *Womens Speaking Justified* (second edition)
      Mary Smith, *These few lines are to all*

Date unclear but from the period:
Priscilla Cotton, *A testimony of truth to all Friends*

Notes

INTRODUCTION: POLITICAL SPEAKING JUSTIFIED

1. I refer throughout to Lady Eleanor Davies as Lady Eleanor. In so doing, I follow her biographer Esther S. Cope who observes that the prophet frequently used "Lady Eleanor" as the signature for her published writings. See Cope's *Handmaid of the Holy Spirit: Dame Eleanor Davies, Never Soe Mad a Ladie* (Ann Arbor: The University of Michigan Press, 1992), 5.

2. Stephen L. Collins, *From Divine Cosmos to Sovereign State* (New York: Oxford, 1989), 5.

3. In her study of English Revolution era female radicals, Hilary Hinds also emphasizes the literariness of these texts but does so in terms of contemporary feminist literary theory. See her *God's Englishwomen: Seventeenth-Century Radical Sectarian Writing and Feminist Criticism* (Manchester: Manchester University Press, 1996). As distinct from Hinds's work, my approach to the literariness of the women prophets' writings is very much influenced by historicist scholarship on Civil War radicals both male and female. See especially Sharon Achinstein, *Milton and the Revolutionary Reader* (Princeton: Princeton University Press, 1994); Clement Hawes, *Mania and Literary Style: The Rhetoric of Enthusiasm from the Ranters to Christopher Smart* (Cambridge: Cambridge University Press, 1996); James Holstun, "Ranting at the New Historicism," *ELR* 19:2 (1989): 189–225 and Introduction to *Pamphlet Wars: Prose in the English Revolution* (London: Frank Cass, 1992), 1–13; and Nigel Smith, *Perfection Proclaimed: Language and Literature in English Radical Religion 1640–1660* (Oxford: Clarendon Press, 1989) and *Literature and the English Revolution 1640–1660* (New Haven: Yale University Press, 1994).

4. Christine Berg and Philippa Berry, " 'Spiritual Whoredom': An Essay on Female Prophets in the Seventeenth Century," in *1642: Literature and Power in the Seventeenth Century: Proceedings of the Essex Conference on the Sociology of Literature, July 1980*, eds. Francis Barker et al., (Colchester: University of Essex, 1981), 38.

5. Margaret Fell, *A Declaration and an Information From us the People of God called Quakers* (London: 1660), 2.

6. Elaine Hobby, *Virtue of Necessity: English Women's Writing 1649–88* (London: Virago, 1988), 26; Phyllis Mack, *Visionary Women: Ecstatic Prophecy in Seventeenth-Century England* (Berkeley: University of California Press, 1992), 1.

7. See the appendix: Provisional Checklist of Women Prophets' Published Writings, 1625–67 on pp. 215–21.

8. Richard Bell and Patricia Crawford, Appendix 2: "Statistical Analysis of

Women's Printed Writings 1600–1700," in *Women in English Society 1500–1800,* ed. Mary Prior (London: Methuen, 1985), 269.

9. According to Bell and Crawford's research, the number of women's published first editions declined markedly in the first two decades of the Restoration but reached the levels of the revolutionary period in the closing decades of the century. See their "Statistical Analysis," 269.

10. Hester Biddle, *The Trumpet of the Lord Sounded forth unto these Three Nations* (London: 1662), 3; Mary Cary, *Little Horns Doom & Downfall* (London: 1651), 42, 46. See also Dan. 7.

11. Biblically inspired prophetic movements continue to play a significant, if frequently overlooked, role in contemporary American politics and culture. Two interesting entries among many on this topic are A. G. Mojtabai's discussion of the "Rapture" movement in her *Blessed Assurance: At Home with the Bomb in Amarillo, Texas* (Boston: Houghton Mifflin, 1986) and Dennis Covington's *Salvation on Sand Mountain:: Snake Handling and Redemption in Southern Appalachia* (Reading, MA: Addison-Wesley, 1995).

12. For Huldah's story, see 2 Kings 22 and 2 Chron. 34.

13. Joseph Besse, *A Collection of the Sufferings of the People called Quakers* (London: 1753), 1: 42–43.

14. Barbara Kiefer Lewalski, *Writing Women in Jacobean England* (Cambridge, MA: Harvard University Press, 1993), 4; Mack, *Visionary Women,* 94; Dorothy Paula Ludlow, "'Arise and Be Doing,' English 'Preaching' Women, 1640–60" (Ph.D. diss., Indiana University, 1978), 33, 342.

15. Dorothy P. Ludlow, "Shaking Patriarchy's Foundations: Sectarian Women in England 1641–1700," in *Triumph over Silence: Women in Protestant History,* ed. Richard L. Greaves (Westport, CT: Greenwood Press, 1985), 104.

16. Ellen A. McArthur, "Women Petitioners and the Long Parliament," *English Historical Review* 24 (1909): 704; N. H. Keeble, "Obedient Subjects? The Loyal Self in Some Later Seventeenth-Century Royalist Women's Memoirs," in *Culture and Society in the Stuart Restoration,* ed. Gerald Maclean, (Cambridge: Cambridge University Press, 1995), 209, 210; Lady Eleanor, *The Restitution of Prophecy,* in *Prophetic Writings of Lady Eleanor Davies,* ed. Esther S. Cope (New York: Oxford University Press, 1995), 365; Dorothy White, *A Diligent Search* (1659), 4.

17. Keith Thomas, "Women and the Civil War Sects," *Past and Present* 13 (1958): 44. For more on the relationship between sectarian ideology and women prophets see Sue Wiseman, "Unsilent Instruments and the Devil's Cushions: Authority in Seventeenth-Century Women's Prophetic Discourse," in *New Feminist Discourses,* ed. Isobel Armstrong, (London: Routledge, 1992), 176–96.

18. George Fox, Epistle CCXCI: "To all the women's meetings, that are believers in the truth" (1672), in *The Works of George Fox* (1831; reprint New York: AMS Press, 1975), 8: 39; Thomas, "Women and the Civil War Sects," 47; Mack, *Visionary Women,* 122.

19. Ludlow, "Shaking Patriarchy's Foundations," 115. For similar developments among a related and contemporary group of female activists, the women petitioners see Ann Marie McEntee, "The [Un] Civill-Sisterhood of Oranges and Lemons: Female Petitioners and Demonstrators, 1642–53," in *Pamphlet Wars: Prose in the English Revolution,* ed. James Holstun (London: Frank Cass, 1992), 109. For more on the women petitioners, see Patricia Higgins, "The Reactions of Women, with Special Reference to Women Petitioners," in *Politics, Religion, and the English Revolution,* ed. Brian Manning, 179–97 (London:

Edward Arnold, 1973); Ann Hughes, "Gender and Politics in Leveller Litera-ture," in *Political Culture and Cultural Politics in Early Modern England*, eds. Susan D. Amussen and Mark A. Kishlansky, (Manchester: Manchester University Press, 1995), 162–88; and Ellen A. McArthur, "Women Petitioners and the Long Parliament," *English Historical Review* 24 (1909): 698–709.

20. Thomas, "Women and the Civil War Sects," 52.

21. Katharine Evans, "To her Husband and Children," in Katharine Evans and Sarah Chevers, *This is a Short Relation of Some of the Cruel Sufferings . . . in the Inquisition in the Isle of Malta* (1662), in *Hidden in Plain Sight: Quaker Women's Writings 1650–1700*, eds. Mary Garman et al. (Wallingford, PA: Pendle Hill Publications, 1996), 204; Sarah Chevers, "To her Husband and Children," in *This is a Short Relation*, 206; Evans, "To her Husband and Children," 205. Rosemary Kegl compellingly argues that Evans and Chevers's use of matrimo-nial language to describe their relationship to one another effectively "unsettles the logic of companionate marriages." See her "Women's Preaching, Absolute Property, and the Cruel Sufferings (For the Truths sake) of Katharine Evans and Sarah Chevers," *Women's Studies* 24 (1994): 70.

22. Rachel Trubowitz has importantly argued that women prophets' words could be appropriated by male sectarians or other interested male authorities. See her "Female Preachers and Male Wives: Gender and Authority in Civil War England," in *Pamphlet Wars: Prose in the English Revolution*, ed. James Hol-stun (London: Frank Cass, 1992), 113–14. One notable exception is the prolific Lady Eleanor who subsidized the publication of her texts herself.

23. Mack, *Visionary Women*, 97. One notable exception is the prolific Lady Eleanor who subsidized the publication of her texts herself.

24. Hugh Peter, preface to *Little Horns Doom & Downfall*, by Mary Cary (London: 1651), a1v–a2r.

25. Assertions of the chosen status of the "middle sort" are a commonplace of much radical sectarian writing. See George Foster, *The Sounding of the Last Trumpet* (1650), 17–18 and John Tillinghast, *Generation-work* (London, 1655), 71–72.

26. Claire Cross, " 'He-goats before the Flocks': a note on the part played by women in the founding of some Civil War churches," in *Popular Belief and Practice*, eds. G. J. Cumming and Derek Baker, 202 (Cambridge: Cambridge University Press, 1972); Cross, " 'Great Reasoners in Scripture': The Activities of Women Lollards," in *Medieval Women*, ed. Derek Baker (Oxford: Basil Blackwell, 1978), 360, 371, 378.

27. Diane Willen, "Women and Religion in Early Modern England," in *Women in Reformation and Counter-Reformation Europe*, ed. Sherrin Mar-shall (Bloomington: Indiana University Press, 1989), 144; John Bale, commen-tary on *The Examinations of Anne Askew*, ed. Elaine V. Beilin (New York: Oxford University Press, 1996), 50.

28. "B. of London. Puretans," in *The Early English Dissenters*, comp. Champlin Burrage (Cambridge: Cambridge University Press, 1912), 2: 15–16; "In the Court of High Commission," in *Early English Dissenters*, 2: 315–16.

29. John Bale, *The Image of Bothe Churches*, in *Select Works of John Bale, D.D.*, ed. Henry Christmas (Cambridge: The University Press, 1849), 252, 344, 404.

30. Richard Bauckham, *Tudor Apocalypse* (Oxford: The Sutton Courtenay Press, 1978), 13 and Bale, *Image of Bothe Churches*, 253.

31. Bale, *Image of Bothe Churches*, 392; Christopher Hill, *Antichrist in Seventeenth-Century England* (London: Verso, 1990), 44; Paul Christianson,

Reformers and Babylon: English Apocalyptic Visions from the Reformation to the Eve of the Civil War (Toronto: University of Toronto Press, 1978), 5.

32. Christianson, *Reformers and Babylon*, 36; Bauckham, *Tudor Apocalypse*, 75.

33. Christianson, *Reformers and Babylon*, 94; John Napier, *A Plaine Discovery of the Whole Revelation of Saint John* (Edinburgh, 1593), 9, 12. See also Rev. 8:7, 11:15, and 16:2, 17.

34. Christianson, *Reformers and Babylon*, 100; Thomas Brightman, *The Revelation of Saint John* (Amsterdam, 1644), 42.

35. For more on this tradition see, in addition to Bauckham, Christianson, and Hill: Katharine R. Firth, *The Apocalyptic Tradition in Reformation Britain 1530–1645* (Oxford: Oxford University Press, 1979); Peter Toon, ed., *Puritans, the Millennium and the Future of Israel: Puritan Eschatology 1600 to 1660* (Cambridge: James Clark, 1970); and Joseph Wittreich, ed., *The Apocalypse in English Renaissance Thought and Literature* (Ithaca: Cornell University Press, 1984).

36. Katherine Chidley, "To the Christian Reader," in *The Justification of the Independent Churches of Christ* (London: 1641); Priscilla Cotton and Mary Cole, *To the Priests and People of England* (1655), 4; Mary Cary, *Little Horns Doom & Downfall* (London: 1651), 17; Cary, *A New and More Exact Mappe Or, Description of New Jerusalems Glory* (London: 1651), 133, 208–9, 213.

37. Cary, *Little Horns Doom*, 17–18. Similarly, Lois G. Schwoerer has observed that women prophets, though they lacked "a classical education," comprehended and integrated into their own writings the ideas found in contemporary political theory. See her "Women's public political voice in England: 1640–1740," in *Women Writers and the Early Modern British Political Tradition*, ed. Hilda Smith (Cambridge: Cambridge University Press, 1998), 65.

38. *The Lambs Defence Against Lyes* (1656), 29.

39. For an early feminist appreciation of the women prophets, see Ethyn Morgan Williams, "Women Preachers in the Civil War," *Journal of Modern History* 1 (1929): 561–69. See also Ellen A. McArthur's appraisal of a related and contemporary group, "Women Petitioners and the Long Parliament," *English Historical Review* 24 (1909): 698–709.

40. Hilda Smith, *Reason's Disciples: Seventeenth-Century English Feminists* (Urbana: University of Illinios Press, 1982), 9.

41. See Joan K. Kinnaird, "Mary Astell and the Conservative Contribution to English Feminism," *Journal of British Studies* 19:1 (Fall 1979): 53–75; Ruth Perry, *The Celebrated Mary Astell: An Early English Feminist* (Chicago: University of Chicago Press, 1986); Catherine Gallagher, "Embracing the Absolute: The Politics of the Female Subject in Seventeenth-Century England," *Genders* 1:1 (1988), 24–39; and Carol Barash, *English Women's Poetry 1649–1714: Politics, Community, and Linguistic Authority* (Oxford: Clarendon, 1996).

42. Barash, *English Women's Poetry*, 32.

43. Smith, *Reason's Disciples*, xi. Keith Thomas similarly observes that the women prophets had little impact on the history of feminism. See his "Women and the Civil War Sects," 56.

44. Smith, *Reason's Disciples*, x.

45. Hobby, *Virtue of Necessity*, 201. Dorothy Ludlow similarly observes that in comparison with the women prophets, "women in the restored Church of England lead much quieter, less anxious (and less exciting) lives." See her "Shaking Patriarchy's Foundations," 117.

46. Hobby, *Virtue of Necessity*, 48, 53.

47. This is also true for Christine Berg and Philippa Berry who represent the women prophets as a bright spot in a cultural milieu generally oppressive to women. They describe the women prophets as bringing about a short-lived "irruption of female speech into the once tabooed domain of public activity." See their "'Spiritual Whoredom,'" 38.

48. Hobby, *Virtue of Necessity*, 203.

49. Mack, *Visionary Women*, 363, 282.

50. Like Mack, Rachel Trubowitz sees elements of rationalism in the Civil War era female prophetic discourse but argues that it serves to limit the radical potential of women's enthusiasm. See her "Female Preachers and Male Wives," 128.

51. Mack, *Visionary Women*, 411.

52. For another approach to how the women prophets appealed to their bodies to authorize their visions, see Diane Purkiss, "Producing the voice, consuming the body: Women prophets of the seventeenth century," in *Women, Writing, History 1640–1740*, eds. Isobel Grundy and Susan Wiseman (Athens: University of Georgia Press, 1992), 139–58. Purkiss does not historicize the female body in the same way that I do but rather explores how the female visionaries invoked tropes of the body to authorize their public speech.

53. Thomas Laquer, *Making Sex: Body and Gender from the Greeks to Freud* (Cambridge, MA: Harvard University Press, 1990), 79–88, 5–6.

54. C. B. Macpherson, *The Political Theory of Possessive Individualism: Hobbes to Locke* (Clarendon: Oxford University Press, 1962), 3, 153.

CHAPTER 1. IN THE NAME OF THE FATHER

1. *Calendar of State Papers Venetian 1655–56*, in *The Right to be King: The Succession to the Crown of England*, Howard Nenner (Chapel Hill: The University of North Carolina Press, 1995), 84.

2. Nenner, *Right to be King*, 84–85. Cromwell never formally accepted the title of king, but, according to Kevin Sharpe, he assumed many of the trappings of monarchy. See his "'An Image Doting Rabble': The Failure of Republican Culture in Seventeenth-Century England," in *Refiguring Revolutions: Aesthetics and Politics from the English Revolution*, eds. Kevin Sharpe and Steven Zwicker, (Berkeley: University of California Press, 1998), 25–56.

3. John Cleveland, "Caroli," in *Monumentum Regale* (1649), 21. The editors of the standard edition of Cleveland's poetry, Brian Morris and Eleanor Withington, do not attribute the *Monumentum Regale* to Cleveland, but in his well-respected edition John M. Berdan does. See Morris and Withington's *The Poems of John Cleveland* (Oxford: Clarendon, 1967) and Berdan's *Poems of John Cleveland* (New Haven: Yale University Press, 1911), 195–98, 248.

4. William Sedgwick, *Justice Upon the Armie Remonstrance* (London, 1649), 12; Marvell, "*An* Horatian *Ode upon* Cromwell's *Return from* Ireland," 63–64, 55–56, 66.

5. Lady Eleanor, *Given to the Elector* (Amsterdam, 1633), 8. While the title page of Harvard's Houghton Library's copy of *Given to the Elector* lists 1633 as the date of publication, marginal comments indicate that it was reissued after Charles's execution in 1649. No extant copies survive of the original 1633 edition. For the story of Belshazzar, see Daniel 5.

6. James I, *The True Lawe of Free Monarchies* (London: 1603; first published 1598), C5. Dorothy Paula Ludlow examines the influence of divine right on the writings of three mid-seventeenth-century women prophets—Mary Pope, Elizabeth Poole, and Elizabeth Warren—in "Crisis of Allegiance," in "'Arise and be Doing,'" 192–240. Carol Barash takes up the same topic in conjunction with later seventeenth-century women writers in *English Women's Poetry.*

7. Lady Eleanor's emphasis on female inheritance, however, runs counter to her contemporaries' attitudes toward women's property rights. According to historian Eileen Spring, women were increasingly seen as incapable of perpetuating the father's line. See her *Law, Land, & Family: Aristocratic Inheritance in England, 1300–1800* (Chapel Hill: University of North Carolina Press, 1993), 19.

8. Donald W. Hanson, *From Kingdom to Commonwealth: The Development of Civic Consciousness in English Political Thought* (Cambridge, MA: Harvard University Press, 1970), 7.

9. These words are taken from Lady Eleanor's transcription of the official account of her trial in 1633 for printing three of her texts in Amsterdam and distributing them in England. See her *The Blasphemous Charge Against Her* (1649), in *Prophetic Writings*, 253. See also the prefiguring of apocalypse in Dan. 12:5–9.

10. Quoted in Cope, *Handmaid of the Holy Spirit*, 162.

11. See S. G. Wright, "Dougle Fooleries," *Bodleian Quarterly Record* 7 (1932–34): 95–98; Theodore Spencer, "The History of an Unfortunate Lady," *Harvard Studies and Notes in Philology and Literature* 20 (1938): 43–59. For another early biographical and bibliographical treatment of Lady Eleanor, see C. J. Hindle, "A Bibliography of the Printed Pamphlets and Broadsides of Lady Eleanor Douglas the Seventeenth-Century Prophetess," *Edinburgh Bibliographical Society Transactions* 1:1 (Edinburgh: R. and R. Clark, 1936): 65–98.

12. See Christine Berg and Philippa Berry, "'Spiritual Whoredom,'"45–47; Hobby, *Virtue of Necessity*, 27–29; Mack *Visionary Women*, 91, 97, 122; Smith, *Perfection Proclaimed*, 32; Wiseman, "Unsilent Instruments and the Devil's Cushions,"192–93.

13. See Beth Nelson, "Lady Elinor Davies: The Prophet as Publisher," *Women's Studies: International Forum* 8 (1985): 403–9.

14. See Megan Matchinske, "Holy Hatred: Formations of the Gendered Subject in English Apocalyptic Writing, 1625–51," *English Literary History* 60 (1993): 349–77.

15. Wright, "Dougle Fooleries," 95; Cope, *Handmaid*, 4; Lady Eleanor, *Tobits Book, A Lesson Appointed for Lent* (1652), 5–6. The full citation for the Pauline text she notes is 1 Cor. 4:5.

16. Lady Eleanor, *The Restitution of Prophecy* (1651), in *Prophetic Writings*, 360. For more on reading strategies for Lady Eleanor's writings, see Richard Pickard, "Anagrams *etc.* The interpretive Dilemmas of Lady Eleanor Douglas," *Renaissance and Reformation* 20:3 (1996): 5–22.

17. Lady Eleanor, *A Warning to the Dragon and All his Angels* (1625) in *Prophetic Writings*, 55–56. Future citations in text. Her signature prediction appears in the following fourteen texts: *A Warning to the Dragon and All His Angels* (1625), *All the kings of the earth shall prayse thee* (Amsterdam, 1633), *The Lady Eleanor, Her Appeale* (1641), *The Star to the Wise* (1643), *Apocalypsis Jesu Christi* (1644), *From the Lady Eleanor, Her Blessing to her Beloved*

Daughter (1644), *Great Brittains Visitation* (1645), *The Lady Eleanor Her Appeal* (1646), *Given to the Elector Prince Charles of the Rhyne* (1648), *The Everlasting Gospel* (1649), *The Blasphemous Charge Against Her* (1649), *The Appearance or Presence of the Son of Man* (1650), *The Dragons Blasphemous Charge against Her* (1651), and *The Restitution of Prophecy* (1651).

18. See for example her *As Not Unknowne* (1645) in *Prophetic Writings*, 139–42.

19. Lady Eleanor, *The Lady Eleanor, Her Appeale* (1641) in *Prophetic Writings*, 81; Isa. 6:1, 8.

20. Cope, *Handmaid*, 40, 41.

21. Here, Lady Eleanor directly invokes Dan. 12:1: "And at that time shall Michael stand up, the great prince which standeth for the children of thy people: and there shall be a time of trouble, such as never was since there was a nation *even* to that same time: and at that time thy people shall be delivered, every one that shall be found written in the book." Another subtext might be the Gunpowder Plot of 1605 in which members of the Catholic nobility as well as, some implied, "the Jesuites" attempted to use force to destroy James and his government.

22. James I, Epistle to *A Paraphrase Upon the Revelation of the Apostle S. John*, in *The Workes of the Most High and Mightie Prince, James* (London, 1616), 2.

23. James I, *Paraphrase*, 2.

24. For a discussion of the four senses—literal, allegorical, tropological, anagogical—articulated by the Catholic Church and the repudiation of this interpretive system by Protestant reformers, see Barbara Kiefer Lewalski, "The Biblical Symbolic Mode: Typology and the Religious Lyric," in *Protestant Poetics and the Seventeenth-Century Religious Lyric* (Princeton: Princeton University Press, 1979), 111–44.

25. Jonathan Goldberg, *James I and the Politics of Literature* (Stanford: Stanford University Press, 1989), 18.

26. Historian Howard Nenner suggests that James succeeded in making "indefeasible hereditary right an orthodoxy that would last for more than another eighty-five years." See his *Right to be King*, 62.

27. See for instance John Cleveland's poem "Caroli" in *Monumentum Regale* (1649), 26.

28. See Joel 2:28–29 and Acts 2:17–18.

29. Lady Eleanor, *The Star to the Wise* (1643) in *Prophetic Writings*, 112.

30. Smith, *Perfection Proclaimed*, 32; Napier, *Plaine Discovery*, 149.

31. For more on Napier, see Firth, *The Apocalyptic Tradition in Reformation Britain*, 132–49.

32. While Lady Eleanor explicitly alludes to Dan. 12:4, she also echoes Bishop John Williams's funeral sermon for James. See his *Great Britain's Salomon* (1625), 52.

33. During the revolutionary period, the conversion of Native Americans would come to be seen as both a matter of state policy and a means for hastening the last days. See, for instance, *Strength out of Weaknesse; Or a Glorious Manifestation Of the further Progresse of the Gospel among the Indians in New-England* (1652).

34. Smith, *Perfection Proclaimed*, 26; Brightman, "To the Holy Reformed Churches," in *Revelation of Saint John*.

35. Brightman, *Revelation of Saint John*, 43. See also Rev. 3:15–16.

36. Hill, *Antichrist in Seventeenth-Century England*, 27.

37. Clement Hawes, *Mania and Literary Style: The Rhetoric of Enthusiasm from the Ranters to Christopher Smart* (Cambridge: Cambridge University Press, 1996), 60, 61; Jackson I. Cope, "Seventeenth-Century Quaker Style," *Publications of the Modern Language Association of America* 71: 4 (1956): 729.

38. Matchinske, "Holy Hatred," 361, 369, 365.

39. Bernard McGinn, "Early Apocalypticism: the ongoing debate," in *The Apocalypse in English Renaissance Thought and Literature*, eds. C. A. Patrides and Joseph Wittreich (Ithaca: Cornell University Press, 1984), 5.

40. See Dan. 9:2; 12:1,4 and Rev. 3:5; 5:1–9; 10:2, 8–10; 13:8; 17:8; 20:12, 15; 21:27; 22:7–10, 18–19.

41. McGinn, "Early Apocalypticism," 5; Joseph Mede, *The Key of the Revelation*, 2nd ed., trans. Richard More (1650), 1. Mede's text was first published in Latin as *Clavis Apocalyptica* in 1627.

42. None of the religious radicals documented in J. C. Davis's *Fear, Myth and History: The Ranters and the Historians* (New York: Cambridge University Press, 1986) and Jerome Friedman's *Blasphemy, Immorality and Anarchy: The Ranters and the English Revolution* (Athens, Ohio: Ohio University Press, 1989) had anything printed prior to the rise of the Long Parliament. This is not to say that Lady Eleanor's treatise antedates any published statement of religious radicalism. Indeed, Peter Heylin recounts how "one *Brabourne* a poor School-master" published a book in 1633 that advanced Sabbatarian ideas. See his *Cyprianus Anglicus*, (London: 1671), 243. Nevertheless, Lady Eleanor appears to be the first of the prominent prophets of the Civil War period to publish her work.

43. Claude Levi-Strauss, *The Savage Mind* (Chicago: The University of Chicago Press, 1966), 18.

44. Peter Heylin, *Cyprianus Anglicus: OR, THE History of the Life and Death, of The most Reverend and Renowned Prelate William* (London, 1671), 251; Lady Eleanor, *The Lady Eleanor Her Appeal* (1646), in *Prophetic Writings*, 188–89.

45. See Lady Eleanor's account of her brother's trial and execution, *The Crying Charge* (1649), in *Prophetic Writings*, 256. She professes to have directed a version of this text "To the High Court of Justice, appointed for the Tryal of CHARLES STUART" as evidence of the King's remissness.

46. Amsterdam was a popular destination for English dissenters who sought to have work printed in their native tongue. The city boasted "several printers, including J. F. Stam, known for publishing books and *corantoes* or newsheets in English." See Cope, *Handmaid*, 59.

Lady Eleanor provides an account of her trip to Amsterdam in *The Everlasting Gospel* (1649). See *Prophetic Writings*, 285–91.

47. Others include Aemelia Lanyer and Dorothy Leigh. In addition, Katherine Philips commemorated Elizabeth's death with the poem "On the Death of the Queen of Bohemia" (1664) that celebrates the Queen's virtue and particularly her fortitude in adverse circumstances. See *The Collected Works of Katherine Philips*, ed. Patrick Thomas (Essex: Stump Cross Books, 1990), 1: 33, 35–36.

Lady Eleanor may also have appealed to Elizabeth because, according to one eyewitness account, her brother Mervin, Earl of Castlehaven, had prayed for the Queen just moments before he was executed. Such a prayer "could have been understood to ally the Earl with a muscular Protestant foreign policy at odds with the accomplishments of Charles I." See Cynthia Herrup, *A House in Gross Disorder: Sex, Law, and the 2nd Earl of Castlehaven* (New York: Oxford University Press, 1999), 94.

48. *All the kings*, 1, Ar.

49. I Kings 17:9. After she was widowed for a second time in 1644, Lady Eleanor would identify her authority with that of the Widow of Zarephath. See her *Elijah the Tishbite's Supplication* (1650) in *Prophetic Writings*, 328.

50. Lady Eleanor records a message she sends to Charles regarding the fate of his servant and her husband, Sir Archibald Douglas: "I would take my course against him, namely Sir *Archibald Dowglas* [sic] that had burnt my papers to purchase his [Charles's] favor, and that he and all should know shortly." See *The Lady Eleanor*, in *Prophetic Writings*, 189.

51. *The Lady Eleanor*, in *Prophetic Writings*, 186, 189; Cope, *Handmaid*, 116.

52. *All the kings*, Av.; Dan. 10:2–3; Sigmund Freud, "Mourning and Melancholia," in *The Standard Edition of the Complete Psychological Works* (London: The Hogarth Press, 1961), 14: 244–45.

53. *All the kings*, Av.

54. "He which testifieth these things saith, Surely I come quickly, Amen. Even so, come, Lord Jesus." See Rev. 22:20.

55. Freud, "Mourning and Melancholia," 244.

56. According to Cope, after Lady Eleanor had personally presented *All the kings* to the Queen of Bohemia (then resident at the Hague), Elizabeth wrote to Charles on her behalf: "she explained that she could not refuse a woman of that quality, and . . . confessed that if the Lady Eleanor's story were true, she was to be 'pitied.'" See *Handmaid*, 63.

57. *All the kings*, Av; 1 Chron. 21:15–16.

58. Psalm 138:4–5; *All the kings*, B3v.

59. For an extended discussion of Carr's role in *The Lady Eleanor*, see below pages 62–64.

60. James I, *Basilikon Doron*, in *The Political Works of James I*, ed. Charles Howard McIlwain (Cambridge, MA: Harvard University Press, 1918), 3. For more on the misogyny of James's poetry, see Goldberg, *Politics of Literature*, 24–26 and Gerald M. MacLean, *Time's Witness: Historical Representation in English Poetry, 1603–1660* (Madison: University of Wisconsin Press, 1990), 89. See also James's "An Elegie written by the King concerning his counsell for Ladies & gentlemen to departe the City of London according to his Majesties Proclamation" (1622), in *The Poems of James VI of Scotland*, ed. James Craigie (Edinburgh: William Blackwood, 1958), 2: 178–81.

61. Lady Eleanor, *Her Appeale*, in *Prophetic Writings*, 76, 80; J. P. Kenyon, *Stuart England* (New York: Penguin, 1978), 125, 129–30.

62. *Her Appeale*, 76; Lady Eleanor, *The Blasphemous Charge Against Her* (1649), in *Prophetic Writings*, 250, 253; Heylin, *Cyprianus Anglicus*, 251.

63. Lady Eleanor, *The Blasphemous Charge*, 254; Hindle, "A Bibliography," 72.

64. On December 17, 1636, the order was signed for her to be committed to Bedlam, but precise data as to her arrival does not exist. Evidence indicates that certainly by February of 1637 she resided at Bedlam. She remained there until April of 1638 when she was transferred to the Tower where she continued a prisoner until her release in September of 1640. See Cope, *Handmaid*, 83–86, 92, 95–96 and Hindle, "A Bibliography," 73. See also *Bethlehem Signifying The House of Bread: or War* (1652) for Lady Eleanor's account of these events.

65. Cope, *Handmaid*, 1. For more on the gendered nature of the allegations of madness that plagued Lady Eleanor, see Roy Porter, "The Prophetic Body: Lady Eleanor Davies and the meanings of madness," *Women's Writing* 1:1(1994): 51–63.

66. *Her Appeale*, 76.

67. *Her Appeale*, 79, 81, 79.

68. Cope, *Handmaid*, 20, 21. That Lady Eleanor's father should make her, a younger child and a daughter, the executor of his will counters the trend of inheritance patterns favoring males and tellingly conveys the extent of his estate's reduced circumstances. Eileen Spring has observed that between 1300 and 1800 "landowners' legal history is much to be seen as the effort to overcome the common law rights of daughters." See her *Law, Land, & Family*, 35.

69. Quoted in Lawrence Stone, *The Crisis of the Aristocracy 1558–1641* (Oxford: Clarendon Press, 1965), 13; *Her Appeale*, 84.

70. Lady Eleanor, *The Appearance or Presence of the Son of Man* (1650), 8–9; Cope, *Handmaid*, 8. For more on James's policy of selling titles to raise money, see Stone, *Crisis of the Aristocracy*, 65–128.

71. *Her Appeale*, 78. For the account of Nebuchadnezzar's dream, see Dan. 2: 31–45.

72. Lady Eleanor, *The Gatehouse Salutation* (1647), in *Prophetic Writings*, 218, 218–19. See also Rev. 4:4.

73. John Goodwin, *The Obstructors of Justice* (London: 1649), 31; Lady Eleanor, *Her Appeal from the Court to the Camp* (1649), in *Prophetic Writings*, 247. See also Matt. 24:45–51 and Luke 16:1–13.

74. Matt. 24:48, 49.

75. John Archer, *The Personal Reign of Christ Upon Earth*, 5th ed. (London: 1661), 2–3, 21–22.

76. For the story of Hezekiah, see 2 Kings 18–20; Lady Eleanor, *A Sign Given Them* (1649), in *Prophetic Writings*, 279, 278. See also Gen. 28:12.

77. Two additional crowns appear in the frontispiece: a crown of thorns that Charles holds in his hands marked *"Gratia"* and a third crown resting at his feet labelled *"Vanitas."* See Charles I (John Gauden, supposed author), frontispiece to *Eikon Basilike: The Pourtracture of His Sacred Majestie in His Solitudes and Sufferings* (1648/9).

78. Henry King, *An Elegy Upon the most Incomparable K. Charles the 1* (1648/9), 18; James Ussher, *The Rights of Primogeniture* (London, 1648), 3.

79. Lady Eleanor, *The Lady Eleanor*, in *Prophetic Writings*, 182, 183. According to Cope, *"The Historie of Friar Rush* (1620) told the tale of a devil who deceived people by representing himself as a friar." See *Prophetic Writings*, 183.

80. For more on Robert Carr, later Earl of Somerset, see Derek Hirst, *Authority and Conflict: England, 1603–1658* (Cambridge, MA: Harvard University Press, 1986), 113–20.

81. This voice and its message appear in the following eleven texts: *The Star to the Wise* (1643), *Apocalypsis Jesu Christi* (1644), *From the Lady Eleanor, Her Blessing to her Beloved Daughter* (1644), *Great Brittains Visitation* (1645), *The Lady Eleanor Her Appeal* (1646), *Given to the Elector Prince Charles of the Rhyne* (1648), *The Everlasting Gospel* (1649), *The Blasphemous Charge Against Her* (1649), *The Appearance or Presence of the Son of Man* (1650), *The Dragons Blasphemous Charge against Her* (1651), and *The Restitution of Prophecy* (1651).

82. *Her Appeale*, 80–81; Rev. 14:1, 4.

83. In the standard reading of this passage, Reformation apologists maintained that the chosen were male and focused on virginity as a spiritual rather than a physical state. See for instance Napier, *Plaine Discovery*, 177.

84. Brightman, *Revelation*, 153. In linking "sodomitry" to Roman Catholic priests, Brightman invokes a common figure of anti-Rome and anti-homosexual rhetoric. See Alan Bray, *Homosexuality in Renaissance England* (London: Gay Men's Press, 1982), 26.

85. Eleanor Davies, *From the Lady Eleanor, Her Blessing to Her Beloved Daughter* (1644), 17–18.

86. "Let the woman learn in silence with all subjection. But I suffer not a woman to teach, nor to usurp authority over the man, but to be in silence" (1 Tim. 2:11–12).

In the early eighteenth century, Mary Astell would interpret Timothy similarly. See her Preface to *Reflections Upon Marriage*, in *The First English Feminist: "Reflections Upon Marriage" and other writings by Mary Astell*, ed. Bridget Hill (New York: St. Martin's Press, 1986), 77.

87. 2 Kings 9:33–34.

88. While I have emphasized Lady Eleanor's use of virginity to articulate the significance of the father-daughter bond, she also uses virginity to express her independence from earthly men's authority. See for instance her *Everlasting Gospel* (1649) and *The Restitution of Prophecy* (1651).

89. Cope, *Handmaid*, 17; Robert Krueger and Ruby Nemser, introduction to *The Poems of Sir John Davies* (Oxford: Clarendon Press, 1975), xlvi. Although Douglas, like Davies, proved a hindrance to her prophetic career, she may have initially been attracted to him because she believed him to be James's illegitimate son. See Cope, *Handmaid*, 46. For Lady Eleanor's accounts of Douglas's supposed kinship with James, see *The New Jerusalem at Hand* (1649) and *Her Jubilee* (1650).

90. Gayle Rubin, "The Traffic in Women: Notes on the 'Political Economy' of Sex," in *Toward an Anthropology of Women*, ed. Rayna Reiter (New York: Monthly Review Press, 1975), 177.

91. T. P. *"The Copy of a letter, as it was sent from* T.P. *a friend of Mrs.* Elizabeth Poole, *To the Congregation of Saints, walking in fellowship with Mr.* William Kiffin," in *An Alarum of War*, by Elizabeth Poole (London: 1649), 8. According to Ludlow, T. P. may have been Thomasine Pendarves, "wife of the dynamic Baptist/ Fifth Monarchist preacher John Pendarves." See "Arise and be Doing," 229.

92. Ian Gentles suggests that she may have been brought before the Council by either Colonel Rich or General Fairfax, both of whom were interested in preserving the king's life. See his *The New Model Army in England, Ireland and Scotland, 1645–1653* (Oxford: Blackwell, 1992), 301.

93. Elizabeth Poole's published works include the aforementioned *A Vision* (London: 1648) and two different versions of a text under the title *An Alarum of War, Given to the Army* (London, 1649). One of these two texts contains a reprint of *A Vision* and a letter from one T. P. (clearly a woman, and possibly Thomasine Pendarves) vindicating Poole who, since speaking before the Army Officers, had been excommunicated from the Baptist congregation led by Mr. William Kiffin. This version of *An Alarum* can be distinguished from the other by the title page which notes the presence of T. P's letter: "Also a letter to the Congregation, in fellowship with Mr. *Kiffin*, in vindication of *E.P.* [Elizabeth Poole] advising them to live lesse in the Letter of the scripture, and more in the

spirit." The other version of *An Alarum* excoriates the Army Officers for failing to heed her advice and preserve the king's life.

For general information on Poole, see Hobby's *Virtue of Necessity* and Mack's *Visionary Women*. Dorothy P. Ludlow discusses Poole's defense of Charles's life in conjunction with those of Mary Pope and Elizabeth Warren. See "Arise and Be Doing," 192–240.

94. Elizabeth Poole, *A Vision: Wherein is manifested the disease and cure of the Kingdome* (London, 1648), 2; Ussher, *Rights of Primogeniture*, 6–7.

95. Poole, *A Vision*, 4.

96. Ibid., 5.

97. Ibid., 3.

CHAPTER 2. SODOMY AND FEMALE AUTHORITY

1. Although I refer to Cope's edition of *Restitution*, I draw the number of pages from the 1651 printed edition found in the Folger Library.

2. Lady Eleanor, *The Restitution of Prophecy* (1651), in *Prophetic Writings*, 355. Future citations in text.

3. Lady Eleanor, *From the Lady Eleanor, Her Blessing*, in *Prophetic Writings*, 128, 129.

4. B. R. Burg, "Ho Hum, Another Work of the Devil: Buggery and Sodomy in Early Stuart England," in *Historical Perspectives on Homosexuality*, eds. Salvatore J. Licata and Robert P. Petersen (New York: Haworth Press, 1981), 72.

5. See Barbara Breasted, "*Comus* and the Castlehaven Scandal," *Milton Studies* 3 (1971): 201–24. For more on the relationship between the Castlehaven Scandal and Milton's *Comus*, see Leah Sinangolou Marcus, "The Milieu of Milton's *Comus*: Judicial Reform at Ludlow and the Problem of Sexual Assault," *Criticism* 25 (1983): 293–327; John Creaser, "Milton's *Comus*: The Irrelevance of the Castlehaven Scandal," *Milton Quarterly* 11 (1987): 24–34; and Nancy Weitz Miller, "Chastity, Rape, and Ideology in the Castlehaven Testimonies and Milton's Ludlow *Mask*," *Milton Studies* 32 (1995): 153–68.

6. Jonathan Dollimore, *Sexual Dissidence* (Oxford: Clarendon Press, 1991), 285; Eve Kosofsky Sedgwick, *Between Men: English Literature and Male Homosocial Desire* (New York: Columbia University Press, 1985), 38.

7. Jonathan Goldberg, *Sodometries: Renaissance Texts, Modern Sexualities* (Stanford: Stanford University Press, 1992), 19; *The Arraignment and Conviction of Mervin Lord Audley* (London: 1642), 9,10.

In this essay, I refer to four different printed versions of the trial: the aforementioned *Arraignment* of 1642; *The Trial of the Lord Audley, Earl of Castlehaven* (London: 1679); *The Tryal and Condemnation of Mervin, Lord Audley Earl of Castle-Haven* (London: 1699); *The Trial of Mervin Lord Audeley, Earl of Castlehaven*, in *Cobbett's Complete Collection of State Trials*, (London: R. Bagshaw, 1809), 3: 401–18.

8. *The Trial of the Lord Audley* (1679), 7.

9. Goldberg, *Sodometries*, 19; Cynthia Herrup, "The Patriarch at Home: The Trial of the 2nd Earl of Castlehaven for Rape and Sodomy,"*History Workshop Journal* 41 (1996): 8.

10. Herrup, *House in Gross Disorder*, 15, 16–17; H. Montgomery Hyde, *The*

Love that Dared not Speak Its Name (Boston: Little, Brown and Company, 1970), 48; Burg, "Ho Hum, Another Work of the Devil," 73.

11. Stone, *Crisis of the Aristocracy*, 668, 671, 669; Herrup, *House in Gross Disorder*, 20.

12. Herrup, "The Patriarch at Home," 8; *The Arraignment and Conviction*, 9–10. According to Broadway's confession from the scaffold (he was hanged for raping the Countess), the Earl had intimated his desire that Broadway have sexual intercourse with his wife before the event took place. See *The Trial of Lawrence Fitz-Patrick and Giles Broadway*, in *Cobbett's Complete Collection of State Trials* (London: R. Bagshaw, 1809), 3: 423–24.

13. *The Arraignment and Conviction*, 8, 6.

14. They unanimously find him guilty of rape while they convict him of sodomy by a bare majority—fifteen of the twenty-seven jurors decide against Castlehaven.

15. Bray, *Homosexuality in Renaissance England*, 49.

16. *The Trial of Mervin Lord Audley*, 413, 412.

17. Lady Audeley testifies that "the Earl himself saw her and Skipwith lie together divers times" and further that he "delighted to see the act done." See *The Trial of Mervin Lord Audley*, 413 and *The Arraignment and Conviction*, 8.

18. *The Arraignment and Conviction*, 8; *The Trial of the Lord Audley*, 5; Herrup, *House in Gross Disorder*, 42–43.

19. *The Arraignment and Conviction*, 8,7,8.

20. On the other hand, Fitzpatrick's more detailed testimony of his sexual relationship with the Earl resulted in his being tried and executed on charges of sodomy.

21. Goldberg, *Sodometries*, 91; *The Arraignment and Conviction*, 11.

22. According to Herrup, "in October, 1630, Lord Audeley [James Touchet] lodged the complaint against his father that eventually resulted in his trial and execution." See "The Patriarch at Home," 2. For a similar account of the chain of events leading to Castlehaven's trial, see Hyde, *The Love that Dared not Speak*, 47. In contradistinction to Herrup and Hyde, Caroline Bingham maintains that Touchet did not engineer the charges against his father but simply followed the lead of his stepmother, the Countess. See her "Seventeenth-Century Attitudes Toward Deviant Sex," *The Journal of Interdisciplinary History* 1:3 (1971): 453.

23. *The Trial of Mervin Lord Audley*, 415; Herrup, "The Patriarch at Home," 12–13.

24. Lady Eleanor excerpts this letter in her *The Word of God, To the Citie of London* (1644), 6.

25. Jon. 4:4,8; Herrup, "The Patriarch at Home," 13.

26. Roland Barthes, *Sade, Fourier, Loyola*, trans. Richard Miller (Berkeley: University of California Press, 1989), 124.

27. Lady Eleanor, *The Crying Charge* (1649), in *Prophetic Writings*, 257.

28. Lady Eleanor, *Woe to the House* (1633), in *Prophetic Writings*, 57. For more on Lady Eleanor's legal battles with the Hastings, see Cope, *Handmaid*, 46–49.

29. Davies is brought into the narrative by virtue of Lady Eleanor noting the date of his death, "Decembris 1626," directly below the anagram on the Countess's name. Correspondingly, the date of Castlehaven's death appears directly below the anagram on his wife's name. See her *Woe*, 57.

30. Lady Eleanor, *Woe*, 57. See also 1 Kings 21:8, 10–11,13.

31. Lady Eleanor, *The Word of God, To the Citie of London* (1644), 8; *From the Lady Eleanor, Her Blessing*, 120, 121.

32. Matt. 25:1–13.

33. Lady Eleanor, *Great Brittains Visitation* (1645), in *Prophetic Writings*, 154; Lady Eleanor, *The New Jerusalem at Hand* (1649), in *Prophetic Writings*, 260.

34. The Earl of Strafford was Charles's Lieutenant General and was associated with the king's repressive, authoritarian policies. He was executed, with Charles's assent, in 1641.

35. On page 11 of the Folger Library's copy of *Restitution*, this word is added in handwriting attributed to Lady Eleanor.

36. Rev. 17:16.

37. Hill, *Antichrist in Seventeenth-Century England*, 76, 79, 88, 133.

38. Lady Eleanor asserts that their brother, Ferdinando Touchet, also conspired Castlehaven's death. She describes Ferdinando as one of "the contrivers of it" and "a perverted Papist wanting no malice" for whom "no aspertion was held too foule." See *The Word of God*, 7–8? (confused pagination). The "perverted Papist" notwithstanding, Lady Eleanor's biographer claims that Ferdinando stood to gain financially from his brother's death. See Cope, *Handmaid*, 54.

39. The image of Castlehaven as martyr sacrificed between two thieves also appears in *The Crying Charge* (1649): "Mervin *Earl of* Castlehaven, *that faithful Martyr, suffering (as it were) between those twain*, one on the right hand, the other on the left, *the honor having to be the first* entred into the joy of his Lord" (6–7). As this passage suggests, Castlehaven was beheaded before (by nearly two months) Broadway and Fitzpatrick were hanged.

40. See Gen. 39.

41. Dollimore, *Sexual Dissidence*, 287.

42. Cope, *Handmaid*, 160.

43. Ironically, one reading of the case against Castlehaven suggests that the prosecution sought to portray the Earl as "unmanned." See Herrup, *House in Gross Disorder*, 74.

44. Cope, *Prophetic Writings*, 365; Dan. 4:25; Lady Eleanor, *Given to the Elector* (1648), in *Prophetic Writings*, 64.

45. Lady Eleanor, *The Crying Charge*, 256. Cope finds irony in the seventeenth-century public's response to these women's problematic relationships with their husbands: "In contrast to Lady Eleanor herself, who had openly predicted her own husband's death and, as a result, had incurred sharp criticism by the king for her apparent treachery, the Countess, who had covertly given evidence that led directly to her husband's conviction and execution, had received public sympathy." See *Handmaid*, 54.

46. One anonymous polemicist contended that women prophets transgressed the bounds of feminine modesty: "presuming to advance themselves before and over men, transgressing the rules of *Nature, Modestie, Divinitie, Discretion, Civilitie*." See *A Spirit Moving in The Women-Preachers: Or, Certaine Quaeres, Vented and put forth unto this affronted, brazen-faced, strange, new Feminine Brood* (London, 1646), 2.

47. *The holy Sisters Conspiracy against their Husbands, and the City of London, designed at their last Farewell of their Meeting-houses in Coleman Street* (1661), 3.

48. Ibid., 5.
49. Ibid., 15, 16.

CHAPTER 3. THE SEMIOTICS OF FASTING

1. Anna Trapnel, title page of *Strange and Wonderful Newes from White-hall* (London: 1654).

Strange and Wonderful Newes appears to be a popularization of her *The Cry of a Stone* (London, 1654) both of which were produced by unnamed editors from a transcription of her words by an unnamed amanuensis. Trapnel herself authored two other texts that appeared in 1654: *Report and Plea Or, A Narrative of her Journey from London into Cornwall* (London) and *A Legacy for Saints* (London). In 1658, two new prophetic tracts were produced, again, by unnamed amanuenses and editors: *A Voice for the King of Saints* (London) and an untitled thousand-page edition of prophecies found in the Bodleian Library.

2. Anna Trapnel, *The Cry of a Stone* (London: 1654), 76. Future citations in text.

3. Trapnel, *Report and Plea*, 58.

4. Margaret Ferguson, "A Room Not Their Own: Renaissance Women as Readers and Writers," in *The Comparative Perspective on Literature: Approaches to Theory and Practice*, eds. Clayton Koelb and Susan Noakes (Ithaca: Cornell University Press, 1988), 97; Purkiss, "Producing the voice," 156, 157.

5. Joan Jacobs Brumberg, *Fasting Girls: The Emergence of Anorexia Nervosa as a Modern Disease* (Cambridge, MA: Harvard University Press, 1988), 2.

6. Henry Jessey, *The Exceeding Riches of Grace* (London, 1647), 19. Future citations in text as *ER*.

7. *The Exceeding Riches of Grace* enjoyed a fairly lengthy publishing run, going through seven editions between 1647 and 1658.

8. Although not as overtly topical as Trapnel's, Wight's message does contain some political content. Indeed, Barbara Ritter Dailey argues persuasively that within the "traditional framework of devotional literature," Wight emerges as "an influential teacher of radical theology." See her "The Visitation of Sarah Wight: Holy Carnival and the Revolution of the Saints in Civil War London," *Church History* 55 (1986): 438. For more on Wight, see also Carola Scott-Luckens, "Propaganda or Marks of Grace? The Impact of the Reported Ordeals of Sarah Wight in Revolutionary London, 1647–52," *Women's Writing* 9:2 (2002): 215–32.

9. A contemporary of Wight and Trapnel, Martha Hatfield also fasts as she delivers her inspired messages. A young girl of eleven years, Hatfield was "stricken dumb, deaf, and blind" and, as a result of her illness, did not eat as she prophesied for some six months in 1652. Her prophecies were published by her uncle James Fisher as *The Wise Virgin* (London, 1653). While we cannot determine Hatfield's religious affiliation with any certainty, some evidence suggests that she may have had Fifth Monarchist leanings. For more on Hatfield, see Nigel Smith, "A Child Prophet: Martha Hatfield as *The Wise Virgin*," in *Children and their Books*, eds. Gillian Avery and Julia Briggs, 79–93 (Oxford: Clarendon Press, 1989).

10. Murray Tolmie, *The Triumph of the Saints* (Cambridge: Cambridge University Press, 1977), 101,119.

11. B. S. Capp, *Fifth Monarchy Men* (London: Faber, 1972), 14; Tolmie, *Triumph of the Saints*, 6.

12. Capp, *Fifth Monarchy Men*, 14.

13. Smith, *Perfection Proclaimed*, 49.

14. Capp, *Fifth Monarchy Men*, 100, 101.

15. *A Directory for the Publique Worship of God* (London: 1644), 74–75; H. R. Trevor-Roper, "The Fast Sermons of the Long Parliament," in *The Crisis of the Seventeenth Century* (New York: Harper and Row, 1968), 306.

16. Ibid., 309, 318.

17. Ibid., 334.

18. Ibid., 342. John F. Wilson, *Pulpit in Parliament: Puritanism during the English Civil War 1640–48* (Princeton: Princeton University Press, 1969), 62.

19. Trevor-Roper, "Fast Sermons," 342.

20. Vavasor Powell, *Christ Exalted above all Creatures By God His Father* (London: 1651), 88, 89, 95. See also Dan. 7.

21. In a related study, Rudolph Bell interprets the extraordinary fasts of religious women in Italy from the thirteenth through the twentieth centuries in terms of modern theories of anorexia nervosa. See his *Holy Anorexia* (Chicago: University of Chicago Press, 1985).

22. Caroline Walker Bynum, *Holy Feast and Holy Fast* (Berkeley: University of California Press, 1987), 191, 294.

23. Ibid., 120. Although not remembered for her self-starvation, the medieval mystic Margery Kempe represents perhaps the most famous English example of a woman expressing her relationship with Christ in terms of erotic union. See *The Book of Margery Kempe*, trans. B. A. Windeatt (New York: Viking Penguin, 1985), 232.

24. Bynum, *Holy Feast and Holy Fast*, 133, 135, 186; Quoted in Hyder E. Rollins, "Notes on Some English Accounts of Miraculous Fasts," *Journal of American Folk-Lore* 34 (1921): 365.

25. Collins, *From Divine Cosmos to Sovereign State*, 5.

26. Quoted in Rollins, "Miraculous Fasts," 366; Bynum, *Holy Feast and Holy Fast*, 68, 115.

27. Quoted in Rollins, "Miraculous Fasts, " 366, 367; "You gallant maidens of the world," in *The Shirburn Ballads 1585–1616*, ed. Andrew Clark (Oxford: Clarendon Press, 1907), st. 15:5–8, st. 16:1–8, st. 17:1–2.

28. For more on fasting in Renaissance drama, see Nancy A. Gutierrez, "Double Standard in the Flesh: Gender, Fasting, and Power in English Renaissance Drama," in *Disorderly Eaters: Texts in Self-Empowerment*, eds. Lilian R. Furst and Peter W. Graham (University Park, PA: The Pennsylvania State University Press, 1992), 79–93.

29. *Love's Cure, or, The Martial Maid*, in *The Dramatic Works in the Beaumont and Fletcher Canon*, ed. George Walton Williams (Cambridge: Cambridge University Press, 1976), 3: V.iii.261, II.i.28–31. See also *News from Plymouth*, in *The Dramatic Works of Sir William Davenant* (Edinburgh: William Paterson, 1873), 4: 114 and Jasper Mayne, *The City Match*, in *A Select Collection of Old Plays*, ed. W. Carew Hazlitt (London: Reeves and Turner, 1875), 13: 236.

30. The identification of food abstinence with sexual abstinence is a commonplace of both early modern and modern discourses of female inedia. See, for

instance, William Davenant's Seawit in *News from Plymouth*, 114 and Hilde Bruch's psychiatric study of anorexia nervosa in *Eating Disorders: Obesity, Anorexia Nervosa, and the Person Within* (New York: Basic Books, 1973), 44.

31. William Shakespeare, *Measure for Measure*, II.ii.153–57, I.iv.4–5, V.i.495.

32. Thomas Robins, *The Wonder of the World* (London: 1669), 9–10, 15.

33. Bynum notes that anatomical observation was a feature of some sixteenth-century hagiographies of fasting women. See *Holy Feast and Holy Fast*, 148.

34. Lescarbot, *A True and admirable Historie of a Mayden of Consolans*, trans. Anthony Munday (1603), 9v–10r, 14r, 51r–51v.

35. Dailey, "Visitation of Sarah Wight," 445, 446.

36. This is not to say, however, that mysticism did not influence Independent and sectarian thought. In his letter commending Jessey for publishing *Exceeding Riches*, John Saltmarsh celebrates, in a rather mystical tone, Wight's words as "that first discovery of God in *love*" (*ER*, a2v). Moreover, he expects that "the Lord will fill this soule with more *discoveries*, then this of glorious grace" (*ER*, a2v).

37. Sue Wiseman has noticed as much: "Trapnel's prophecies use Biblical language extensively. The text allies itself linguistically to that of the canonical prophecies." See her "Unsilent Instruments and the Devil's Cushions," 187.

38. On yet another occasion when she amazingly reproduces a feature of the Greek translation of the Bible, her editors confirm that she does not know Greek: "*As I live saith the Lord, I will not the death of a sinner. He hath sworn it; he hath sworn it, that he delights not in the death of a sinner. He hath said, Ile never leave thee, no, Ile never forsake thee, no.* [Thus shee added the *Emphasis, No*; that is more in the Greek, then in our Translation: though shee be no Grecian.]" (*ER*, 21).

39. Patricia Caldwell, *The Puritan Conversion Narrative* (Cambridge: Cambridge University Press, 1983), 25, 9–13.

40. Quoted in Caldwell, *Puritan Conversion Narrative*, 12. White's experience of grace compares with that of John Bunyan in the classic conversion narrative, *Grace Abounding to the Chief of Sinners*, ed. Roger Sharrock (Oxford: Clarendon Press, 1962), 80.

41. Trapnel also recalls that during her period of despair, she entertained suicidal thoughts: "I was strongly tempted to destroy my self, which had not divine power prevented, I had been a murderer of my own life . . . I have been waked in the night by the devill for this very purpose, and directed where to have the knife." See her *Legacy*, 2–3.

42. According to Smith, Thomas Bromley and Morgan Llwyd do the selfsame thing. See *Perfection Proclaimed*, 222.

43. 2 Cor. 3:6, 3.

44. According to B.S. Capp, the emphasis on scriptural authority was a cornerstone of Fifth Monarchist belief. Nevertheless, "there was a pronounced mystical element in Fifth Monarchist thought, shown by the saints' emphasis on inward illumination, usually through dreams and visions." Indeed, some of Trapnel's own visionary experiences and pronouncements (particularly those regarding Cromwell) bore only the barest resemblance to scriptural texts. See his *Fifth Monarchy Men*, 185,186. I concentrate on her reliance on Scripture as a counterpoint to Wight and as a way of highlighting her privileging of textual forms of knowledge.

45. "After two days will he revive us: in the third day he will raise us up, and we shall live in his sight" (Hos. 6:2).

46. Anna Trapnel, *A Legacy for Saints* (London, 1654), 27, 9.

47. "And the destruction of the transgressors and of the sinners *shall be* together, and they that forsake the Lord, shall be consumed. For they shall be ashamed of the oaks which ye have desired, and ye shall be confounded for the gardens, that ye have chosen. For ye shall be as an oak whose leafe fadeth, and as a garden that hath no water" (Isa. 1:28–30). The marginal commentary of the Geneva Bible offers insight into these cryptic passages and into Trapnel's interpretation of them. According to the commentary, the oaks and gardens represent the "trees & pleasant places" where idolatry was committed. Those who worship such false gods, the commentary insists, can expect to be consumed together with the "transgressors" and "sinners."

48. Rev. 2:3.

49. Michel Foucault, *Discipline and Punish*, trans. by Alan Sheridan (New York: Vintage, 1979), 55.

50. See especially *Exceeding Riches*, 6–7, 13–14, 19.

51. The Fifth Monarchist John Tillinghast defines the term "generation-work" in his 1655 treatise *Generation-work*. According to Tillinghast, "generation-work" is *"that work, or those works which the way or manner of God's dispensations in the age a Saint lives in, calls him unto"* (5).

52. Judges 8:23.

53. Bynum, *Holy Feast and Holy Fast*, 172.

54. Quoted and translated in Bynum, *Holy Feast and Holy Fast*, 173.

55. Fisher, *Wise Virgin*, 127–28.

56. Ann Kibbey, *The Interpretation of Material Shapes in Puritanism* (Cambridge: Cambridge University Press, 1986), 42–64.

57. Ibid., 47, 47–48, 53.

58. Max Weber, *The Protestant Ethic and the Spirit of Capitalism*, trans. Talcott Parsons (London: Unwin, 1930), 81, 176–77.

59. Thomas Hobbes, *Leviathan*, ed. Richard Tuck (Cambridge: Cambridge University Press, 1991), 117, 120.

60. Christopher Hill, "Covenant Theology and the Concept of 'A Public Person,'" in *Powers, Possessions, and Freedom: Essays in Honour of C.B. Macpherson*, ed. Alkis Kontos (Toronto: University of Toronto Press, 1979), 3, 6. For more on the intricacies of covenant theology, see Perry Miller's landmark essay, "The Marrow of Puritan Divinity," in *Errand into the Wilderness* (Cambridge, MA: The Belknap Press of Harvard University Press, 1956), 48–98.

61. Hill, "Covenant Theology," 7–8; David Zaret, *The Heavenly Contract: Ideology and Organization in Pre-Revolutionary Puritanism* (Chicago: The University of Chicago Press, 1985), 165, 163.

62. Hill, "Covenant Theology," 20–21; Cary, *Little Horns Doom*, 30; Alfred Cohen, "Mary Cary," *Biographical Dictionary of British Radicals in the Seventeenth Century*, eds. Richard L. Greaves and Robert Zaller (Sussex: The Harvester Press, 1982), 1: 128. For more on Cary, see Alfred Cohen, "The Fifth Monarchy Mind: Mary Cary and the origins of Totalitarianism," *Social Research* 31 (1964): 195–213.

63. Trapnel's assertion of a limited authority over God is consistent with the principles of early modern covenant theology. As Perry Miller puts it, "if a man can prove that he has faith, he has then done his part and can hold God to account, hale Him into court and force Him to give what has become the man's just and legal due." See his "Marrow of Puritan Divinity," 72.

64. Hill, "Covenant Theology," 22, 21, 21–22; Hobbes, *Leviathan*, 122.

65. Ibid., 220–21; Richard Helgerson suggests that Hobbes's identification of his state with Leviathan is one way in which his text appropriates apocalyptic—a powerful discursive form associated with radical sectarianism. See his *Forms of Nationhood* (Chicago: The University of Chicago Press, 1992), 292.

66. Hill, "Covenant Theology," 22.

67. Helgerson, *Forms of Nationhood*, 297, 295–98; Catherine A. MacKinnon, *Toward a Feminist Theory of the State* (Cambridge, MA: Harvard University Press, 1989), 249.

68. In addition to MacKinnon's *Feminist Theory of the State*, see Carole Pateman, *The Sexual Contract* (Stanford: Stanford University Press, 1988).

69. Macpherson, *Political Theory of Possessive Individualism*, 30.

70. J. G. A. Pocock has famously argued that Hobbes does create a political role for historical thinking. Pocock argues that he does this through the eschatological content of books three and four of *Leviathan*. When I say history does not contribute to *Leviathan*'s image of the public realm, I mean that it does not influence the principles which found the commonwealth. Pocock himself agrees that in this philosophical sense Hobbes's theory of the state "can very properly be said" to be "unhistorical." See his "Time, History and Eschatology in the Thought of Thomas Hobbes," in *Politics, Language and Time: Essays in Political Thought and History* (London: Methuen, 1972), 160, 158.

71. Hobbes, *Leviathan*, 139, 140; Pateman, *Sexual Contract*, 36, 102.

72. Ibid.; Ibid., 93–94.

73. Hobbes, *Leviathan*, 235.

74. Ibid., 140; Sharon W. Tiffany and Kathleen J. Adams, *The Wild Woman: An Inquiry into the Anthropology of an Idea* (Cambridge, MA: Schenkman Publishing, 1985), 59; Pateman, *Sexual Contract*, 11.

75. Hobbes, *Leviathan*, 140.

76. Ibid., 163. For a related reading of this passage, see Keith Thomas, "The Social Origins of Hobbes's Political Thought," in *Hobbes Studies*, ed. K. C. Brown (Cambridge, MA: Harvard University Press, 1965), 188,189.

77. B. S. Capp reports that in "the church lists which survived, women easily outnumbered men." See *Fifth Monarchy Men*, 82.

78. Mack, *Visionary Women*, 34.

79. See Bynum, *Holy Feast and Holy Fast*, 230 and Dailey, "Visitation of Sarah Wight," 438.

80. For a discussion of the relationship between death and the literary authority of late sixteenth- and early seventeenth-century women writers, see Wendy Wall's "Isabella Whitney and the Female Legacy," *ELH* 58 (1991): 35–62.

81. Trapnel, *Legacy*, 27.

82. Hobbes, *Leviathan*, 28–29.

83. These very words would return to her later in 1654 when she was imprisoned in Bridewell, but this time they would figure in Satan's efforts to tempt her. In *Report and Plea* she remembers: "I was much assaulted by Satan and my own heart; who said, to be so forward for God, see what thou hast got by it, thy mother little thought this would have befallen thee, when she prayed that God would double his spirit on thee, now thou mayest see what her prayer is come to; I then was tempted to murmure at that prayer, and the Tempter bid me speak against that prayer" (39).

84. Dan. 5:6.

85. Kempe, *Book of Margery Kempe*, 104.

86. Anna Trapnel, *A Voice for the King of Saints* (London, 1658), 91.

87. Trapnel, *Legacy*, 26; John 14:16, 1:14.

88. Diane Purkiss also contends that Trapnel's mother's dying speech "associates" her "with the power of words." Further, Purkiss insists that her mother's command to God "represents the full subversive power of the woman prophet, for it inverts the most basic of all hierarchical relations, the relationship between God and the believer. The woman commands, and commands God." See "Producing the voice," 143.

89. Pateman, *Sexual Contract*, 58; MacKinnon, *Feminist Theory of the State*, 239, 244.

90. MacKinnon, *Feminist Theory of the State*, 243, 248.

91. Margaret Fell, *Womens Speaking Justified* (London:1667), 16, 14; Luke 1:41, 42.

CHAPTER 4. *WOMENS SPEAKING JUSTIFIED*

1. Margaret Fell, *A Relation of Margaret Fell*, in *A Brief Collection of Remarkable Passages and Occurences Relating to . . . Margaret Fell* (London: 1710), 1.

2. See Anna Trapnel, "A Defiance to all reproachfull, scandalous, base, horrid, defaming speeches," in *Report and Plea*, 49–59.

3. "The Examination of Margaret Fell," in *A Brief Collection of Remarkable Passages and Occurences*, 279; Bonnelyn Young Kunze, *Margaret Fell and the Rise of Quakerism* (Stanford: Stanford University Press, 1994), 143. For another biography of Fell, see Isabel Ross, *Margaret Fell: Mother of Quakerism* (London: Longmans, 1949).

Because of her role within the sect, the life and works of Fell figure prominently in general studies of Quaker women: See Mabel R. Brailsford's *Quaker Women, 1650–1690* (London: Duckworth and Co., 1915); Phyllis Mack's *Visionary Women* (Berkeley: University of California Press, 1992); and Christine Trevett's *Women and Quakerism in the 17th Century* (York: Ebor Press, 1991).

Articles devoted to Fell include: Barbara Ritter Dailey, "The Husbands of Margaret Fell: An Essay on Religious Metaphor and Social Change," *The Seventeenth Century* 2:1 (1987): 55–71; Judith Keegan Gardiner, "Re-Gendering Individualism: Margaret Fell Fox and Quaker Rhetoric," in *Privileging Gender in Early Modern England*, ed. Jean R. Brink (Kirksville, MO: Sixteenth Century Journal Publishers, 1993), 205–24; Gardiner, "Margaret Fell Fox and Feminist Literary History: A 'Mother in Israel,'" in *The Emergence of Quaker Writing: Dissenting Literature in Seventeenth-Century England*, eds. Thomas N. Corns and David Loewenstein, (London: Frank Cass, 1995), 42–56; Achsah Guibbory, "Conversation, Conversion, Messianic Redemption: Margaret Fell, Menasseh ben Israel, and the Jews," in *Literary Circles and Cultural Communities in Renaissance England*, eds. Claude J. Summers and Ted-Larry Pebworth (Columbia, MO: University of Missouri Press, 2000), 210–24; and Marilyn Serraino Luecke, " 'God Hath Made No Difference Such As Men Would': Margaret Fell and the Politics of Women's Speech," *Bunyan Studies* 7 (1997): 73–95.

4. Mack, *Visionary Women*, 215–35.

5. *Womens Speaking Justified* appears in a significant number of anthologies: See Patricia Bizzell and Bruce Herzberg, eds., *The Rhetorical Tradition: Readings from Classical Times to the Present*, 2nd ed. (Boston: Bedford, 2001),

753–60; Moira Ferguson, ed., *First Feminists: British Women Writers 1578–1799* (Bloomington: Indiana University Press, 1985), 114–27; Charlotte Otten, ed., *English Women's Voices 1540–1700* (Miami: Florida International University Press, 1992), 363–78; Suzanne Trill, Kate Chedgzoy, and Melanie Osborne, eds., *Lay by Your Needles Ladies, Take the Pen: Writing Women in England 1500–1700* (London: Arnold, 1997), 217–20; and Robert W. Uphaus and Gretchen M. Foster, eds., *The "Other" Eighteenth Century: English Women of Letters 1660–1800* (East Lansing: Colleagues Press, 1991), 17–22. Two modern reprints of the tract have been published: one under the auspices of the New England Yearly Meeting of Friends (Amherst: Mosher Book and Tract Committee, 1980) and another by the Augustan Reprint Society, Publication Number 194 (Los Angeles: William Andrews Clark Memorial Library, 1979).

6. Smith, *Reason's Disciples*, 96, 95, 4; Margaret Olofson Thickstun, " 'This was a Woman that taught': Feminist Scriptural Exegesis in the Seventeenth Century," *Studies in Eighteenth-Century Culture* 21 (1991): 149–50; Hobby, *Virtue of Necessity*, 40, and "Handmaids of the Lord and Mothers in Israel: Early Vindications of Quaker Women's Prophecy," in *The Emergence of Quaker Writing*, 92, 94.

7. Hobby, *Virtue of Necessity*, 45. Like Hobby, Christine Trevett also finds Fell's treatise rather staid: "In my view, however, *Womens Speaking Justified* lacks the charm and wit that we find in some other writings by women Friends." See her *Women and Quakerism in the 17th Century*, 54.

8. Hobby, "Early Vindications," 88. In addition to Hobby and Mack, Margaret J. M. Ezell considers the broad range of early Quaker women's writing in "Breaking the Seventh Seal: Writings by Early Quaker Women," in *Writing Women's Literary History* (Baltimore: The Johns Hopkins University Press, 1993), 132–60.

9. Acts 2:17–18. See also Joel 2:28–29.

10. Mack, *Visionary Women*, 9, 173.

11. Catherine M. Wilcox, *Theology and Women's Ministry in Seventeenth-Century English Quakerism* (Lewiston, NY: Edwin Mellen Press, 1995), 237; Hester Biddle, *The Trumpet of the Lord sounded forth*, in *Hidden in Plain Sight*, 131.

12. Anne Audland, *A True Declaration Of The suffering of the Innocent* (London, 1655), 1, 5.

13. Priscilla Cotton and Mary Cole, *To the Priests and People of England* (London, 1655), 2, 6. For a more detailed analysis of this tract, see Hilary Hinds's " 'It's weakness that is the woman': readings of Priscilla Cotton and Mary Cole's *To the Priests and People of England* (1655)," in *God's Englishwomen*, 180–208.

14. 1 Cor. 14:34–35; Cotton and Cole, *Priests and People*, 7–8.

15. Ibid., 13. See also 1 Cor. 11:3: "But I would have you know, that the head of every man is Christ; and the head of the woman is the man; and the head of Christ is God."

16. 1 Cor. 11:7. See also 1 Cor. 11:4–6.

17. Blackborow, *Just and Equall Ballance*, 13. See also Phil. 4:3: "And I intreat thee also, true yokefellow, help those women which laboured with me in the gospel, with Clement also, and *with* other my fellow labourers, whose names *are* in the book of life."

18. 1 Tim. 2:11–12; 1 Cor. 11:9–10; Blackborow, *Just and Equall Ballance*, 14.

19. *The Geneva Bible: The New Annotated New Testament 1602 Edition*, ed.

Gerald T. Sheppard (New York: Pilgrim Press, 1989), 85; William F. Orr and James Arthur Walther, eds., I Corinthians, The Anchor Bible, vol. 32 (Garden City, NY: Doubleday, 1976), 264. 1 Cor. 11:11.

20. Richard Farnworth, *A Woman Forbidden to Speak in the Church* (London: 1655), 2, 3, 7.

21. George Fox, *Concerning Sons and Daughters*, 2nd ed. (London: 1661), 5. The first edition of this text was published in London in 1656.

22. Fox, *Sons and Daughters*, 2, 11, 3–4.

23. Ibid., 5.

24. Ma-her-shal-al-hash-baz is one of Isaiah's symbolically named sons. His mother was a prophetess: "And I went unto the prophetess; and she conceived, and bare a son. Then said the Lord to me, Call his name Ma-her-shal-al-hash-baz. For before the child shall have knowledge to cry, My father, and my mother, the riches of Damascus and the spoil of Samaria shall be taken away before the king of Assyria" (Isa. 8:3–4).

25. Fox, *Sons and Daughters*, 1, 7.

26. Ibid., 4; Wilcox, *Theology and Women's Ministry*, 169.

27. Fox, *Sons and Daughters*, 4–5.

28. Wilcox, *Theology and Women's Ministry*, 170; Fox *Concerning Sons and Daughters*, 4. 2 Pet. 3:16 reads: " As also in all *his* [Paul's] epistles, speaking in them of these things; in which are some things hard to be understood, which they that are unlearned and unstable wrest, as *they do* also the other scriptures, unto their own destruction."

29. Fox, *Sons and Daughters*, 11, 5–6, 7. For the story of Anna, see Luke 2:22–38.

30. Besse, *Collection of the Sufferings,* I: 84–85; Mack, *Visionary Women,* 127–28, 215.

31. Keith Thomas, *Religion and the Decline of Magic* (London: Weidenfeld and Nicolson, 1971), 562–63, 556; Mack, *Visionary Women,* 128.

32. Some twelve years after the publication of *Womens Speaking Justified,* Isabel Yeamans, one of Fell's daughters, would also appeal to the women messengers of Christ's resurrection to justify female visonary authority. For Yeamans, however, these female messengers are not central to the redemption of humankind but rather serve as biblical types for contemporary Quaker women who announce Christ's "inward and spiritual Appearance" and who are not believed. See her *An Invitation of Love* (1679), 7–8.

33. See Mark 16:11 and Luke 24:11.

34. See Matt. 28:10 and John 20:17–18.

35. See Matt. 28:16–17, Mark 16:14, Luke 24:36, and John 20:19.

36. Elaine Scarry, *The Body in Pain: The Making and Unmaking of the World* (New York: Oxford University Press, 1985), 219.

37. Matthew 26:10–12.

38. Fox, *Sons and Daughters*, 3.

39. Influenced by the writings of both Fell and Fox, Elizabeth Bathurst's *The Sayings of Women,* first published in 1683, is completely devoted to compiling instances of women's inspired speech. For a reprint of the 1695 edition, see *Hidden in Plain Sight,* 430–40.

40. See 2 Kings 22:15–20.

41. "But the younger widows refuse: for when they have begun to wax wanton against Christ, they will marry; Having damnation, because they have cast off their first faith. And withal they learn *to be* idle, wandering about from house

to house; and not only idle, but tattlers also and busybodies, speaking things which they ought not" (1 Tim. 5:11–13).

42. Anne Docwra, *An Epistle of Love* (1683), 5; Bettris, *Lamentation*, 7.

43. See Gen. 1:27.

44. Appearing in the same year that Cotton and Cole's tract did (1655), Farnworth's treatise on women's speaking also considers the topic of female weakness. Like Cotton and Cole, Farnworth identifies women's inspired speech as separate from their bodies; his particular emphasis being on the capacity of God's spirit to transcend women's bodily weakness. See his *A Woman Forbidden*, 4.

45. See Rev. 19:8.

46. Ibid., 22:20.

47. Prior to 1671, two Quaker women's meetings had existed in London. In 1659, Sarah Blackborow founded (at the prompting of Fox) the London Box Meeting. This meeting "was composed entirely of women, and got its peculiar name from the fact that it gathered money into a box, and disbursed it for the relief of the poor." The second women's meeting in London, the Two Weeks' Women's Meeting, became the model for the sect-wide system of women's meetings Fox would inaugurate in 1671. Formed shortly after the London Box Meeting, the Two Weeks' Women's Meeting "worked in association with the Two Weeks' Men's Meeting, and its first work was the visiting of the sick and the prisoners, and in looking after the poor, the widows and the fatherless. Its work developed very soon to include the moral care of women Friends, the stopping of false reports or difficulties tending to disunity among Friends. It found places for Quaker maid-servants, and dealt with women who married non-Friends or who went to a 'priest' to be married." See Ross, *Margaret Fell: Mother of Quakerism*, 284, 285.

The literature on the formation of Quaker women's meetings is extensive. For more on the topic, see Brailsford, "The Women's Meeting," *Quaker Women*, 268–89; William C. Braithwaite, "Women's Meetings and Central Organization," in *The Second Period of Quakerism*, 2nd ed. (Cambridge: Cambridge University Press, 1961), 269–89; Irene L. Edwards, "The Women Friends of London: The Two-Weeks and Box Meetings," *Journal of the Friends Historical Society* 47:1(1955): 3–21; Kunze, "'Walk as Becomes Truth': Margaret Fell and Women's Meetings," in *Margaret Fell and the Rise of Quakerism*, 143–68; Arnold Lloyd, "The Quaker Women's Meetings," in *Quaker Social History* (1950; reprint, Westport, CT: Greenwood Press, 1979), 107–20; Mack,"The Snake in the Garden: Quaker Politics and the Origin of the Women's Meeting" and "The Mystical Housewife," in *Visionary Women*, 265–350; and Christine Trevett, "'This is My Friend': Marriage, children, education and the Women's Meetings," in *Women and Quakerism in the 17th Century*, 75–131.

48. George Fox, circular letter of June 16, 1671 quoted in Braithwaite, *The Second Period of Quakerism*, 273. Prior to the circular letter of 1671, Fox wrote on the subject in 1666 in his epistle 248: "An Exhortation to Set Up Women's Meetings." For a copy of the epistle, see *Early Quaker Writings 1650–1700*, eds. Hugh Barbour and Arthur O. Roberts (Grand Rapids, MI: Eerdmans, 1973), 491–92.

49. "*A few Words to the* Magistrates" (1684), in *Sufferings,* I: 544; John Lane et al., "*To the* Knights *and* Burgesses" (1685), in *Sufferings,* I: 550.

50. Mack, *Visionary Women*, 274, 276.

51. Ibid., 303.

52. See also Braithwaite on this topic: "it is clear from . . . the epistles of Fox that the question whether the women should be given less or more authority was not in his mind. What he was concerned with was to give them their place, their right place, and to stir them up to take it." See *Second Period of Quakerism*, 273.

53. Fox's writings on women's meetings include the following: Epistle 248: "An Exhortation to Set Up Women's Meetings" (1666) in *Early Quaker Writings 1650–1700*, 491–92; Epistle CCXCI: "To all the women's meetings, that are believers in the truth," (1672), in *The Works of George Fox* (1831; reprint, New York: AMS Press, 1975) 8: 39–41; Epistle CCXCVI (1673), in *Works*, 8: 45–45; *This is an Encouragement to All the Women's-Meetings in the World* (1676); Epistle CCCXLIV: "An epistle to be read in the men and women's meetings," (1677), in *Works*, 8: 139–42; Epistle CCCLX: "To all the men and women's meetings every where," (1679), in *Works*, 8: 169–75. The subject of women's meetings also forms part of his "Wheeler Street Sermon" (1680), in *Early Quaker Writings*, 501–12.

54. George Fox, *This is an Encouragement to all the Womens-Meetings in the World* (1676), 25. Future citations in text as *Encouragement*.

55. George Fox, Epistle CCXCI: "To all the women's meetings, that are believers in the truth" (1672), in *Works*, 8: 39.

56. Ibid.

57. Ibid.

58. Gayle Rubin, "Traffic in Women,"159.

59. George Fox, "To the Men and Womens Monthly and Quarterly Meetings" n.d., quoted in Mack, *Visionary Women*, 286.

60. See Exod. 35:22, 25–26.

61. George Fox, Epistle CCCLX: "To all the men and women's meetings every where" (1679), in *Works*, 8: 170–71; Fox, Epistle CCXCI: "To all the women's meetings," 41. See also Titus 2:3–5.

62. George Fox, Epistle CCCXLIV: "An epistle to be read in the men and women's meetings" (1677), in *Works*, 8: 141.

63. John Wilkinson and John Story were "two northern Quakers who were angered by the . . . criticism of Friends who protected themselves from arrest by meeting in the woods and fields rather than in public buildings." They also opposed "the establishment of autonomous women's meetings, except as a means of administering poor relief in large towns." See Mack, *Visionary Women*, 293.

64. Mack, *Visionary Women*, 294.

65. Ibid., 296–97.

66. Theophila Townsend, *An Epistle of Love To Friends in the Womens Meetings in London* (1680?), 4.

Townsend's reference to "comly Order" may be an allusion to Paul's explanation for the different rules about headwear that apply to men and women: "Judge in yourselves: is it comely that a woman pray unto God uncovered? Doth not even nature itself teach you, that if a man have long hair, it is a shame unto him? But if a woman have long hair, it is a glory to her: for *her* hair is given her for a covering" (I Cor. 11:13–15). Paul's comments on the comeliness of women praying with covered heads amplify Townsend's attempt throughout her treatise to assure her female readers that women's meetings, far from being hotbeds of female insubordination, serve to reenforce traditional female traits such as "meekness." See Townsend, *Epistle of Love*, 3.

67. Mary Foster et al., *A Living Testimony* (1685), 2.
68. William Loddington, *The Good Order of Truth Justified* (London, 1685), 5.
69. Exod. 1:19.
70. Ross, *Mother of Quakerism*, 218; Mack, *Visionary Women*, 227.
71. Quoted in Braithwaite, *Second Period of Quakerism*, 263.
72. Ross, *Mother of Quakerism*, 214.
73. Quite surprisingly, however, Mack has located a 1670 letter from Elizabeth Bowman to William Penn which "implies that Margaret Fell Fox believed she was pregnant at one time." See *Visionary Women*, 227.
74. Milton D. Speizman and Jane C. Kronick, "A Seventeenth-Century Quaker Woman's Declaration," *Signs*, 1 (1975): 233.
75. Sarah Fell, "From our Country Women's meeting in Lancashire to be Dispersed abroad, among the Women's meetings every where," in "A Seventeenth-Century Quaker Woman's Declaration," 242.
76. Ibid., 235, 235–36, 235.
77. Ibid., 240, 238, 239.
78. Ibid., 235, 245.
79. Ibid., 244, 255.

Epilogue

1. Smith, *Reason's Disciples*, 9.
2. For the philosophical connection between Restoration Quaker women and Astell, see Mack, *Visionary Women*, 408.
3. In her *Little Horns Doom & Downfall* of 1651, Cary claims that some nine years previous she had understood the vision of the little horn in Dan. 7 to signify the overthrow and death of Charles. See Cary, *Doom & Downfall*, 46.
4. Mary Astell, *A Fair Way with the Dissenters and their Patrons*, in *Political Writings*, ed. Patricia Springborg (Cambridge: Cambridge University Press, 1996), 125; Thickstun, "Feminist Scriptural Exegesis," 153.
5. Mary Astell, The Preface to *Some Reflections upon Marriage*, in *Political Writings*, ed. Patricia Springborg (Cambridge: Cambridge University Press, 1996), 23, 9. Future citations in text.
6. Smith, *Reason's Disciples*, 131.
7. Mary Astell, *A Serious Proposal to the Ladies*, ed. Patricia Springborg (London: Pickering and Chatto, 1997), 16.
8. Ruth Perry, "Radical Doubt and the Liberation of Women," *Eighteenth-Century Studies* 18:4 (1985): 491; Astell, *Serious Proposal*, 179–80; Astell, *Reflections*, in *Political Writings*, 62, 52, 56.
9. Ruth Perry, *The Celebrated Mary Astell* (Chicago: The University of Chicago Press, 1986), 210.
10. Perry, *Celebrated Mary Astell*, 214.
11. Astell, *Serious Proposal*, 14; *Fair Way*, 90.
12. Fittingly, the rise of party politics has been deemed by historian Mark Kishlansky to be an outgrowth of the Civil War Astell so vehemently despised. See his *The Rise of the New Model Army* (Cambridge: Cambridge University Press, 1979), 106,120.
13. Mary Astell, "Prefatory Discourse to Dr. D'Avenant," in *Moderation truly Stated* (London, 1704), xxvi, ix.

14. Ibid., xlix, li.

15. Ibid., lii, liv, lv.

16. Ibid., liii.

17. Astell, *Fair Way with the Dissenters*, 112.

18. Swift lampoons the dissenters' working-class membership: "IT is therefore upon this *Mechanical Operation of the Spirit*, that I mean to treat, as it is at present performed by our *British Workmen*" and observes the special, implicitly sexual, affection women have for sectarian preachers: "all Females are attracted by Visionary or Enthusiastick Preachers, tho' never so contemptible in their *outward Men*." Swift, *A Discourse Concerning the Mechanical Operation of the Spirit*, in *A Tale of the Tub with other Early Writings*, ed. Herbert Davis (Oxford: Basil Blackwell, 1957), 175, 189.

19. Astell, "Prefatory Discourse," in *Moderation truly Stated*, xlix; title page of *A Spirit Moving in The Women-Preachers* (London, 1646).

20. Perry, *Celebrated Mary Astell*, 202. For a similar observation, see also Ludlow, "Shaking Patriarchy's Foundations," 117.

21. Astell, "Prefatory Discourse," in *Moderation truly Stated*, l.

22. In common with Fell, Astell considers Paul's assertion of men's headship of women in 1 Cor. 11:3–15 and his teachings on women's subordinate role in the church in 1 Tim. 2:9–15.

23. Milton, *Samson Agonistes*, 982–83.

24. For the story of Miriam's questioning of Moses's authority, see Num. 12.

25. See for instance, Aemilia Lanyer's 1611 *Salve Deus Rex Judaeorum*, in *The Poems of Aemilia Lanyer: Salve Deus Rex Judaeorum*, ed. Susanne Woods (New York: Oxford University Press, 1993), lines 1497–98.

26. Laquer, *Making Sex*, 150, 153–54.

27. See Isa. 65:17, 19. Astell alludes directly to Isa. 65:25: "The wolf and the lamb shall feed together, and the lion shall eat straw like the bullock: and dust shall be the serpent's meat. They shall not hurt nor destroy all in my holy mountain, saith the Lord." For more on Third Isaiah, see Gerhard von Rad, *The Message of the Prophets*, trans. D. M. G. Stalker (New York: Harper & Row, 1965), 245–47 and Joseph Blenkinsopp, *A History of Prophecy in Israel* (Philadelphia: Westminster Press, 1983), 242–51.

28. Cary, *New and More Exact Mappe*, 237.

29. See Revelation 12 for the account of the woman. For more on the relationship between the woman and the plight of the Protestant church, see Napier, *Plaine Discovery*, 33, 163.

Bibliography

PRIMARY SOURCES

The Arraignment and Conviction of Mervin Lord Audley. London: 1642.

Astell, Mary. "Prefatory Discourse to Dr. D'Avenant." In *Moderation truly Stated.* London: 1704.

———. *The First English Feminist: "Reflections Upon Marriage" and other writings by Mary Astell.* Edited by Bridget Hill. New York: St. Martin's Press, 1986.

———. *Political Writings.* Edited by Patricia Springborg. Cambridge: Cambridge University Press, 1996.

———. *A Serious Proposal to the Ladies.* Edited by Patricia Springborg. London: Pickering and Chatto, 1997.

Audland, Anne. *A True Declaration Of The suffering of the Innocent.* London: 1655.

Bathurst, Elizabeth. *The Sayings of Women.* In *Hidden in Plain Sight: Quaker Women's Writings 1650–1700,* edited by Mary Garman et al. Wallingford, PA: Pendle Hill Publications, 1996.

Bettris, Jeane. *A Lamentation for the Deceived People of the World.* London: 1657.

Biddle, Hester. *The Trumpet of the Lord Sounded forth unto these Three Nations.* London: 1662.

Blackborow, Sarah. *The Just and Equall Ballance Discovered.* London: 1660.

Cary, Mary. *Little Horns Doom & Downfall.* London: 1651.

———. *A New and More Exact Mappe Or, Description of New Jerusalems Glory.* London: 1651.

Chidley, Katherine. *The Justification of the Independent Churches of Christ.* London: 1641.

Cobbett's Complete Collection of State Trials. Vol. 3. London: R. Bagshaw, 1809.

Cotton, Priscilla and Mary Cole. *To the Priests and People of England.* London, 1655.

Davies, Lady Eleanor. *Prophetic Writings of Lady Eleanor Davies.* Edited by Esther S. Cope. New York: Oxford University Press, 1995.

———. *All the kings of the earth shall prayse thee.* Amsterdam: 1633.

———. *Given to the Elector.* Amsterdam, 1633.

———. *The Lady Eleanor, Her Appeale.* 1641.

———. *Apocalypsis Jesu Christi.* 1644.

———. *From the Lady Eleanor, Her Blessing to Her Beloved Daughter.* 1644.

————. *The Word of God, To the Citie of London.* 1644.

————. *The Crying Charge.* 1649.

————. *The Appearance or Presence of the Son of Man.* 1650.

————. *The Dragons Blasphemous Charge against Her.* 1651.

————. *The Restitution of Prophecy.* 1651.

————. *Bethlehem Signifying The House of Bread: or War.* 1652.

————. *Tobits Book, A Lesson Appointed for Lent.* 1652.

Docwra, Anne. *An Epistle of Love.* 1683.

Evans, Katharine, and Sarah Chevers. *This is a Short Relation of Some of the Cruel Sufferings . . . in the Inquisition in the Isle of Malta.* In *Hidden in Plain Sight: Quaker Women's Writings 1650–1700*, edited by Mary Garman et al. Wallingford, PA: Pendle Hill Publications, 1996.

Farnworth, Richard. *A Woman Forbidden to Speak in the Church.* London, 1655.

Fell, Margaret. *A Declaration and an Information From us the People of God called Quakers.* London: 1660.

————. *Womens Speaking Justified.* London: 1667.

————. *Womens Speaking Justified.* 1667. Augustan Reprint Society, no. 194. Los Angeles: William Andrews Clark Memorial Library, 1979.

————. *Womens Speaking Justified.* 1667. Reprint, Amherst: Mosher Book and Tract Committee, 1980.

————. *Womens Speaking Justified.* In *The Rhetorical Tradition: Readings from Classical Times to the Present*, eds. Patricia Bizzell and Bruce Herzberg. 2nd ed. Boston: Bedford, 2001.

————. *Womens Speaking Justified.* In *First Feminists: British Women Writers 1578–1799*, edited by Moira Ferguson. Bloomington: Indiana University Press, 1985.

————. *Womens Speaking Justified.* In *English Women's Voices 1540–1700*, edited by Charlotte Otten. Miami: Florida International University Press, 1992.

————. *Womens Speaking Justified.* In *Lay by Your Needles Ladies, Take the Pen: Writing Women in England 1500–1700*, edited by Suzanne Trill, Kate Chedgzoy, and Melanie Osborne. London: Arnold, 1997.

————. *Womens Speaking Justified.* In *The "Other" Eighteenth Century: English Women of Letters 1660–1800*, edited by Robert W. Uphaus and Gretchen M. Foster. East Lansing: Colleagues Press, 1991.

————. "The Examination of Margaret Fell." In *A Brief Collection of Remarkable Passages and Occurences Relating to . . . Margaret Fell.* London, 1710.

————. *A Relation of Margaret Fell.* In *A Brief Collection of Remarkable Passages and Occurences Relating to . . . Margaret Fell.* London: 1710.

Fell, Sarah. "From our Country Women's meeting in Lancashire to be Dispersed abroad, among the Woman's meetings every where." In "A Seventeenth-Century Quaker Woman's Declaration," Milton D. Speizman and Jane C. Kronick. *Signs* 1 (1975): 231–45.

Foster, Mary et al. *A Living Testimony.* 1685.

Fox, George. *Concerning Sons and Daughters.* 2nd ed. London, 1661.

————. Epistle 248: "An Exhortation to Set Up Women's Meetings." In *Early*

Quaker Writings 1650–1700, edited by Hugh Barbour and Arthur O. Roberts. Grand Rapids, MI: Eerdmans, 1973.

———. Epistle CCXCI: "To all the women's meetings, that are believers in the truth" (1672). In *The Works of George Fox*. Vol. 8. 1831. Reprint, New York: AMS Press, 1975.

———. Epistle CCXCVI (1673). In *The Works of George Fox*. Vol. 8. 1831. Reprint, New York: AMS Press, 1975.

———. *This is an Encouragement to All the Women's-Meetings in the World*. 1676.

———. Epistle CCCXLIV: "An epistle to be read in the men and women's meetings" (1677). In *The Works of George Fox*. Vol. 8. 1831. Reprint, New York: AMS Press, 1975.

———. Epistle CCCLX: "To all the men and women's meetings every where." (1679). In *The Works of George Fox*. Vol. 8. 1831. Reprint, New York: AMS Press, 1975.

———. "Wheeler Street Sermon" (1680). In *Early Quaker Writings 1650–1700*, edited by Hugh Barbour and Arthur O. Roberts. Grand Rapids, MI: Eerdmans, 1973.

Hobbes, Thomas. *Leviathan*. Edited by Richard Tuck. Cambridge: Cambridge University Press, 1991.

The holy Sisters Conspiracy against their Husbands, and the City of London, designed at their last Farewell of their Meeting-houses in Coleman Street. 1661.

Jessey, Henry. *The Exceeding Riches of Grace*. London: 1647.

[Pendarves, Thomasine (supposed author).] *"The Copy of a letter, as it was sent from T.P. a friend of Mrs. Elizabeth Poole, To the Congregation of Saints, walking in fellowship with Mr. William Kiffin."* In *An Alarum of War*, by Elizabeth Poole. London, 1649.

Poole, Elizabeth. *A Vision: Wherein is manifested the disease and cure of the Kingdome*. London: 1648.

———. *An Alarum of War, Given to the Army* (London: 1649).

———. *An Alarum of War, Given to the Army* . . . "Also a letter to the Congregation, in fellowship with Mr. *Kiffin*, in vindication of *E.P.* [Elizabeth Poole] advising them to live lesse in the Letter of the scripture, and more in the spirit." (London, 1649).

Townsend, Theophila. *An Epistle of Love To Friends in the Womens Meetings in London*. 1680?.

Trapnel, Anna. *The Cry of a Stone*. London, 1654.

———. *A Legacy for Saints*. London, 1654.

———. *Report and Plea Or, A Narrative of her Journey from London into Cornwall*. London, 1654.

———. *Strange and Wonderful Newes from White-hall*. London, 1654.

———. *A Voice for the King of Saints*. London: 1658.

The Trial of the Lord Audley, Earl of Castlehaven. London, 1679.

The Tryal and Condemnation of Mervin, Lord Audley Earl of Castle-Haven. London, 1699.

White, Dorothy. *A Diligent Search amongst Rulers, Priests, Professors, and People.* 1659.

———. *This is to be delivered to the Counsellors.* 1659.

———. *Upon the 22 day of the 8th Month, 1659, A Lamentation Unto this Nation.* 1660.

———. *Unto All Gods Host in England.* 1660.

———. *Alarm Sounded To England's Inhabitants.* 1661.

———. *An Epistle of Love.* 1661.

———. *A Salutation of Love.* ca. 1684.

Yeamans, Isabel. *An Invitation of Love.* 1679.

SECONDARY SOURCES

Early Modern

Archer, John. *The Personal Reign of Christ Upon Earth.* 5th ed. London, 1661.

Bale, John. *The Image of Bothe Churches.* In *Select Works of John Bale, D.D.,* edited by Henry Christmas. Cambridge: The University Press, 1849.

———. Commentary on *The Examinations of Anne Askew,* edited by Elaine V. Beilin. New York: Oxford University Press, 1996.

Beaumont, William and John Fletcher. *Love's Cure, or, The Martial Maid.* In *The Dramatic Works in the Beaumont and Fletcher Canon,* edited by George Walton Williams. Vol. 3. Cambridge: Cambridge University Press, 1976.

Besse, Joseph. *A Collection of the Sufferings of the People called Quakers.* Vol. 1. London: 1753.

Brightman, Thomas. *The Revelation of Saint John.* Amsterdam, 1644.

Bunyan, John. *Grace Abounding to the Chief of Sinners.* Edited by Roger Sharrock. Oxford: Clarendon Press, 1962.

Burrage, Champlin, comp. *The Early English Dissenters.* Vol. 2. Cambridge: Cambridge University Press, 1912.

Charles I (John Gauden, supposed author). *Eikon Basilike: The Pourtracture of His Sacred Majestie in His Solitudes and Sufferings.* 1648/9.

Cleveland, John. *Monumentum Regale.* 1649.

Davenant, William. *News from Plymouth.* In *The Dramatic Works of Sir William Davenant.* Vol. 4. Edinburgh: William Paterson, 1873.

A Directory for the Publique Worship of God. London, 1644.

Fisher, James. *The Wise Virgin.* London, 1653.

Foster, George. *The Sounding of the Last Trumpet.* 1650.

Goodwin, John. *The Obstructors of Justice.* London, 1649.

Heylin, Peter. *Cyprianus Anglicus: OR, THE History of the Life and Death, of The most Reverend and Renowned Prelate William.* London: 1671.

James I, *The True Lawe of Free Monarchies.* London: 1603.

———. *A Paraphrase Upon the Revelation of the Apostle S. John.* In *The Workes of the Most High and Mightie Prince, James.* London, 1616.

————. *Basilikon Doron*. In *The Political Works of James I*, edited by Charles Howard McIlwain. Cambridge, MA: Harvard University Press, 1918.

————. *The Poems of James VI of Scotland*. Edited by James Craigie. Edinburgh: William Blackwood, 1958.

Kempe, Margery. *The Book of Margery Kempe*. Translated by B. A. Windeatt. New York: Viking Penguin, 1985.

King, Henry. *An Elegy Upon the most Incomparable K. Charles the 1*. 1648/9.

The Lambs Defence Against Lyes. 1656.

Lanyer, Aemilia. *The Poems of Aemilia Lanyer: Salve Deus Rex Judaeorum*. Edited by Susanne Woods. New York: Oxford University Press, 1993.

Lescarbot. *A True and admirable Historie of a Mayden of Consolans*. Translated by Anthony Munday. 1603.

Loddington, William. *The Good Order of Truth Justified*. London, 1685.

Marvell, Andrew. "*An* Horatian *Ode upon* Cromwell's *Return from* Ireland." In *The Poems and Letters of Andrew Marvell*, edited by H. M. Margoliouth. 3rd ed. Vol. 1. Oxford: Clarendon Press, 1971.

Mayne, Jasper. *The City Match*. In *A Select Collection of Old Plays*, edited by W. Carew Hazlitt. Vol. 13. London: Reeves and Turner, 1875.

Mede, Joseph. *The Key of the Revelation*. Translated by Richard More. 2nd ed. 1650.

Milton, John. *Samson Agonistes*. In *Complete Poems and Major Prose*, edited by Merritt Y. Hughes. New York: Macmillan, 1957.

Napier, John. *A Plaine Discovery of the Whole Revelation of Saint John*. Edinburgh, 1593.

Peter, Hugh. Preface to *Little Horns Doom & Downfall*, by Mary Cary. London, 1651.

Philips, Katherine. *The Collected Works of Katherine Philips*. Edited by Patrick Thomas. Essex: Stump Cross Books, 1990.

Powell, Vavasor. *Christ Exalted above all Creatures By God His Father*. London, 1651.

Robins, Thomas. *The Wonder of the World*. London, 1669.

Sedgwick, William. *Justice Upon the Armie Remonstrance*. London, 1649.

Shakespeare, William. *Measure for Measure*. Edited by G. Blakemore Evans. The Riverside Shakespeare. Boston: Houghton Mifflin, 1974.

Swift, Jonathan. *Mechanical Operation of the Spirit* . In *A Tale of the Tub with other Early Works, 1696–1707*, edited by Herbert Davis. Oxford: Basil Blackwell, 1957.

Tillinghast, John. *Generation-work*. London, 1655.

Ussher, James. *The Rights of Primogeniture*. London, 1648.

Williams, John. *Great Britain's Salomon*. 1625.

"You gallant maidens of the world." In *The Shirburn Ballads 1585–1616*, edited by Andrew Clark. Oxford: Clarendon Press, 1907.

Modern

Achinstein, Sharon. *Milton and the Revolutionary Reader*. Princeton: Princeton University Press, 1994.

Barash, Carol. *English Women's Poetry 1649–1714: Politics, Community, and Linguistic Authority*. Oxford: Clarendon, 1996.

Barbour, Hugh. "Quaker Prophetesses and Mothers in Israel." In *Seeking the Light: Essays in Quaker History in Honor of Edwin M. Bronner*, edited by J. William Frost and John M. Moore. Wallingford, PA: Pendle Hill Publications, 1986.

Barthes, Roland. *Sade, Fourier, Loyola*. Translated by Richard Miller. Berkeley: University of California Press, 1989.

Bauckham, Richard. *Tudor Apocalypse*. Oxford: The Sutton Courtenay Press, 1978.

Bell, Richard, and Patricia Crawford. "Statistical Analysis of Women's Printed Writings 1600–1700." Appendix 2 to *Women in English Society 1500–1800*, edited by Mary Prior. London: Methuen, 1985.

Bell, Rudolph. *Holy Anorexia*. Chicago: University of Chicago Press, 1985.

Berdan, John M., ed. *Poems of John Cleveland*, by John Cleveland. New Haven: Yale University Press, 1911.

Berg, Christine, and Philippa Berry. "'Spiritual Whoredom': An Essay on Female Prophets in the Seventeenth Century." In *1642: Literature and Power in the Seventeenth Century: Proceedings of the Essex Conference on the Sociology of Literature, July 1980*, edited by Francis Barker et al. Colchester: University of Essex, 1981.

Bingham, Caroline. "Seventeenth-Century Attitudes Toward Deviant Sex." *The Journal of Interdisciplinary History* 1:3 (1971): 447–72.

Blenkinsopp, Joseph. *A History of Prophecy in Israel*. Philadelphia: Westminster Press, 1983.

Brailsford, Mabel R. *Quaker Women, 1650–1690*. London: Duckworth and Co., 1915.

Braithwaite, William C. *The Second Period of Quakerism*. 2nd ed. Cambridge: Cambridge University Press, 1961.

Bray, Alan. *Homosexuality in Renaissance England*. London: Gay Men's Press, 1982.

Breasted, Barbara. "*Comus* and the Castlehaven Scandal." *Milton Studies* 3 (1971): 201–24.

Bruch, Hilde. *Eating Disorders: Obesity, Anorexia Nervosa, and the Person Within*. New York: Basic Books, 1973.

Brumberg, Joan Jacobs. *Fasting Girls: The Emergence of Anorexia Nervosa as a Modern Disease*. Cambridge: Harvard University Press, 1988.

Burg, B. R. "Ho Hum, Another Work of the Devil: Buggery and Sodomy in Early Stuart England." In *Historical Perspectives on Homosexuality*, edited by Salvatore J. Licata and Robert P. Petersen. New York: Haworth Press, 1981.

Bynum, Caroline Walker. *Holy Feast and Holy Fast*. Berkeley: University of California Press, 1987.

Caldwell, Patricia. *The Puritan Conversion Narrative*. Cambridge: Cambridge University Press, 1983.

Capp, B. S. *Fifth Monarchy Men*. London: Faber, 1972.

Christianson, Paul. *Reformers and Babylon: English Apocalyptic Visions from the Reformation to the Eve of the Civil War*. Toronto: University of Toronto Press, 1978.

Cohen, Alfred. "The Fifth Monarchy Mind: Mary Cary and the origins of Totalitarianism." *Social Research* 31 (1964): 195–213.

———. "Mary Cary." In *Biographical Dictionary of British Radicals in the Seventeenth Century*, edited by Richard L. Greaves and Robert Zaller. Vol. 1. Sussex: The Harvester Press, 1982.

Collins, Stephen L. *From Divine Cosmos to Sovereign State*. New York: Oxford University Press, 1989.

Cope, Esther S. *Handmaid of the Holy Spirit: Dame Eleanor Davies, Never Soe Mad a Ladie*. Ann Arbor: The University of Michigan Press, 1992.

Cope, Jackson I. "Seventeenth-Century Quaker Style." *Publications of the Modern Language Association of America* 71:4 (1956): 725–54.

Covington, Dennis. *Salvation on Sand Mountain: Snake Handling and Redemption in Southern Appalachia*. Reading, MA: Addison-Wesley, 1995.

Creaser, John. "Milton's *Comus*: The Irrelevance of the Castlehaven Scandal." *Milton Quarterly* 11 (1987): 24–34.

Cross, Claire. "'He-goats before the Flocks': a note on the part played by women in the founding of some Civil War churches." In *Popular Belief and Practice*, edited by G. J. Cumming and Derek Baker. Cambridge: Cambridge University Press, 1972.

———. "'Great Reasoners in Scripture': The Activities of Women Lollards." In *Medieval Women*, edited by Derek Baker. Oxford: Basil Blackwell, 1978.

Dailey, Barbara Ritter. "The Visitation of Sarah Wight: Holy Carnival and the Revolution of the Saints in Civil War London." *Church History* 55 (1986): 438–55.

———. "The Husbands of Margaret Fell: An Essay on Religious Metaphor and Social Change." *The Seventeenth Century* 2:1 (1987): 55–71.

Davis, J. C. *Fear, Myth and History: The Ranters and the Historians*. New York: Cambridge University Press, 1986.

Dollimore, Jonathan. *Sexual Dissidence*. Oxford: Clarendon Press, 1991.

Edwards, Irene L. "The Women Friends of London: The Two-Weeks and Box Meeetings." *Journal of the Friends Historical Society* 47: 1(1955): 3–21.

Ezell, Margaret J. M. "Breaking the Seventh Seal: Writings by Early Quaker Women." In *Writing Women's Literary History*. Baltimore: The Johns Hopkins University Press, 1993.

Ferguson, Margaret. "A Room Not Their Own: Renaissance Women as Readers and Writers." In *The Comparative Perspective on Literature: Approaches to Theory and Practice*, edited by Clayton Koelb and Susan Noakes. Ithaca: Cornell University Press, 1988.

Firth, Katharine R. *The Apocalyptic Tradition in Reformation Britain 1530–1645*. Oxford: Oxford University Press, 1979.

Foucault, Michel. *Discipline and Punish*. Translated by Alan Sheridan. New York: Vintage, 1979.

Freud, Sigmund. "Mourning and Melancholia." In *The Standard Edition of the Complete Psychological Works*. Vol. 14. London: The Hogarth Press, 1961.

Friedman, Jerome. *Blasphemy, Immorality and Anarchy: The Ranters and the English Revolution*. Athens, Ohio: Ohio University Press, 1989.

Gallagher, Catherine. "Embracing the Absolute: The Politics of the Female Subject in Seventeenth-Century England." *Genders* 1:1 (1988): 24–39.

Gardiner, Judith Keegan. "Re-Gendering Individualism: Margaret Fell Fox and Quaker Rhetoric." In *Privileging Gender in Early Modern England*, edited by Jean R. Brink. Kirksville, MO: Sixteenth Century Journal Publishers, 1993.

———. "Margaret Fell Fox and Feminist Literary History: A 'Mother in Israel.'" In *The Emergence of Quaker Writing: Dissenting Literature in Seventeenth-Century England*, edited by Thomas N. Corns and David Loewenstein. London: Frank Cass, 1995.

Gentles, Ian. *The New Model Army in England, Ireland and Scotland, 1645–1653*. Oxford: Blackwell, 1992.

Gillespie, Katharine. *Domesticity and Dissent in the Seventeenth Century*. Cambridge: Cambridge University Press, 2004.

Goldberg, Jonathan. *James I and the Politics of Literature*. Stanford: Stanford University Press, 1989.

———. *Sodometries: Renaissance Texts, Modern Sexualities*. Stanford: Stanford University Press, 1992.

Guibbory, Achsah. "Conversation, Conversion, Messianic Redemption: Margaret Fell, Menasseh ben Israel, and the Jews." In *Literary Circles and Cultural Communities in Renaissance England*, edited by Claude J. Summers and Ted-Larry Pebworth. Columbia, MO: University of Missouri Press, 2000.

Gutierrez, Nancy A. "Double Standard in the Flesh: Gender, Fasting, and Power in English Renaissance Drama." In *Disorderly Eaters: Texts in Self-Empowerment*, edited by Lilian R. Furst and Peter W. Graham. University Park, PA: The Pennsylvania State University Press, 1992.

Hanson, Donald W. *From Kingdom to Commonwealth: The Development of Civic Consciousness in English Political Thought*. Cambridge: Harvard University Press, 1970.

Hawes, Clement. *Mania and Literary Style: The Rhetoric of Enthusiasm from the Ranters to Christopher Smart*. Cambridge: Cambridge University Press, 1996.

Helgerson, Richard. *Forms of Nationhood*. Chicago: The University of Chicago Press, 1992.

Herrup, Cynthia. *A House in Gross Disorder: Sex, Law, and the 2nd Earl of Castlehaven*. New York: Oxford University Press, 1999.

———. "The Patriarch at Home: The Trial of the 2nd Earl of Castlehaven for Rape and Sodomy." *History Workshop Journal* 41 (1996): 1–18.

Higgins, Patricia. "The Reactions of Women, with Special Reference to Women Petitioners." In *Politics, Religion, and the English Revolution*, edited by Brian Manning. London: Edward Arnold, 1973.

Hill, Christopher. *Antichrist in Seventeenth-Century England*. London: Verso, 1990.

———. "Covenant Theology and the Concept of 'A Public Person.'" In *Powers, Possessions, and Freedom: Essays in Honour of C. B. Macpherson*, edited by Alkis Kontos. Toronto: University of Toronto Press, 1979.

Hindle, C. J. "A Bibliography of the Printed Pamphlets and Broadsides of Lady Eleanor Douglas the Seventeenth-Century Prophetess." *Edinburgh Bibliographical Society Transactions* 1:1 (1936): 65–98.

Hinds, Hilary. *God's Englishwomen: Seventeenth-Century Radical Sectarian*

Writing and Feminist Criticism. Manchester: Manchester University Press, 1996.

Hirst, Derek. *Authority and Conflict: England, 1603–1658.* Cambridge, MA: Harvard University Press, 1986.

Hobby, Elaine. *Virtue of Necessity: English Women's Writing 1649–88.* London: Virago, 1988.

———. "Handmaids of the Lord and Mothers in Israel: Early Vindications of Quaker Women's Prophecy." In *The Emergence of Quaker Writing: Dissenting Literature in Seventeenth-Century England,* edited by Thomas N. Corns and David Loewenstein. London: Frank Cass, 1995.

Holstun, James. "Ranting at the New Historicism." *English Literary Renaissance* 19:2 (1989): 189–225.

———. Introduction to *Pamphlet Wars: Prose in the English Revolution.* London: Frank Cass, 1992.

Hughes, Ann. "Gender and Politics in Leveller Literature." In *Political Culture and Cultural Politics in Early Modern England,* edited by Susan D. Amussen and Mark A. Kishlansky. Manchester: Manchester University Press, 1995.

Hyde, H. Montgomery. *The Love that Dared not Speak Its Name.* Boston: Little, Brown and Company, 1970.

Keeble, N. H. "Obedient Subjects? The Loyal Self in Some Later Seventeenth-Century Royalist Women's Memoirs." In *Culture and Society in the Stuart Restoration,* edited by Gerald MacLean. Cambridge: Cambridge University Press, 1995.

Kegl, Rosemary. "Women's Preaching, Absolute Property, and the Cruel Sufferings (For the Truths sake) of Katharine Evans and Sarah Chevers." *Women's Studies* 24 (1994): 51–83.

Kenyon, J. P. *Stuart England.* New York: Penguin, 1978.

Kibbey, Ann. *The Interpretation of Material Shapes in Puritanism.* Cambridge: Cambridge University Press, 1986.

Kinnaird, Joan K. "Mary Astell and the Conservative Contribution to English Feminism." *Journal of British Studies* 19:1 (1979): 53–75.

Kishlansky, Mark. *The Rise of the New Model Army.* Cambridge: Cambridge University Press, 1979.

Krueger, Robert, and Ruby Nemser, eds. *The Poems of Sir John Davies,* by John Davies. Oxford: Clarendon Press, 1975.

Kunze, Bonnelyn Young. *Margaret Fell and the Rise of Quakerism.* Stanford: Stanford University Press, 1994.

Laquer, Thomas. *Making Sex: Body and Gender from the Greeks to Freud.* Cambridge, MA: Harvard University Press, 1990.

Levi-Strauss, Claude. *The Savage Mind.* Chicago: The University of Chicago Press, 1966.

Lewalski, Barbara Kiefer. "The Biblical Symbolic Mode: Typology and the Religious Lyric." In *Protestant Poetics and the Seventeenth-Century Religious Lyric.* Princeton: Princeton University Press, 1979.

———. *Writing Women in Jacobean England.* Cambridge, MA: Harvard University Press, 1993.

Lloyd, Arnold. "The Quaker Women's Meetings." In *Quaker Social History*. 1950. Reprint, Westport, CT: Greenwood Press, 1979.

Ludlow, Dorothy Paula. "'Arise and Be Doing,' English 'Preaching' Women, 1640–60." Ph.D. diss., Indiana University, 1978.

———. "Shaking Patriarchy's Foundations: Sectarian Women in England 1641–1700." In *Triumph over Silence: Women in Protestant History*, edited by Richard L. Greaves. Westport, CT: Greenwood Press, 1985.

Luecke, Marilyn Serraino. "'God hath made no difference such as men would': Margaret Fell and the Politics of Women's Speech." *Bunyan Studies* 7 (1997): 73–95.

Mack, Phyllis. *Visionary Women: Ecstatic Prophecy in Seventeenth-Century England*. Berkeley: University of California Press, 1992.

MacKinnon, Catherine A. *Toward a Feminist Theory of the State*. Cambridge, MA: Harvard University Press, 1989.

MacLean, Gerald M. *Time's Witness: Historical Representation in English Poetry, 1603–1660*. Madison: University of Wisconsin Press, 1990.

Macpherson, C. B. *The Political Theory of Possessive Individualism: Hobbes to Locke*. Clarendon: Oxford University Press, 1962.

Marcus, Leah Sinangolou. "The Milieu of Milton's *Comus*: Judicial Reform at Ludlow and the Problem of Sexual Assault." *Criticism* 25 (1983): 293–327.

Matchinske, Megan. "Holy Hatred: Formations of the Gendered Subject in English Apocalyptic Writing, 1625–51." *English Literary History* 60 (1993): 349–77.

McArthur, Ellen A. "Women Petitioners and the Long Parliament." *English Historical Review* 24 (1909): 698–709.

McEntee, Ann Marie. "The [Un] Civill-Sisterhood of Oranges and Lemons: Female Petitioners and Demonstrators, 1642–53." In *Pamphlet Wars: Prose in the English Revolution*, edited by James Holstun. London: Frank Cass, 1992.

McGinn, Bernard. "Early Apocalypticism: the ongoing debate." In *The Apocalypse in English Renaissance Thought and Literature*, edited by C. A. Patrides and Joseph Wittreich. Ithaca: Cornell University Press, 1984.

Miller, Nancy Weitz. "Chastity, Rape, and Ideology in the Castlehaven Testimonies and Milton's Ludlow *Mask*." *Milton Studies* 32 (1995): 153–68.

Miller, Perry. "The Marrow of Puritan Divinity." In *Errand into the Wilderness*. Cambridge, MA: The Belknap Press of Harvard University Press, 1956.

Mojtabai, A. G. *Blessed Assurance: At Home with the Bomb in Amarillo, Texas*. Boston: Houghton Mifflin, 1986.

Morris, Brian, and Eleanor Withington, eds. *The Poems of John Cleveland*, by John Cleveland. Oxford: Clarendon, 1967.

Nelson, Beth. "Lady Elinor Davies: The Prophet as Publisher." *Women's Studies: International Forum* 8 (1985): 403–9.

Nenner, Howard. *The Right to be King: The Succession to the Crown of England*. Chapel Hill: The University of North Carolina Press, 1995.

Orr, William F., and James Arthur Walther, eds. I Corinthians. Vol. 32 of *The Anchor Bible*. Garden City, NY: Doubleday, 1976.

Pateman, Carole. *The Sexual Contract*. Stanford: Stanford University Press, 1988.

Patrides, C. A. and Joseph Wittreich, eds. *The Apocalypse in English Renaissance Thought and Literature*. Ithaca: Cornell University Press, 1984.

Perry, Ruth. *The Celebrated Mary Astell: An Early English Feminist*. Chicago: University of Chicago Press, 1986.

———. "Radical Doubt and the Liberation of Women." *Eighteenth-Century Studies* 18:4 (1985): 472–93.

Pickard, Richard. "Anagrams *etc*. The interpretive Dilemmas of Lady Eleanor Douglas." *Renaissance and Reformation* 20:3 (1996): 5–22.

Pocock, J. G. A. "Time, History and Eschatology in the Thought of Thomas Hobbes." In *Politics, Language and Time*. New York: Atheneum, 1971.

Porter, Roy. "The Prophetic Body: Lady Eleanor Davies and the meanings of madness." *Women's Writing* 1:1 (1994): 51–63.

Purkiss, Diane. "Producing the voice, consuming the body: Women prophets of the seventeenth century." In *Women, Writing, History 1640–1740*, edited by Isobel Grundy and Susan Wiseman. Athens: University of Georgia Press, 1992.

Rollins, Hyder E. "Notes on Some English Accounts of Miraculous Fasts." *Journal of American Folk-Lore* 34 (1921): 357–76.

Ross, Isabel. *Margaret Fell: Mother of Quakerism*. London: Longmans, 1949.

Rubin, Gayle. "The Traffic in Women: Notes on the 'Political Economy' of Sex." In *Toward an Anthropology of Women*, edited by Rayna Reiter. New York: Monthly Review Press, 1975.

Scarry, Elaine. *The Body in Pain: The Making and Unmaking of the World*. New York: Oxford University Press, 1985.

Schwoerer, Lois G. "Women's public political voice in England: 1640–1740." In *Women Writers and the Early Modern British Political Tradition*, edited by Hilda Smith. Cambridge: Cambridge University Press, 1998.

Scott-Luckens, Carola. "Propaganda or Marks of Grace? The Impact of the Reported Ordeals of Sarah Wight in Revolutionary London, 1647–52." *Women's Writing* 9:2 (2002): 215–32.

Sedgwick, Eve Kosofsky. *Between Men: English Literature and Male Homosocial Desire*. New York: Columbia University Press, 1985.

Sharpe, Kevin. "'An Image Doting Rabble': The Failure of Republican Culture in Seventeenth-Century England." In *Refiguring Revolutions: Aesthetics and Politics from the English Revolution*, edited by Kevin Sharpe and Steven Zwicker. Berkeley: University of California Press, 1998.

Smith, Hilda. *Reason's Disciples: Seventeenth-Century English Feminists*. Urbana: University of Illinios Press, 1982.

Smith, Nigel. *Perfection Proclaimed: Language and Literature in English Radical Religion 1640–1660*. Oxford: Clarendon Press, 1989.

———. "A Child Prophet: Martha Hatfield as *The Wise Virgin*." In *Children and their Books*, edited by Gillian Avery and Julia Briggs. Oxford: Clarendon Press, 1989.

———. *Literature and the English Revolution 1640–1660*. New Haven: Yale University Press, 1994.

Speizman, Milton D., and Jane C. Kronick. "A Seventeenth-Century Quaker Women's Declaration." *Signs* 1 (1975): 231–45.

Spencer, Theodore. "The History of an Unfortunate Lady." *Harvard Studies and Notes in Philology and Literature* 20 (1938): 43–59.

Spring, Eileen. *Law, Land, & Family: Aristocratic Inheritance in England, 1300–1800.* Chapel Hill: University of North Carolina Press, 1993.

Stone, Lawrence. *The Crisis of the Aristocracy 1558–1641.* Oxford: Clarendon Press, 1965.

Thickstun, Margaret Olofson. " 'This was a Woman that taught': Feminist Scriptural Exegesis in the Seventeenth Century." *Studies in Eighteenth-Century Culture* 21 (1991): 149–57.

Thomas, Keith. "Women and the Civil War Sects." *Past and Present* 13 (1958): 42–62.

———. "The Social Origins of Hobbes's Political Thought." In *Hobbes Studies*, edited by K. C. Brown. Cambridge, MA: Harvard University Press, 1965.

———. *Religion and the Decline of Magic.* London: Weidenfeld and Nicolson, 1971.

Tiffany, Sharon W., and Kathleen J. Adams. *The Wild Woman: An Inquiry into the Anthropology of an Idea.* Cambridge, MA: Schenkman Publishing, 1985.

Tolmie, Murray. *The Triumph of the Saints.* Cambridge: Cambridge University Press, 1977.

Toon, Peter, ed. *Puritans, the Millennium and the Future of Israel: Puritan Eschatology 1600 to 1660.* Cambridge: James Clark, 1970.

Trevett, Christine. *Women and Quakerism in the 17th Century.* York: Ebor Press, 1991.

Trevor-Roper, H. R. "The Fast Sermons of the Long Parliament." In *The Crisis of the Seventeenth Century.* New York: Harper and Row, 1968.

Trubowitz, Rachel. "Female Preachers and Male Wives: Gender and Authority in Civil War England." In *Pamphlet Wars: Prose in the English Revolution*, edited by James Holstun. London: Frank Cass, 1992.

Von Rad, Gerhard. *The Message of the Prophets.* Translated by D. M. G. Stalker. New York: Harper & Row, 1965.

Wall, Wendy. "Isabella Whitney and the Female Legacy." *English Literary History* 58 (1991): 35–62.

Weber, Max. *The Protestant Ethic and the Spirit of Capitalism.* Translated by Talcott Parsons. London: Unwin, 1930.

Wilcox, Catherine M. *Theology and Women's Ministry in Seventeenth-Century English Quakerism.* Lewiston, NY: Edwin Mellen Press, 1995.

Willen, Diane. "Women and Religion in Early Modern England." In *Women in Reformation and Counter-Reformation Europe*, edited by Sherrin Marshall. Bloomington: Indiana University Press, 1989.

Williams, Ethyn Morgan. "Women Preachers in the Civil War." *Journal of Modern History* 1 (1929): 561–69.

Wilson, John F. *Pulpit in Parliament: Puritanism during the English Civil War 1640–48.* Princeton: Princeton University Press, 1969.

Wiseman, Sue. "Unsilent Instruments and the Devil's Cushions: Authority in Seventeenth-Century Women's Prophetic Discourse." In *New Feminist Discourses*, edited by Isobel Armstrong. London: Routledge, 1992.

Wright, S. G. "Dougle Fooleries." *Bodleian Quarterly Record* 7 (1932–34): 95–98.

Zaret, David. *The Heavenly Contract: Ideology and Organization in Pre-Revolutionary Puritanism.* Chicago: The University of Chicago Press, 1985.

Index

Aaron, 160, 183–84

Abbot, George, Archbishop of Canterbury, 41, 44

Achinstein, Sharon, 222 n. 3

Acts, 114, 151, 152, 158, 167

Adams, Jane, 23

Adams, Kathleen, 137

Agrippina, 203, 206

Ahab, 49, 85, 105

Amsterdam, 38, 46, 49, 55, 227 n. 9, 229 n. 46

Anna (or Hannah; biblical prophet), 162–64, 170, 209

Anne, Queen, 200, 203, 205, 212–13, 214

Antichrist, 25, 27, 46

apocalypticism, 15, 19, 26–28, 38, 44–48, 53, 58–61, 72, 88–89, 151, 159, 176, 212–14, 225 n. 35, 227 n. 9, 228 n. 33, 230 n. 65, 247 nn. 27 and 29

Archer, John: *The Personal Reign of Christ Upon Earth*, 60

aristocracy, 24, 25, 49, 57–58, 77, 89–90, 92, 93

Aristotle, 112

Askew, Anne, 25–26

Astell, Mary, 16, 17, 29, 30, 33, 150, 197–214, 246 n. 2, 247 n. 27; ambivalence toward scripture as source on women of, 206–11, 232 n. 86, 246 n. 22; argument for naturalness of female authority of, 202–6; concerns with class and hierarchy of, 199, 201–2, 205; and dislike of party politics, 202–4, 246 n. 12; as early feminist 16, 17, 29, 30, 150, 197, 214; and emphasis on education, 17, 30, 150, 198–200, 201; evocations of women prophets and divine sanction of female authority, 197–98, 200–201, 203–9, 214; and literary authority, 200–201; and Occasional Conformity controversy, 200, 201–2, 205; and the politics of sexual difference and negation of the female body, 33, 210–11; and Queen Anne as model of female power, 200, 203, 205, 212–13, 214; and rationalist philosophy, 17, 150, 198–200, 211; Tory/High Church affiliations of, 197, 201. Works: *A Fair Way with the Dissenters*, 201; *Moderation Truly Stated*, 201, 202–6; Preface (1706) to *Some Reflections Upon Marriage*, 17, 197–98, 199–202, 206–14, 232 n. 86; *A Serious Proposal to the Ladies*, 198, 201, 205; *Some Reflections on Marriage*, 197, 198–200, 201

Audeley, Lady Elizabeth, 74, 79, 80, 81, 82, 91, 234 n. 17

Audeley, Lord (James Touchet), 79, 80, 234 n. 22

Audland, Anne: *A True Declaration Of The suffering of the Innocent*, 153

Balan, Jane, 111–12

Bale, John, 25, 28; *The Image of Bothe Churches*, 26–27

Baptists, 22, 68, 100, 102, 113, 232 n. 91, 232–33 n. 93

Barash, Carol, 29–30, 227 n. 6

Barebones Parliament, 104

Barthes, Roland, 82–83

Bathurst, Elizabeth: *The Sayings of Women*, 243 n. 39

Bauckham, Richard, 225 n. 35

Beaumont, William: *Love's Cure, or, The Martial Maid*, 110

Bell, Richard, 223 n. 9

Bell, Rudolph, 237 n. 21

Belshazzar, 36, 51, 142, 226 n. 5

Berdan, John M., 226 n. 3